"If reality is the greatest ally of God, then this realistic and balanced book is surely its helpmate. Anyone struggling with how to offer their love life to God will find wisdom and hard won experience in this honest book. This is mature Christian faith, and from a down to earth lay perspective. Many vowed celibates will find their own experience and helpful guidance here also."

Fr. Richard Rohr, O.F.M.
Center for Action and Contemplation
Albuquerque, New Mexico

"Here Jean Sheridan, discusses with vivid and sincere illustrations what it means to find oneself suddenly single and challenged by the church to live a celibate lifestyle. No such change in life is ever easy. No such commitment precludes the pain and confusion of change, but this book approaches this new style of community, friendship, hospitality, and service with depth, humor, and a keen sense of reality. Most original is the author's treatment of living a personal rule of life and relishing in sabbatical time."

Susan Muto, Ph.D.
Author, *Celebrating the Single Life*

"This is a great guide around the loneliness that often comes from the single life. Simultaneously practical and spiritual, the author's gift is in combining these two. Reflective living is the author's answer to the invisibility singles often feel."

Donna Schaper
Author, *Alone But Not Lonely*

"*The Unwilling Celibates* is a wonderful book especially suited to our frenetic and stress-filled times. Jean Sheridan gives voice to the pain and isolation of those marginalized in our church simply because they are single. Yet she does so in a way that speaks to all of us who struggle to find meaning and God in our lives. Her wisdom and candor make the book at once a healing and revealing read. She warms one's heart and illumines one's mind by telling her story and sharing what can only be called a truly authentic 'lay' spirituality. This is a book you don't want to miss."

Dick Westley
Author, *Good Things Happen* and *Redemptive Intimacy*

The
UNWILLING
Celibates

A Spirituality for Single Adults

JEAN SHERIDAN

TWENTY-THIRD PUBLICATIONS
BAYARD Mystic, CT 06355

Twenty-Third Publications/ Bayard
185 Willow Street
P.O. Box 180
Mystic, CT 06355
(860) 536-2611
(800) 321-0411

ISBN:1-58595-092-0
Library of Congress Catalog Card Number: 00-131184
Printed in the U.S.A.

Table of Contents

"Prophets are not honored in their own country. Truly, I say to you, there were many widows in Israel in the days of Elijah, when the heavens withheld rain for three years and six months and a great famine came over the whole land. Yet Elijah was not sent to any of them, but to a widow of Zarepath, in the country of Sidon. There were also many lepers in Israel at the time of Elisha the prophet, and no one was healed except Naaman, the Syrian."

On hearing these words, the whole assembly became indignant. They rose up and brought him out of the town to the edge of the hill on which Nazareth is built, intending to throw him down the cliff. But he passed through their midst and went his way.

—LUKE 4:24–30

Introduction

It is a warm June day in Oregon and I am sitting happily in my daughter's backyard enjoying the sun and reading Dorothy Day's autobiography, *The Long Loneliness*. I am so enchanted by her words and stories and by her facile writing that the pages fly through my fingers. But mostly I am captured by the honesty with which she reveals the events of her life. I am reading now about her houses of hospitality in the period following World War II, when suddenly my attention is arrested by the following sentence.

> The voluntary apostolate was for the unwilling celibate and for the unemployed as well as for the men and women, willing celibates, who felt that running hospices, performing the works of mercy, working on farms, was their vocation, just as definitely a vocation as that of the professed religious.

In one swift moment Dorothy, skilled wordsmith that she was, has completed a task which I, in twenty years, have been unable to accomplish for myself. She has put a name to my "station in life."

Married for twenty years, suddenly left, and subsequently divorced, I had lived the next twenty years trying to redefine myself in a world that had no definition of me. My family of origin hovered anxiously, hoping that every relationship I entered into would be "the one," that surely I would soon be safely removed from my limbo state and returned to the legitimate one of marriage.

1

(I hoped so too.) Society pegged me as a divorcee, as "single," and tried to entice me into what were for me, a child of the fifties, weird mating rituals. My children, thank God, let me be, but they grew up and went away, taking with them their noisy and joyful society.

And my church, my beloved church, had not known what to do with me either. I found myself no longer on the playing fields, one of the team, but relegated to the sidelines, marginalized. She never ostracized me, but neither did she hug me to her bosom as she did her married people and her young single people whom she hoped might one day embrace the life of a priest or professed religious.

Only in recent years have I come to some sort of peace with the circumstances of my life. Now retired and a grandmother, I can contemplate with pleasure and gratitude a serene life filled with family activities, creative pursuits, and volunteer opportunities. In short, I have finally come to accept the life I have so reluctantly led.

But not until this moment in the sun did I finally know who I was and who I am. I am one of Dorothy Day's "unwilling celibates."

Who Are the Celibates?

An odd juxtaposition of words, these—unwilling and celibate. I know who celibates are; that's obvious. They are the church's professed religious women and men, its monks and nuns, sisters and brothers, and priests. Then there are the widows and widowers. But are they celibate? Always? And what about the divorced, like me, and the never-married? What about gays and lesbians? How many are celibate? How many aren't? Are they always? Are they by choice? Do they embrace their celibacy, or endure it? Do the divorced, the widowed, the never-married, the gay and lesbian even think about it, whether they are willingly or unwillingly celibate? And if one is not celibate what is the flip side of the coin, what is one called? I scratched my head, but could not retrieve a word to describe the opposite.

Finally, I opened the pages of my trusty thesaurus and looked up the word. Synonyms such as abstinence, constancy, chastity, modesty, elegance—lovely words—presented themselves. But what about the opposite? Tracing one of the synonyms, I came up with this list: self-indulgent, unrestrained, profligate, wanton, promiscuous. I literally drew back, startled, almost as if I had been slapped in the face. Wow. Now there was a message. Little wonder that the church was disinclined to deal with the "uncelibate." Such people, clearly, would be untrustworthy if not downright dangerous. I nearly blushed for shame.

I began to wonder why I was spending so much time on this question. What does it matter if one is celibate or not, or if one's celibacy is a willing choice or a default in today's sexually open world? So what?

The answer is that it does matter to people like me, professed and practicing Roman Catholics, it matters a lot; for lifestyle strongly affects the way in which one is perceived by the church. From my place on the edges, I have seen her look fully, openly, and lovingly at her married members, her professed religious, her widows and widowers, but lower her eyes when she looks at me and others like me who are not safely contained within the bonds of a marriage contract, who, quite possibly, may be sexually active in an "illegitimate" way.

Consciously or unconsciously, she makes those of us who do not match these neat categories feel like outcasts. Church bulletins on any given Sunday, for example, carry announcements about meetings for the recently bereaved, for parents of children being initiated into the sacraments, for families, for unmarried singles who might have a vocation to the religious life. There are dinner dances and hay rides and ski trips, and the signs say, "Come one, come all," but the message is clear. If the unmarried adult, the young single parent, the lesbian, the gay, do not show up, they will not be missed.

True, ministry to the divorced, single, remarried, and widowed (SDRW) is active, and I have been to these meetings over the years. But what I found there was a clear division between the widowed and the divorced, the "good" and the "bad." At one meeting I attended I was told that the divorced met separately from the widowed and that I should go to their meeting instead. Widowers do not attend SDRW meetings for very long.

We Are Disenfranchised

Again, I wish to repeat that I do not believe it is the intention of the church to disenfranchise us. But she does. Why this is so I am not exactly sure. It may simply be a fallout, a byproduct of the church's discomfort when it comes to sexual issues. It may be that she is embroiled in too many internal struggles at this time (not the least of which, I might add, is her inability to define and model a healthy sexuality for the faithful) and, consequently, unable to confront an issue that may seem irrelevant and even impertinent to her. There may be other reasons; the net has many holes.

In her employment of benign neglect, however, she drops a veil of illegitimacy over her less favored children, children who are already deeply wounded. This is a sad situation for all involved. The church suffers because many of us drift away, and when we do, we take with us considerable charisma and financial power. We single adults suffer because we need as much support and affirmation as possible in a world in which few affirm us. It is not only about the church.

Families do not affirm us; their question always seems to be, "Met anyone interesting lately?" Then, after a few years, they lose interest and relegate the unmarried person to a status somewhere between loser and profligate, depending on their individual perception of the single state. At this point in my personal history, my mother laughingly asked me what I thought was my "fatal flaw." The implication behind her question—that I had somehow failed—deflated and wounded me.

And families are only a part of the treacherous highways and byways trod by the single person. Some of our own kind, others like ourselves, will prey upon the particularly vulnerable, offering a cheap imitation of love although incapable of fulfilling glibly made promises. Without the support of an intimate partner, without a grounded sense of self-esteem, in pursuit of genuine permanent relationships, we may become victims of this predatory behavior time and time again. After a while we may turn inward, become bitter, and set up barriers to intimacy. Consciously or unconsciously, we decide to live life at the edges, avoiding active engagement with those who have wounded us, crawling along sideways like a crab, getting somewhere perhaps, but not very quickly and not very directly, unsure of our destination. Living on hold and killing time waiting for Ms. or Mr. Right to appear, we reduce our opportunities to grow and develop personal power.

Not the Only Hazards

And these are not the only hazards the single adult encounters. Modern culture also conspires to undermine our morale. We live in a "material world," awash in commercial enticements. They subvert and agitate the soul by providing more things to buy, which encumber, and a surfeit of things to do, which overstimulate. Young professionals and the retired are especially vulnerable. Seen as a lucrative market segment, they are bombarded by the advertising world, defined only by their usefulness as consumers. Upgrade your wardrobe and your technological toys, take another cruise, buy a second home.

Those who do buy into the messages from the media and other commercial interests provide us with caricatures: the old man who roams the beaches, over-tanned and musclebound; the middle-aged man who prides himself on his prowess at the singles party and on the cruise ship; the harpy woman, keeping up with the latest fashions, tilting at windmills, fighting career wars, or involved to an obsessive degree in the lives of her children and grandchildren. Many others, unable to compete financially, fall into mild depressions wondering why they haven't "made it" and questioning the meaning of their lives. (This, of course, is a universal problem, I hasten to add.)

While there is little single adults can do to change the perceptions and attitudes of family, church, and society-at-large, they do have the power to change how they perceive themselves. They have the power to shrug off the timid—or bold—persona that they have assumed as a way to protect themselves. They have the power to refuse to tramp out their lives on a treadmill.

Instead, I invite single adults to take a bold step and embrace a lifestyle I call "focused living." This is a way of living that encourages and develops spiritual depth, personal effectiveness, and social consciousness. It demands the adoption of unique values and commitments. These include, among others: a habit of self-reflection, a commitment to deep prayer, participation in intentional community, friendship with silence and solitude, proper balance in work, the study of sacred and spiritual resources, a preferential option for the poor, reverence for one's body, home as a sacred place, hospitality as a way of life, stability in relationships, and disciplines in daily living, all of which culminate in the creation of a personal "rule." Adopting such a way of life, which is countercultural to say the least, is an intimidating and rigorous process, but stimulating throughout and highly rewarding at its conclusion. Once embraced, it will serve to liberate and empower people in ways unimaginable. Thus empowered, such individuals will make significant lasting contributions to worlds beyond themselves, worlds both large and small.

What this Book Covers

In the first four chapters of this book, I will describe through memory and reflection my own experience as a single person in relation to church, family, and society. It sets the tone for chapters 5 through 17 in which I present suggestions and guidelines for those who wish to live as intentionally focused individuals. Reflective living, commitment to prayer, and participation in intentional community form the grounding for the focused life as I see it. Reflective living is what Socrates was talking about when he said, "The unconsidered life is not worth living." And he was not the only one. Emerson said it, too—and Thoreau and other sages. You may have said it yourself from time to time. Jesus' own life is an example of reflective living; that is what he constantly prodded those around him to do, asking the same questions over and over again. What are you doing? What are you not doing? Why? Isn't it time to change?

This way of being is the subject of chapter 6. It suggests an unwavering and disciplined commitment to self-reflection and the development of a conscious interior life. For some, this is a natural inclination, for others an unpleasant, even abhorrent task. Nevertheless, it is an essential ingredient in any personal growth project. No serious endeavor can succeed without self-reflection.

Chapter 7 concerns prayer. In times past, laypersons were not aware of the many ways to approach God. Only the "tried and true," such as the rosary, attendance at Mass, and the prayers that were printed in devotional books were options. Now we understand that we can pray through nature, in our interactions with others, with our bodies, in silence, and in social action. There are many choices and we will consider a number of them.

Community, specifically intentional community, the topic of chapter 8, is a built-in benefit for vowed celibates, especially those who belong to religious orders. Married couples have a form of community as well, but for the unwilling celibate, community is often missing. Sadly, it is what we need most. Standing at the margins of the "official" church, the single adult envies those who appear to have community: the married, the ordained, the professed religious—and he or she wonders how to get there.

What we need to realize is that community is expressed in many ways and with many different intents. Some communities are loosely joined, and we fit into them by happenstance. We happen to belong to a certain family, workplace, parish, and local, national, or global community. Others are intentional; we decide to join with others in a mutually stated resolve to engage in a supportive relationship. This is the nature of the community we are looking for.

Chapter 9 is about silence and solitude, the floorboards if you will of the house of prayer. Only when there is sufficient quiet in one's life can the voices of God, the Spirit, and the Self be heard. If it is our desire to hear these voices, then there is no alternative but to invite silence into our lives. Television, the radio, and the flow of information from books, newspapers, periodicals, and the Internet must be controlled or reduced. These are the daemons of modern life and can easily overload and overstimulate us. Those who would create a focused life must censor all stimuli that agitate the listening heart.

In chapter 10 we turn our attention to our home space. Home for single people can be a storeroom for the castoff furniture of family and friends or the remnants of college dorm rooms. It can be a single room shared in an apartment with a changing cast of characters, or the place we stop off before going somewhere else. But it should be more than that, much more. Home should be the visual expression of our dreams and visions, a work of art expressed in color, texture, decoration, fragrance, in gardens, and table settings. Within our homes we can create a special space where we meet God in prayer.

It was Henri Nouwen who suggested to me the progression from solitude to hospitality which we look at in chapter 11. And it makes a lot of sense. Solitude settles us; once comfortable there, we begin to befriend our innermost selves and the God who dwells at our core. We become saturated with a peace that frees us to welcome others into our renewed private space. We find ourselves wanting to open ourselves and our homes to others, offering peace along with the casseroles.

Chapter 12 addresses the complicated issue of work. The question here, for the creator of a focused life, is the nature of one's work, and the amount of time and energy devoted to it. Too often lonely, not involved in the ordinary, time-consuming activities associated with family or married life, single people may find a certain solace in work and spend entirely too much time there. Instead, it can and should be put aside to make room for other essential aspects of life. In creating a focused life we become aware of how to bring balance into our lives and realize that our work is only one of the many important ways we use our time.

At the time of "profession," Benedictine monks and nuns make a commitment to one monastery for the remainder of their lives. This little known vow of stability is what we turn our attention to in chapter 13. Surprisingly, this commitment also carries meaning for our day. Although the exigencies of contemporary life will not allow most of us to promise to stay in one place forever, an examination of the concept of stability can make us think about some healthy ways of functioning within that reality. When many choose to be rootless, to reject what came before, to seek out the new and the unusual, and when society encourages this attitude, stability asks us to curb this impulse and to make an effort to stick with our commitments to a particular place, job, family, church, friend.

Chapter 14 is about study. Benedict incorporated into each monk's day a time for the study of sacred and spiritual literature, and we can do this too. There is much worthwhile material available in bookstores and libraries, not only in book form but on tape and video as well, and more to come on the Internet. To be committed to study is really to be alert to the many ways spiritual "information" comes to us.

Like Jesus, we live with and among, not apart from, human society. As a result, our spirituality must embrace everyone in our worldwide family; it cannot stop—even though it must begin there—with self-reflection and private prayer. The dilemma of how to become appropriately involved is a difficult one for middle-class Americans. In chapter 15 we will consider some of the ways.

Chapter 16 focuses our attention on self-discipline. While hair shirts and immoderate fasting are out of fashion today, and rightly so, it is also true that the authentically focused life is a disciplined one; living indulgently is inconsistent with the basic premise. There are some core disciplines that we should all observe: being sure that our intake of food and alcohol is moderate, getting proper exercise and sufficient rest and recreation, living as simple a lifestyle as possible. At the proper time and when it seems appropriate, some may want to add additional practices, such as observance of the monastic hours of prayer, or keeping the Sabbath in a more traditional sense.

Chapter 17 brings all the elements of the focused life together as I invite readers to create their own personal rule. Unique for each individual, it will incorporate whatever elements in chapters 5-17 that seem relevant or special to one's life situation and one's personal vision of the future. This is a matter of great significance, the soul's opus as it were, and should be undertaken reverently and with the support of one's intentional community and the guidance of one's spiritual director. Therefore, I suggest in chapter 18 that anyone who has reached this point in developing a focused life might want to seriously consider taking sabbatical time to make a specific life plan.

And when that great work is concluded, it is time to celebrate our new covenant with ritual and within the warm circle of our intentional community. Ritual makes the intangible concrete and calls upon God to consecrate it. It has been defined as words, gestures, and movements that communicate a message about the spiritual world. Either alone or with the help of our intentional community, we will design our celebration. In it we declare our intention to follow our own personal rule and name the promises we wish to make, our vows (chapters 19 and 20). Thus consecrated, we enter a new life.

So, join me on this journey if you wish, first through the pages of this book and then into action. There is much to do; the kingdom of God is waiting.

CHAPTER ONE

Social Life

A poignant moment in the gospels, and one that has always spoken to me, is this question Jesus put to his friends: Who do you say that I am? He must have been rattled by the recent scrutiny of the Pharisees and Sadducees, who had asked him for a sign to prove his claims of divinity, for he warned those who were with him to be watchful about their influence: "Beware of the leaven of the Pharisees and Sadducees." But he could not stop there; he needed to know something. What did the people themselves think of him, he wondered aloud, knowing that his disciples had their ears open to the voices in the crowds that formed around him. And he seemed to accept the answer— John, Elijah, or one of the prophets. But he was not satisfied; his soul cried out for affirmation from those closest to him, and he took the question still deeper. "But you," he pressed, "who do *you* say that I am?" And when Peter gave him the answer he sought, he was so grateful that he gave him the world.

We all want affirmation from those closest to us: our friends and families, the institutions we belong to, the places where we work. Jesus would be misunderstood over and over again by those closest to him and by the community in which he grew up. It was part of his life experience. The return to and rejection at Nazareth must have felt like a thousand stinging arrows. Of course, it was not so much about what he was doing as about who he was being.

These stories told about Jesus, I think, are stories about us, the single adults in the church, the people who don't fit into neat lifestyle slots. Since leadership influences the people in the pews, neither do parishioners really pay attention to the single

11

adults who sit among them—or, sadly, not among them. So, in this part of our discussion we will consider the question of who the people we love say we are and examine some of the ways we, the "unwilling celibates," experience life within our families, parishes, and the culture in which we live.

Single adults in today's society operate in a kind of "demimonde," a word defined in Webster's as "a class of women on the fringes of respectful society" or "a group engaged in activity of doubtful legality or propriety." It recalls a time, principally in European cultures, when it was customary for prominent men to keep mistresses. A culture grew up around these women, many of whom came to exert powerful influence in the arts and politics. Nevertheless, their place in society was unquestionably tenuous and their claims on their benefactors unsanctioned; the stories of pathos and tragedy that often accompanied this half-life are a part of literary folklore.

I am playing a bit when I use the word to describe the place of the single adult in our times, but the word itself, which translated means "half-world," is evocative. Those who inhabit a half-world are not fully honored by the dominant culture; thus I find it applicable to our situation as single adults in contemporary times. Let me introduce you to some people who inhabit the demimonde. Perhaps you are one of them.

Who Are These Single Adults?

Nancy is a school guidance counselor in her late thirties, a dynamic woman with a vibrant personality. Too vibrant perhaps? Her several relationships have been with quiet men, one of whom was a candidate in a religious order for a few years. Being a deeply spiritual person herself, Nancy thought this would be an ideal relationship; after all, she told a friend, she had been hoping to find someone "tall, dark, and spiritual." Her boyfriend was all those things, but the relationship didn't last.

She prayed through her anguish and finally gathered herself together to realize her dream of buying an ark of a Victorian house in an old city neighborhood. She would like to see it filled with children running up and down the stairs, but that dream is fading. On weekends, she runs it as a bed and breakfast. Sometimes she is able to get to Mass in the big old church on her block, the same parish where she made her first communion and confirmation.

James is a young man in his early thirties, and like his brother who recently died, gay. He acknowledges his sexual orientation and bears his crosses with grace and composure. Too wounded to attend the church of his childhood, he finds spiritual sustenance in the company of his family, who are supportive of him, and his friends in the gay men's choir. He always says that he misses church and remembers with a sense of loss the feeling of belonging he felt there as a child. A shy person, he tentatively and hopefully waits for the appearance in his life of someone to love.

Ellen and her boyfriend have an on-again, off-again relationship that keeps her on edge. She is uncertain about adopting, something she has always wanted to do, but, between renovating the house she bought a year ago, commuting long distance to work, and keeping up with her difficult relationship, her life is pretty complicated.

Linda and Jane are career women in their mid-thirties. Although they live in the same cozy neighborhood, they do not know each other. While the men to whom they were once engaged now have new girlfriends, Jane and Linda are in relationships with the houses they have just bought. They find comfort in hanging wallpaper and selecting fabrics for the curtains they will put up in their living rooms. They are "getting back to religion" and thinking about going to the Catholic church in their neighborhood someday.

Rosemary and Mike are not long out of college. Brought up in traditionally Catholic homes and educated in Catholic schools and colleges, they feel a little lost in a world that seems to have no spiritual grounding. Both considered religious life for a time, but eventually rejected the idea. Like their friends, they date, but often find that they are considered "prudish." The church they sometimes attend in the city where they work—one is a teacher, one works for an agency that provides support for refugees— seems strange and boring after the lively liturgies they attended in college. It's a lonely time for them, but they don't know where to look for support.

Charlie is recovering from alcohol addiction and the termination of a long-term marriage. He has recently moved into an apartment and is struggling to furnish it from what remains of a meager salary after he has paid his rent, car loan, and other basic necessities. His children live elsewhere. On some Sundays he makes his way to the Catholic church in his neighborhood, but there, looking around at all the married couples and young families, he feels even more sad and lonely. It's better, he tells his AA group, for him to take a walk on the beach or hang out in a coffee shop and read the paper.

Terry lives in a condominium very near Charlie's apartment building. Her life, unlike his, is very tidy. She has been an office manager with the same firm for twenty years and spends many evenings at her computer preparing reports and agendas. She travels quite a bit as an officer in her professional association. Her only regret about her life is having to board her dog, Tyke, whenever she travels. Tyke provides her with a lot of love. Between taking her for walks, watching videos, and having a few glasses of wine on weekend evenings, the time goes pretty quickly, she says. If she's in the mood, she may catch a Mass on Sunday, but more often than not, she reads the paper and watches news programs. Keep moving, that's her motto.

Sally spends most of her time with her five-year-old Sarah, the joy of her life. She never married Sarah's father, and now doesn't know where he lives, but she has been able to make ends meet by taking temp jobs. She teaches yoga, her real love, two evenings a week. Men don't often come into her life, but there have been one or two hopeful relationships; one lasted two years. After it was over, she buried herself in her work and forgot. Maybe someday, she speculates when she allows herself the thought. Sarah will be making her first communion in the spring. Sally goes to the parent meetings, but is shy about saying too much. People may want to know more about her than she is prepared to tell.

Joe is in his sixties and is a widower. He is no longer interested in finding a soulmate; the several relationships he has had since his wife's death ended unhappily and he doesn't want to jeopardize his serenity again. After retirement, he moved to the city to be near two of his children, but he wants to find friends his own age. He goes to the coffee hours at church, but everyone seems to be married, and he often leaves there feeling lonely and depressed.

Nancy and James, Ellen, Jane and Linda, Sally and Charlie, Rosemary and Mike, Terry, Sally, and Joe: at times celibate, at times in intimate relationships, all practicing their faith to one degree or another, all struggling with loneliness and sadness, questions of identity, masking their pain in indifference or addiction to work. And the irony of it is that they all belong to the same parish but don't know it, the church on the block with Nancy's bed and breakfast.

Living in a Half-World

In the first years after my divorce, I came to the slow realization that I lived in a demimonde of sorts. After I had lived in my new community for a year, I decided to give a Christmas party and invited some of the people I had met as I walked the dog or traipsed around the village with my children. It was an enjoyable evening and I paid no particular attention to the fact that one of my neighbors had come to the party without his wife. Later, however, when he began to stop by alone more frequently, I did begin to pay attention. He felt compassion toward me, but wished to express it romantically. So much for socializing.

When I did start to date, it was in the hope of returning to married life with all its requisite expectations—the obvious comfort and solace of having a companion and having more opportunities to be a social presence in my family and my community. But I quickly learned, that to the families of the men you are dating, to their friends and colleagues, you are "the girlfriend," probably one of a string, one never knows.

Soon I realized that I had to put away any hope of belonging to the coupled society in the town. Not only was I excluded from their gatherings, but the wives were cautious about developing friendships. I didn't blame them; when I was married, I knew few divorced women and those I did know were not included in our social life. But it was a bitter pill to swallow when I realized that I was on the other side now and simply did not "belong" any more. The friendships to which I had access were among the group of single people who lived in the town.

I struggled for a new identity even within my own family. My mother, of course, belonged to an earlier generation and had been brought up in kinder and gentler times in terms of premarriage customs. Unaware of the harsh realities of modern life, she found it hard to believe, once she had accepted my status as a divorced woman, that I could not reclaim my position in society as a married woman, the only "legitimate" lifestyle she could imagine for me. Even when I was experiencing anguish in my relationships, she urged me always to forgive; understanding was always the woman's task. No matter how deeply I had been wounded, she encouraged me to overlook the pain and return to the relationship.

My brothers, too, expressed concern and gave me advice on how to conduct my social life, and my children worried about my "being alone," as if their constant presence wasn't enough. Eventually I "got the picture" and realized that I would have to add another task to the already pressing ones of beginning a career in mid-life and taking care of four children in a home without a father. I had to find a man. Little wonder that a therapist I consulted at one time likened my situation to that of a quarterback on a football team. There I was running down the field clutching the ball while the stands were full of people watching my progress. It was enough to make me want to quit the team.

"Have you met anyone interesting lately?" my mother would query during our phone conversations, meaning men, of course. "Are you getting out? Remember, you have to flirt a little." As my mother well knew, I had indeed met "interesting" people, quite a few of them in fact. They were interesting in many ways. One I met at yoga class and frequently at the local supermarket. Later, I learned that this was his "style"; he had discovered that, to meet women, one needs to go where women hang out. There was another who was so attached to the country club to which he had belonged since childhood that he wondered aloud one day if it would be possible for him to change to a new one if he moved to be near me. He would need to give it some thought. Another friendship ended when I discovered that this particularly interesting person, who had told me he was separated from his wife, was still living in their house, sleeping in the den. Yet another excused himself from a prior engagement because he had fallen for someone he had met at an astrology lunch. When I inquired what such a thing was, he told me that it was a group of singles who got matched according to the astrological sign under which they were born.

These are funny anecdotes, but a lot of unfunny things happened. In the process of bringing up four children I had missed the sexual revolution and the beginnings of the feminist one (although I had read *The Feminist Mystique* and particularly enjoyed the chapter, "Housewifery Expands to Fill the Time Available"). I had likewise missed the sixties revolution, the Twist, and Fleetwood Mac. Uneducated in the mores of the new "single" society which met me as I exited the door called marriage, and reeling from the wounds I had suffered in the process, I floundered badly. Eventually I found solace with the bird-watchers.

A Welcoming Group

My friend Joanne, whom you will meet later, took me to my first event, a winter walk to investigate mosses and what was left of bird life after the first snows of December had fallen. We drove a long way into the scruffy southern Rhode Island woods and found our way to a small building topped by a tiny chimney out of which billowed pungent woodsy smoke. The house itself reminded me of the witch's hut Hansel and Gretel found themselves trapped in, but it was different for us. Once inside, we were greeted with the warm smell of soup which was simmering in an old iron pot on a wood-burning stove and an odd assemblage of "swamp Yankees," a name applied to genuine locals in southern Rhode Island, and patricians, once the mainstay of Audubon.

The people in the room, six or eight at most, were for the most part in their seventies and early eighties. In the way of true Yankees—and true birders—they had known one another for years, but their welcome to us was warm and genuine. They were delighted to share their knowledge and love of the natural world with neophytes.

Sustained by bowls of warm bean soup, we ventured out into the surrounding woods and slowly made our way down the well-trod paths on which they had traveled together for many years. There I discovered what was to become a favorite pastime for me, eavesdropping on their reminiscences as I accompanied them on innumerable walks on beaches and in woodlands over the next few years. I heard of children who had moved on, succeeded in life, or met with calamity, the one or two who had died, the husbands and wives who were ill or had "passed on." Gently and carefully, they spoke to one another of these realities, not denying, only accepting, and then they moved on into the present.

"Look, there he goes. See, up there in the top left hand branches, about 10 o'clock." Another warbler for the list.

Welcomed without question into their company, I often escaped to them, fleeing the treacherous bog of "the single life" or the loneliness that engulfed me on the weekends when the children were with their father. They asked no questions, and I revealed little of myself. No matter, I think they understood. I wonder now, as I recall how they spoke among themselves of this person or that who no longer came on the walks, if other lost souls had filtered in and out of their midst over the years, taking strength for a time from their stability. Perhaps now others have taken my place in their ranks; I would like to think so. I still think of them wandering about the woods of southern Rhode Island exclaiming with delight over a hidden lady-slipper or the rare sighting of the fabulous ruby-crowned kinglet.

What this reminiscence tells me is that, in those days, there was no place for me to find safety and comfort. In the normal course of things a woman in her early forties, still young, should not be hiding out with octogenarians. She should not have to escape from life because she finds it treacherous and lonely. And she should not have to dodge the weekly phone call, "Meet anyone interesting lately?"

Our families, represented by my mother whose promptings reminded me of this story, often do us harm by putting unrealistic demands on us. My situation in life as a divorced woman grieved her, and she was compassionate toward me, but also unconsciously insensitive. Once, when I told her I was anxious because I was about to move into a small conservative community as a single parent, she consoled me by saying that I shouldn't worry, I was "no redheaded hussy." Oops.

Our friends, too, even if unwittingly, can cause us pain. I recall one instance particularly. I am at the summer home of dear friends sitting around a big old table having morning coffee and looking out over the lovely mess of a Martha's Vineyard marsh. "Would you like to see the blueprints?" asks Evelyn, speaking of the plans she and her husband Ted are developing for their retirement home. For a year now, ever since they started talking about retirement I had been hearing about this house. Spare and lean it will be, to grow as if organically in the middle of a lovely woods, the expression, the culmination of their shared visions, developed in a spirit of mutual love and respect for thirty years now, or is it thirty-five?

The heavy sheets are rolled out onto the table, the coffee cups pushed aside, and Evelyn indicates with her long graceful fingers how the kitchen and dining room will complement each other beautifully and efficiently, how the terrazzo floors will be heated, and, outside, how the Japanese garden will eventually continue the simple but elegant flow of their house and of their lives. I can hardly breathe I feel so sad, and I murmur my approval only softly because I fear I may burst out crying and spoil it all for them. It is a sadness that has been building ever since they began to talk about the house, exacerbated now by the recent failure of a relationship in which I had placed much hope.

It is not only our families, our friends, our social groups who wound us unintentionally; our own selves betray us, too. There is a story that goes around our family concerning a granny who lived into her nineties, and every day of her life up to the week before she died, she made an apple pie. The story was told to hold her up as an example of feisty determination, and I can see her still, a short stocky woman who lived, to enhance the story even further, in a third floor walk-up until her final days. Why this story has stuck in my mind I do not know, but I never thought it was such a wonderful tale. Didn't she have better things to do, I wanted to challenge the storyteller, than make pies all day?

Another story that sticks with me is about another older relative who discovered that she could place orders at her favorite department store—the women in my family love department stores—by telephoning at any time of the day or night. And she did. An insomniac after menopause, she ordered draperies, breadmakers and, one time, a rocking chair at two a.m. Poor woman.

A Remarkably Sad Story

At one time I worked in a college for older adult students, a lovely place to be, and there I met some remarkable people. One of them was a wonderful woman, then in her seventies, a career accountant throughout her long life. When she retired, she did something amazing, something that put her in the spotlight and made her famous. She got her high school equivalency diploma (GED). She had been taken out of school during the

Great Depression to be trained in accounting so she could support her widowed mother. She had never returned to school. Now she had—and with a vengeance.

When the newspapers got hold of her story, her picture was on the front page and the college approached her and said, Now, what about a bachelor's degree? Why not, she said, I have always loved to read, and so she enrolled. When she was finished with that, she went on to complete a master's degree. That's when I met her. She spent a lot of time in the library where I worked, and we became friends.

"Let's meet for lunch," I would suggest, but she was too busy.

"Wait until I finish the BA, Mrs. Sheridan," she said. (She belonged to the generation where anyone in the field of education was fitted out with all the appurtenances of authority; although she was twenty-five years my senior, she could never call me by my first name.) "Wait until I get through this master's."

The English department loved her. She was making it, and the college, too, for that matter, famous. Every time she completed a degree, the newspapers swarmed all over the place.

"Well, Agnes," said the chair of the English department, with a winning smile as she was awarded her master's degree, "what about a Ph.D.?" Agnes blushed, and agreed. What else could she do in the face of such an invitation from such an important person?

She was getting on in years now and everything was more difficult. I could tell that the reading was overwhelming her, and the prospect of writing a thesis was terrifying. But she persevered, and the great day for her "defense," that culmination point when the candidate for the highest degree in academia submits to an interrogation by the smartest heads in the business, finally arrived.

I cajoled a friend in the department to let me sit in on this great event, and there I found out what a silly business it had become. Agnes arrived befuddled and baffled and stayed that way. She had chosen to research Jane Austen because she liked her novels and related to the domestic life depicted in them.

Interrogated by the committee, she gave back the same answer to every question directed to her, that the family life depicted in Austen's novels was remarkably similar to her own, and it was not nervousness that made her answer this way. Agnes didn't get any of it; she was unable either to synthesize any of the critical theory she had studied or to apply theory to the many novels she had read. In all of them she saw only the one theme that spoke to her experience; she was unable to draw any further inferences. She was an accountant, after all, who liked to read.

Undaunted, the chair of the committee, beamed benignly on her, and she was roundly applauded when the awful hour ended. The newspapers loved her all the more, then, and she was toasted at banquets and even appeared on television.

Shortly afterwards, I went on to another position and left the school. I lost touch with Agnes. I heard a few years later that she had died. I wonder if she ever made the trip to Bermuda she had often dreamed of.

"Don't let your lives be driven by prayer wheels," said a well-known spiritual leader during a conference I was attending. "Break out of your old patterns, surrender to the spirit."

"What do you mean by prayer wheels?" someone in the audience asked.

"A prayer wheel," he responded, "is anything you can't stop doing. It is any habitual practice that keeps you from experiencing intimacy with yourself or another, or from experiencing the presence of God."

I think that these stories—of the pie lady, the shopper, and of Agnes the perennial student—stay with me because they speak of the entrapment of prayer wheels, an image that reminds me of the medieval torture rack. "Stop," I want to say, "you don't have to keep on doing things that no longer have meaning. Be new, be different." And I know that I would be yelling at myself as well. I, too, get caught up in compulsive behavior. Lots of people get spread out on prayer wheels—not only single people—but getting hooked on some one thing, I think, is a *particular* trap for those who are single. Too much time alone, left too much to our own devices, we risk becoming eccentric and narrowly focused.

That is not to say that many single people aren't happy and well-adjusted. Surely, many are. Without any sanctioned models from history, they are successfully designing new kinds of lives. But just as surely, many are not. They bury their disappointments and fears in activity, spend time exclusively with others who share their lifestyle, and at the end of most days, tired after long hours at work, they park their cars, walk up the stairs, and close the doors behind them to spend the evening and night alone.

No "Sunset" For Us

My moment with Evelyn and Ted was a difficult one for me because everywhere I look these days, especially in television advertisements and promotional flyers for financial services, couples my age are planning for retirement, setting off into the proverbial sunset together. I, however, and the other single people I know, are not. We are still struggling with issues of loneliness, with financial constrictions, and with the fatigue and energy loss of aging. It is a time, we commiserate with one another, when it would be awfully nice—as it would have been during any part of our lives—to have a companion.

But it is not only the older single person who weeps inwardly as contemporaries who are coupled move through the "normal" stages of life. Younger people in their twenties, thirties, forties, who wait on the periphery watching their friends marry, have children, and move into first homes, feel this sadness, and anger, too, even more acutely. I am especially touched by the plight of these younger people, whose numbers are increasing at a surprisingly rapid rate.

While planning a program for a professional workshop recently, I set up meetings with several women in their early thirties. Each had her own house, recently bought. I sat with them at their newly purchased dining room tables, and after our business was completed we talked about wallpaper and color schemes. These were little starter homes, situated in slightly shabby neighborhoods where the householders were primarily older couples and young beginner families. As I sat and talked with these single young women, I could look out the window and see mothers their age walking by with their babies in strollers. And I wondered about the attractive young woman sitting across from me. Why was she planning a trip with her sister's family? Why was she changing careers yet again? Why had she just bought a rare and expensive dog? Why was she talking about adopting?

This is the fallout of the sexual revolution, which has challenged the reigning phenomenon of the nuclear family and is now forcing us to accept new models of family. Rarely now do men and women in their early twenties marry and begin to have children. Not that young people do not meet and fall in love just as they always did. It's just that they do not marry; when troubles arise, they split.

Whether or not marriage would have held these relationships together, as some people speculate, is an interesting question. The generation of their fathers and mothers, my generation, divorced in great numbers, collapsing under the stresses of too much early responsibility (my interpretation). But of those who remained "intact," I wonder how many, either unaware of or not interested in the recent breakthroughs in psychological counseling, barely managed to hobble along, classically dysfunctional, but still putting on a face for the public to see—and for the churches to applaud. It begs a question for me. Should the church not be in the business of annulling families, just as it annuls those marriages that it declares invalid according to its sound definition? Just as there are marks of a true marriage, are there not also marks of a true family?

While it strikes me as primarily a woman's predicament, this remaining single when all around are married, it is also true that many men, young and older, are equally adrift and searching for a definition of their lives. My own son, at thirty-five, single and more or less adjusted to his present situation, will soon buy a house; he wants a backyard for his cat and intends to buy her a companion as soon as he is settled. He speaks more often with me now of other men in his age group and the experiences they share—the difficulties experienced as they grow older, of sharing living quarters with roommates, the anger they find in many of the woman they date, the children some of these women bring along with them into relationships. Better to take up golf. In our family, Mark and I have more in common with each other in some ways than either of us does with his three sisters, all of whom are married.

A young gay man I know seems to suffer as many women do, passively waiting and wishing for a loving relationship to develop, but uncertain about how to adjust his life in the void. As a Roman Catholic he is pleased on the one hand by the church's newly open acceptance of homosexuality, but confused on the other by its adamant refusal to condone its sexual expression. Furthermore, unlike the single heterosexual who may ultimately enjoy the sanction of the sacrament of marriage, gays and lesbians are not allowed to celebrate their unions within the church.

All three: the older divorced or never-married adult, the younger "single," the gay, the lesbian—are caught in a time warp. Never in the history of the world has there been such an awareness of the homosexual orientation and public acknowledgment of its numbers, never have there been so many middle-aged and older single people and so many young adults living unattached lives. And yet, church bulletins of all denominations continue to report on the business of programs and committees devoted to "family" issues, whether they be sacramental initiations of the children or the annual parish dinner dance. Elitist and exclusive, the churches plod on, living in a world that no longer exists.

A New Minority

The two young women I met while planning a workshop, my son, and myself are part of the "new minority," added to the cast of characters we met earlier in this chapter. Change my name to Joe, and I could be he; change Mark's to James—although Mark is not gay—and you have someone who is waiting passively for "Ms. Right" to come along. The two young women could be a younger Terry, a potential Sally, an Ellen. We are many. We struggle, mostly alone, with our issues and either keep up a good front or find a comfortable defensive posture. Both are masks behind which to hide our pain and isolation.

What we need, just as Jesus did, is affirmation, understanding, comfort, and the company of others willing to help us resolve our existential issues of isolation and identity. Yet, our church does not offer us a hand. Sure, there is the consolation of liturgy and the rich spiritual heritage of Roman Catholicism from which to draw sustenance, and sure, we can get involved in all sorts of committee and ministry work, which many of us do. But no one ministers to us; we are left to our own devices.

The antidote for isolation and all its many entrapments, of course, is community, but only community of a special kind. Families, friendships, and workplace relationships all constitute community and they support us in their unique ways, but what the single person needs is a community that promotes growth to wholeness by developing a heightened awareness of the spiritual aspect of everyday life. Strengthened by such a community of like-minded persons, the single adult is better prepared to withstand the vicissitudes inherent in the single state. Later, we will investigate more fully what this community could look like.

CHAPTER TWO

Sex Life

The portly priest sat back in his chair and pulled on a good cigar, rightfully enjoying a feeling of immense satisfaction. He and the other members of his committee were celebrating the successful conclusion of an intensive weekend workshop for the separated, divorced, remarried, and widowed (SDRW) ministry. I had attended the weekend and found it a healing one for me. Now I felt especially pleased to have been included in this inner circle, invited because I was a friend of one of the presenters. I was the only layperson there.

The priest blew some smoke rings, and smiling wickedly, said, "I guess you could call that oral. See, I can speak their language."

Their language. Their.

I will never forget the chill that went through me at that moment. With a sudden cold realization I saw that no matter how much lip service the clergy gives to the ministry to the divorced, no matter how hard they try to make us believe that they understand and respect the life of the layperson, they speak with forked tongues. For him to say, "their language" was to demean, to belittle, and, ultimately, to reveal his personal perspective on the single life.

The gulf is wide. And why is this so? Didn't Vatican II mandate that the role of the laity be elevated? It did indeed, but by some sleight of hand, the hierarchical model of clergy leadership did not change; it still remains intact almost universally, and with it, the implication that the celibate life is the better one. For this reason, and for none other, I believe, the church is unable to meet the laity on equal footing.

Even married people must sense the division. Take for example the comment made by a priest who visited the home of a parishioner. His host invited him on a tour of the house. When they entered the bedroom, the priest said, "And this is the playroom." It was an embarrassing moment for the host and displayed an adolescent self-consciousness on the part of the priest. Perhaps, to give him credit, he thought that he was displaying a sophisticated camaraderie. It sounded, however, more like something a thirteen-year-old would say.

Of course, there are those among the clergy who have determined, with the help of enlightened spiritual guides and thinkers, to engage in the difficult task of integrating their celibate state of life with an understanding of themselves as sexual beings. Kathleen Norris has paid attention to this process of integration in her book *Cloister Walk,* but even here, the women religious were apparently more willing than the men to reveal the stories of their true passages. Or perhaps the author was reticent about asking these questions of men.

For those many vowed religious who do enter the journey faithfully and with good intentions, there are myriad others who simply block it out. This, of course, is a strategy that simply does not work. Someone once said that there is no such thing as an unsexual person, that the celibate is either heterosexual or homosexual, there is no other way. If we try to disregard whole parts of our psyche, we are bound to become distorted in our behaviors. We have seen evidence of this in the horrors of pedophilia, but the subtle manifestations of sexual denial are also damaging. The issue hangs in the air, at best invisibly, often palpably. Many of my women friends say that they can never have true friendships, or even genuine conversations, with priests because of the posture of protective distance they maintain at all times. It's as if women are to be avoided, as if they are all temptresses.

A Nice Catholic Girl

We women used to view ourselves this way too. I have a memory in my head that never leaves. I have even given it a name and written it as a short story. I call it, "Adam and Eve in the Freshman Dorm."

I was a freshman in college in the mid-fifties, an outsider as a commuter student in an Ivy League school. Coming out of the protective environment of a Catholic education, I felt an additional vulnerability, and, certainly a resistance to any "challenges to the faith" I was told to expect from the powerful "secular" forces I would now have to encounter. My intention was to remain just as I was, a nice religious Catholic girl.

I met another like myself, a girl from out-of-state who lived in one of the dorms, and we spent many happy hours in her room discussing our new adventure. She had a boyfriend at home; they had gone to companion Catholic high schools, his for boys, hers for girls. They were "pre-engaged" she told me in a tone of voice which implied that I was not to inquire further about the implications of this agreement, and that she held secret information to which I was not privy.

Eventually, my friend had another secret; she thought she might be pregnant. She asked me for the name of my family doctor and he indeed did confirm the awful truth. We ruminated for hours about her situation and its implications as she went down the inevitable road to dropping out of school to marry.

Our thought process went something like this. It was all her fault. Over a long weekend, she had agreed to go with her boyfriend to a party at somebody's beach house. She should have refused, but willingly—she admitted it—she had entered into an "occasion of sin," and by her proximity, had been the provocateur, the cause of both their downfalls.

We both knew that, somehow, we as females were "temptations of sin" for our male counterparts and, therefore, responsible for helping them keep their passions under control. This had been instilled in us by our educators. It was a heavy responsibility and related somehow to "the curse of Eve," who was the conduit through which evil had entered the world—and stayed there. Just look at the results of her betrayal: sickness, death, pain, hard labor, all so potently mirrored in our own personal "curse," our menstrual flow and its attendant cramps. Only by conducting ourselves like Mary, the Virgin Mother, the one who had retrieved humankind from the consequences of Eve's betrayal, could we be redeemed. We carried a heavy load, and, unfair though it was, we deserved everything we got. But we could bear it. We had prayer, the sacraments, and visits to the Blessed Sacrament to sustain us. This, as Catholic girls, was our belief.

My friend went home between semesters and didn't return when classes began again. A month or so later, I received an announcement of her marriage. On the bottom she had written, "If I had it to do all over again...."

There is a postscript to this story. After college, I found myself living for a time in the city where she lived, and we visited. I had a new baby and she was, by that time, the mother of three. She looked good, perky and fresh-faced as I always remembered her, and she loved her children. She didn't say much about her husband. Years went by and it was our twentieth reunion year, and there were her name and address in the reunion booklet. Strangely, she was no longer in the city but living on an island off the Atlantic coast, a bleak and barren place in winter, a bustling resort community during the summer months. I called her up.

The voice on the other end was hearty and rich just as I remembered. She had been full of laughter, and she still was, but there was an additional huskiness to it now. Cigarettes, perhaps? Was the slight slur in her voice an indication that she had been drinking? She told me her story. Having divorced "the jerk" after eighteen years of "hell," she had visited several of her children one summer when they had jobs on the island. She fell in love with the free life there, and stayed on to buy the restaurant/bar they were working in. In effect she "dropped out."

"It's my Bimini," she croaked with a gravelly laugh, referring to the sixties phenomenon of men who traded in their grey flannel suits for cutoffs and took off for tropical islands. But I knew that life on her island was no Bimini. Winters there were harsh, and the small population fraught with problems of poverty, domestic violence, and alcoholism. But better perhaps than being married to "the jerk."

She did not remember me; sorry, but my name did not ring a bell. And, no—another hearty laugh here—she was certainly not interested in going to the reunion.

Baffled, and not a little wounded by her lapse in memory, as she was fixed so clearly in mine, I hung up. But I was not finished, and when I next visited the island, I found out where her place was and went there. It was a grimy hole, a favorite on season and off with the "locals," and smelled badly of smoke and stale beer. A pool table dominated the room where a half dozen tables were set up for diners, and up a few stairs from that space, a long bar, famous on the island, stretched the length of the building and faced plate glass windows that overlooked the rolling Atlantic. On that July afternoon it was packed and noisy. I sat at a table and waited.

Her arrival was an occasion. She swept in the door, a full-bodied woman in a tent-shaped flowery dress, her grey hair still in the twenties bob she wore in college. An uproar of voices greeted her and she laughed right back and stopped briefly to enjoy the moment before she made her way to the end of the bar, patting the rear-ends of the stool-sitters as she went. Once in place she lit up a cigarette and took a sip of the drink which had been set there for her.

End of story. I did not introduce myself to her, and the few other times I saw her on the island on my infrequent trips there, she always seemed to be having a grand time with the other island residents; she had become something of a local character it seemed. When I returned one summer, I heard that, when she died of lung cancer during the winter, there was a great outpouring of affection at her memorial service.

Looking For Guidelines

When I was freshly separated from my husband, I was working in the library of a local Catholic college. Hoping that my husband would return, I was still not telling anyone about the crisis and, to avoid break-time chatter, spent quiet times browsing through the stacks. There I came upon a book called *The Sexual Celibate* by Donald Goergen, a Dominican priest. It addressed the efforts at that time, the mid-seventies, for vowed religious to come to terms with their sexuality. I know that I was grateful to find it as I was looking for some "Catholic" guidelines to help me in my new state in life as a celibate and probably, in all honesty, for some official sanction for masturbation. (What did "they" do? If "they" could do it, then so could I.) As I recall, I was disappointed in my search and had to endure, at least a few times, the ignominy of going to confession at the age of forty-two to confess a sexual sin.

My mother thinks that it is improper for girls to be on the altar as they may tempt the priest, likewise for women lectors and eucharistic ministers who have large breasts. When priests leave to marry, it is invariably the fault of some designing woman.

When I was a young bride and mother I was embarrassed to be in the company of my pastor because he, all powerful and all knowing, would obviously know that I was engaging in sexual activities. It was enough to make me blush. When I told a young priest of my acquaintance about the idea for this book and who it would be about, he whispered in my ear, "Don't forget to add some of us," and turned red all the way to the tips of his ears. Whatever shall we do?

Out of curiosity, I recently returned to a reading of *The Sexual Celibate* and was greatly rewarded. It is the most comprehensive, intelligent, realistic, and sensitive treatment on the subject of human sexuality that I, a layperson and not a student of the subject, have ever encountered. Scholarly in his approach, Goergen scans history and current research for cultural, religious, psychological, and moral attitudes and beliefs. He presents a viewpoint that makes sense for any sexual human (which includes all of us, of course, celibate or not) by separating the affective expressions of sexuality from the genital. (And, by the way, he writes about masturbation and suggests that depending on the circumstances, psychological health, and spiritual aspirations of the person, it is not necessarily sinful. In the copy I read, which was loaned from the library of a Catholic college, the sections on masturbation were heavily underlined. I guess people are still wondering.)

Throughout history, all religious traditions have alleged that the sexually active person (invariably designated as married) has neither the time nor the disposition to devote to the contemplative life, considered to be the only true expression of spirituality. Consequently, celibacy became a prerequisite of the monastic life and replaced martyrdom as the highest expression of Christian belief. There are few married folk in the sainthood.

Augustine and Paul, of course, are the scapegoats for critics of current church attitudes toward sex, but Goergen, in an impressive scholarly survey from earliest biblical times, to the gospels, to Paul and Augustine, points out how the cultures of the times have affected theological thought and attitudes toward sex. In the time of Augustine, for example, marriage was considered sinful by certain groups such as the Encratites and Manicheans. Thus, Goergen claims, Augustine, "in defending marriage, ...helped save sexuality from total rejection." Nice try, Fr. Goergen, but we later learn that Augustine also declared sexual intercourse, even in marriage, a sin unless its motivation was to procreate.

Goergen makes six major points as he concludes his discussion on theology and sexuality, and I think they are worth paraphrasing here. First, he says there is no evidence of a negative attitude toward sex in either the Old or the New Testaments. It is sin, not sex, which is to be avoided. Second, sexuality is not linked to procreation—until Augustine. Before then, it was seen as an expression of relational love. When linked to love, third, it is sacramental and, therefore, fourth, an incarnational expression of the coming Kingdom. Goergen closes his discussion of the theological aspects of sexuality by reiterating that neither abstinence nor sexual intercourse is valued one over the other, that what is valued is the constancy and the quality of the commitment.

He derives his final comments from Derrick Bailey's 1959 book, *Sexual Relations in Christian Thought*, in which he questions the validity of the vow of celibacy except in the most extraordinary—and temporary—circumstances. His claim is that celibacy "hinder[s] free and healthy partnership between the sexes," a partnership that is grounded in the details of the Genesis story. In the normal course of events, this human relationship may progress to the point of sexual expression, even outside of marriage. This is not an apologia or argument for "free sex," but for the validity of healthy—and I emphasize the word healthy—sexual expression. It is legitimate for celibates to choose their unique lifestyle of abstention, says Bailey, if they do not avoid this "free and healthy partnership" between the sexes. Somehow, however, the vow of celibacy has actually impeded rather than enhanced the potential give and take that would empower the church. This is exactly what lies at the heart of the difficulties that continue to surround the relationship between clergy and laity. Rather than making these relationships free and open, it has served to shut them down. The vow of celibacy, except perhaps for the monastic, has backfired.

Part of the dilemma lies in naming the vow "chastity," a word that has a different meaning from celibacy, although the two have come to be used interchangeably. As Goergen explains in his discussion of Aquinas and temperance, chastity is about temperance for both the sexually active person and the celibate. Celibacy is about a life without genital sexual expression. Married people as well as celibates are both vowed to the virtue of chastity, making it possible to talk about pre-conjugal or pre-celibate chastity.

If celibates, however, could embrace Goergen's thesis—a delicate and subtle one to be sure—that they can learn to express their sexuality in affective ways, much of our uneasiness could be overcome. Who has not been comforted by the twinkling eye of a priest or sister, the pat on the back, the warm hug, the complicitous wink? Such gestures give the message, "We are in this together. You and I are the same, equals, not different. We are both touchable." Too often, however, the message is the opposite and what we experience is standoffishness, hesitancy, a defensive holding back. *The Sexual Celibate* should be on the required reading list for all seminarians. Clearly, it isn't.

Intimate Human Creatures

The church is putting its head in the sand when it refuses to face the fact that its mature single men and women, old or young, gay or lesbian, are going to be sexually active. Not always, not, it is to be hoped, in a promiscuous way, but as an expression of their orientations as social, intimate human creatures. Once they find themselves in a relationship that seems to promise permanency, there are few who will abstain from sexual expression; it is, after all, the incarnation of love and hope embedded in the Genesis story. Thus has it always been, thus will it ever be.

But it is all too easy to make mistakes, often bad mistakes. In this day and age, the traditional supports that prevent many from making bad decisions have themselves crumbled. In this I include our families of origin. As a psychotherapy culture, we are only too well aware that fathers have failed daughters by not modeling good unconditional love, that mothers have failed sons, that mothers have misdirected daughters, that fathers have berated their sons or set impossible standards for them. Wobbling about in life with few good models and much misinformation, many of us are simply ill equipped to make proper decisions. I have heard this called "damaged intuition"; in religious terminology, it may be called an "uninformed conscience." Whatever it is, it causes well-meaning people to inflict untold harm on others unwittingly and others to be naive and gullible victims.

For most people, indeed for anyone who is not a saint, there will be times, when, for one reason or another, they fail to act rightly. They hurt another or they are rejected by another, sometimes both. These experiences can become patterns of repeated behavior for those in the single life. What is needed in the context of this reality, of course, is the exercise of good judgment, which only comes with maturity. It is our responsibility, then, to engage in thoughtful reflection about our personal issues, for that is the only path to wholeness. Only the whole person, or one who is on an intentional path to wholeness, can be a good partner.

The path to wholeness is most productive and efficient when accompanied by a spiritual guide or therapist, or both. Another less often realized consolation and support for the single adult is membership in an intentional community. It is my firm belief that, when we are comforted by the presence in our lives of others who are committed to giving us affectionate and caring guidance, we will be less likely to go off on unhealthy tangents, including painful love relationships. This is not about licking wounds; this is about being grounded in something genuine and real at the root of our lives, something that models right and wholesome love. Intentional community is where we can find it.

CHAPTER THREE

Parish Life

I trembled as I approached the priest after Mass on a sunny Saturday afternoon in late summer. He was closing the stained glass windows with a long hooked rod. I remember that his shoelaces were untied.

"I'm divorced," I blurted out after explaining that I would be moving into the community with my children and joining the parish. Best to put my cards on the table right up front.

"Oh?" he said in the absent-minded way I would come to know well. His kindly myopic brown eyes peered at me through thick lenses. "That's too bad. Well, just give your name to the secretary so we can send you envelopes.

"And don't forget to sign the children up for religion classes," he called to me as I left the church.

Piece of cake.

The next hurdle was the welcoming committee. I arranged to meet the current chair, a pleasant strait-laced young woman, in the parish hall after Mass on a Sunday. Surrounded by the din of parishioners who sat at round tables munching on doughnuts and sipping coffee, we talked about religion classes and parish committees.

"And what does your husband do?" she eventually asked as I knew she would.

"I'm divorced," I answered.

"Oh, that's too bad," she said, pausing only briefly before continuing to go down her checkoff list. I volunteered to facilitate a confirmation preparation class and looked around for an empty space at one of the buzzing tables. Finding none, I gathered up the children and departed.

Home free again.

"You ought to meet Joanne," said the priest, "she's divorced too." So I called her up. A bold and fearless person who joked about her "husband once removed," she showed me the ropes. We shared a lectoring slot and drove each other's children to choir practice and religion classes.

I thought it would be a good idea to get the lectors together to learn more about the Scriptures and pray together. Joanne was skeptical.

"It won't work," she said.

"Well, we could give it a try,"

"You'll see," she said.

We proposed the idea. Great, they said, but we must include our spouses, and we must have a potluck, and we really need to go to a house instead of a parish meeting room so there will be room enough for everyone. Someone's wife, since Joanne and I "had enough to do with our jobs and all," organized the potluck. She made sure that there were the right number of salads and desserts and main dishes. So we got together and talked about religious education classes and parish politics. After dinner one of the husbands started to tell jokes about married sex, so Joanne and I made a hasty retreat. We never did get to talk about Scripture, let alone pray.

"See?" said Joanne.

At the end of my first year in the parish I decided to go to the appreciation dinner dance.

"No thanks," said Joanne, "once was enough for me."

Undaunted, I looked forward to the first social evening since my divorce, put on my best dress, and showed up at the parish hall on the night of the dinner. Just like the coffee and dough-nuts social hour, it seemed as if everyone knew everyone else and no one knew me. Most of the tables were filled, but I found one with two empty seats and joined the three couples already there. The seat next to me remained empty; everyone, it seemed, had come in twos except for the widows, who were embraced by old friends, and me. I was warmly welcomed by the other couples at the table as they were also parents of children the ages of mine. We found common ground, and I was having a good time—until the dancing started.

Then the couples, one by one, abandoned the table to the dance floor and then to visits with friends at other tables or back to ours where they sat until the wives dragged the men out once more. Increasingly uncomfortable, I sat alone and tried to look interested in the shenanigans. Eventually one of the men at the table, a dancing fool who had exhausted the energies and good disposition of his wife, invited me to dance. He was a very good dancer (and so am I), and we stayed on the dance floor for quite a while. What a treat! I hadn't danced in two years and was having a wonderful time, until, coming up from a deep dip—we were doing a tango—I saw out of the corner of my eye the faces of his wife and the other couples at our table turned toward us with looks of consternation. Shortly afterwards, I excused myself from the festivities and scurried home. Cinderella leaves the ball.

"How was the Appreciation Dinner?" asked Joanne the next time we met.

"Oh, pretty good," I answered.

"Hmmm," she said.

Families Are Welcome

Years went by, and I found my way. But one weekend when the children were away with their father, I found myself at a Saturday afternoon Mass and in a bad mood. It was a sultry day in early September, hurricane weather, and the weekend had become long and lonely. "Welcome Back Sunday," announced the banner over the door of the church, and on the lawn outside sat booths set up by the parish committees. After Mass I wandered among them. The one with the "family life" sign over it caught my eye, and I went up to the man who was tending it.

"Do you ever do anything for single parents?" I asked, trying to look friendly but not really succeeding, not really trying. I could see that my question had startled him, and he looked away before answering. Sure, he said, all the activities were for anyone with children. I knew this to be true as I had gone with mine on a ski weekend the previous winter. The children had had a wonderful time—they speak of it still—but I was left to fend for myself while the couples who were there socialized among themselves. For me it had been an uncomfortable and unpleasant experience.

"But, do you ever say explicitly in your announcements, 'Single parent families are welcome'?" I pursued. Well, no, he didn't recall that they had, but he would bring it up to the committee. I would be happy to make a presentation to them, I volunteered. He took my name and phone number but I never heard from him again.

Only recently, the church had proclaimed a "year of the family" which I felt was an ill-concealed attempt to join the conservative backlash affecting the country at the time. I was deeply offended by the implication that the ills of our society could be attributed to the proliferation of "broken homes," of which my children and I were examples. Our home, like the home of my friend Joanne and her children and the homes of other single parents I knew, was a stable and secure place that provided love, intellectual stimulation, and proper supervision. Who was to say that "intact" families provided better environments for children than we did? How many of these homes were dysfunctional, even abusive; how many children were damaged by domestic hostilities? Why should the two-parent family be held up as the only model? Why was no respect shown for the extraordinary efforts good single parents were making to provide proper homes for their children?

I watched the bulletin for a few months, nudged the family life committee a little, but saw no offerings that specifically invited single parents. Finally, with the permission of the pastor, I placed an announcement in the bulletin inviting single parents to a meeting after a Sunday Mass. The new assistant pastor, who had written his master's thesis on the subject, agreed to attend as did the head of the adult education committee.

They straggled in one by one, all women, faces mostly new

to me. We went around the circle so everyone could speak. They were distraught, confused, sad, bitter. Nearly every one said that until she saw the bulletin notice, she didn't think the church cared. Some thought their children did not qualify to take the sacraments or enroll in religious education classes. Some expressed uncertainty about their status in the church, mistakenly thinking that the ruling regarding remarriage and excommunication applied as well to those who were "only" divorced. Some were grandparents, grieving at being separated from their grandchildren and worried about their religious upbringing.

One woman who had been divorced for many years and was a pillar of the church community burst into tears when she introduced herself and told why she had come. "I'm not bad," she wailed, "just because I'm divorced. I'm a very good person." These tears, this plea, after fifteen years as a eucharistic minister!

They wanted to talk further about what to tell their children about their place in the church, how to deal with visitations with the other parent, the need for support groups. There were many questions, many issues. We were ready to move ahead, on the verge of creating a vital link between this distressed group and a caring parish. But the opportune moment slipped past and was never recaptured. This is what happened.

First Father took the floor. He expressed compassion for their difficulties; after all he had done his master's work with them. To prove his sincerity, he opened his briefcase, removed the thesis, and began to read from it. He read, and he read, and he read. The children who were there got itchy and some of the women had to leave to meet other commitments; the group began to disperse, the focus, the energy was lost.

I met with the chair of the adult education committee to block out a "unit" for single parents. After our sixth turgid meeting, I pleaded with her. "Just get them together. Let them set their own agenda." But she had to present a plan to the parish council, something concrete.

Lack of Interest

I was scheduled for a sabbatical and left town before we had completed our task. When I returned, I read in the minutes of the parish council meetings that the project had failed. The reason: "lack of interest." Lack of interest? I challenged the parish council. Apparently, the adult education chair had called the few names we had managed to collect at our first meeting, was unable to find a meeting time and date to please everyone, and had left it at that. There had been no attempt to call another open meeting through a bulletin announcement. End of discussion. And so, these women continued to sit alone in the back of the church, hoping they wouldn't be singled out as "sinners." Or they did not come at all. And their children?

I reported the sequence of events to Joanne who wasn't coming to church much anymore.

"Why do you wear yourself out trying?" she said. "Nothing will ever change."

If you speak to most of the people still living in my then parish, they will tell you that everything is just swell. The Masses are full and the coffers are full, too. There are plenty of programs, good liturgies, lots of children enrolled in religious education classes. Most of the parishioners speak about and behave liberally toward gays and lesbians, and they feel compassion for the divorced or single.

But theirs is only one reality. Another is that these segments of the parish population are, in fact, marginalized, invisible for the most part to the mainstream who would not mind if they would just quietly slip away and mind their own business. Better for them, good Christians that they are, to include us with the widows and orphans of biblical renown and shower us with kindnesses.

I have heard that some parishes do have programs for single people. However, from what I have gathered, these are set up to provide social opportunities, and this is not a bad idea. Some of the other groups can be like battlegrounds; being with people with whom one shares a common heritage is more relaxing.

Opportunities for socializing, however, are readily available. If the parishes were to take on the loving responsibility of providing support and encouragement for single adults, I would suggest that they create opportunities for spiritual growth and community building. Spiritual growth helps to define us interiorly. Community serves to connect us beyond ourselves and helps us remain stable in spite of the fluctuations we experience in other areas of our lives. In an impermanent world, it is spirituality and community that endure. I will have more to say in later chapters on both these issues.

CHAPTER FOUR

Feeling Invisible

One day I discovered that I had become invisible. Although it happened twenty years ago, I remember it as clearly as if it were yesterday. It was a day in early January, and the flurry of Christmas activity had passed. Before that, in early December on St. Nicholas Day, my choice, the children and I had made our big move from suburban Connecticut to village Rhode Island. The hyperactivity of winding up life there, of selling the house and signing the papers (which ended the life my husband and I had shared with our four children, then aged eleven to eighteen), dominated every waking moment. Sleep was nirvana. In short, the past year had been nothing if not exciting.

But on this January morning, several weeks before I was to begin graduate school at the University of Rhode Island, life was calmer. I was standing at an upstairs front window watching the two youngest go up the street on their way to their first day of classes at the middle school. I watched as they stood waiting at the corner and then I saw the yellow flash that meant that they were safely on the bus. Suddenly, all was still and quiet. And for the first time in my entire life, I found myself alone.

My window faced the house across the street, a street so narrow that I could see my neighbor in this early morning hour, interacting in her living room with her two children, a baby and a toddler. Without feeling at all like a voyeur, I watched them for a few minutes, remembering my own experiences as a young mother, living a secure and happy life, times gone forever, and my eyes filled with tears. Who was I now? Not the contented young mother I had once been. Not a wife, that I knew for sure. And, with one child already in college, I knew somewhere in my heart, that the others would be saying their good-byes before long. My neighbor did not know me, no one in this town knew me, no one in the entire state of Rhode Island, except my mother, knew me. If I stood at that window until the children came home from school, no one would know it. No one would know if I were in the house or out of it, if I went to the store or stayed home, if I sat in a chair all day and stared at the walls, no one. Unless I went out and presented myself in some way to the world, I would cease to exist.

It was a frightening moment, and the fear of it has never quite left me. I see it now as an existential moment, one that all con-scious people will, or should, face at one time or another in their lives, even though it is a moment that can be postponed. Others have experienced such times: widows and widowers separated permanently from the mirroring person; divorced men who are facing not only the fact of separation from familiar relationships with their wives and children but also the daunting task of cre-ating domestic space for the first time; certainly gays and les-bians trying to insinuate themselves in the midst of families or work associates who deny their sexual orientations. How do they cope, how do they move beyond or engage with the exis-tential questions facing them?

Or do they? One can ignore or deny the moment by being in a new or demanding relationship, a busy work environment, or on a crowded cruise ship, or by moving. Being outwardly active can enable a person to push the moment back indefinitely. By keeping busy, many do not face it until they are well along in years, and even then some never face it, choosing instead to remain "distracted from distraction by distraction," to use a phrase from T. S. Eliot.

I think that single people, the "unwilling celibates" of our dis-cussion, if they are willing, meet the invisible moment early on. And it either makes them or breaks them. It breaks them if they flee from it and allow themselves to be prodded along by the demons of modern society, learning to keep up until they reach the point where they march along at the same frenzied pace as everyone else. It "makes" them if they can take a deep breath and slow down to the point where they can hear the "still, small voice of God" which is breathing as they breathe and telling them that they are not invisible, that, although others may not see them, God beholds them with a constant loving gaze. At this point, if the opportunity presents itself (and this should be the responsibility of the church, of course, to make these opportunities available) they can begin to intensify their spiritual journey and make community with others like themselves.

Others Who Have Survived

Another way to break through the invisible moment is to identify with those who have gone before, healthy models who have survived a similar experience. In our religious tradition, however, these are few and far between. As Mary Oliver McPherson pointed out in great detail and with some humor in her interesting book, *Conjugal Spirituality,* the overwhelming majority of the saints, our models of the spiritual life, were celibate and introverted, and many were professed religious: priests, founders of religious orders, virgin martyrs. Renunciation of sexuality, it would appear, is a significant prerequisite for the granting of sainthood. The few married saints in the lineup have little or nothing to say about their intimate lives with their spouses and seem to have escaped from married life as soon as they were able. And so we must canonize our own saints. I have found a few models, a few unwilling celibate saints.

For starters I propose Dorothy Day, founder of the Catholic Worker movement. She tells a story in a section of her autobiography, *The Long Loneliness,* called simply "Family" which speaks eloquently to me. A priest once told her that her views would be taken more seriously by the church if she were a married woman. This comment unsettled her, but she apparently took it at face value, as she responded by saying, "it gave me an excuse to dally with the idea of marriage." Then she goes on to give an anguished apologia for her lifestyle as the single parent of her beloved daughter, Tamar. "But I *am* a woman of family," she said, "I have had husband and home life—and I have a daughter...."

Continuing, she poignantly talks about her yearning to be married once again. "A woman does not feel whole without a man," she says, "and for a woman who has known the joys of marriage, yes, it was hard. It was years before I awakened without that longing for a face pressed against my breast, an arm around my shoulder." And yet, she managed to turn the realities of her own life into a vision that has transformed American Catholicism.

Thomas Merton, of whom we will speak later in the chapters on prayer and reflective living, himself fell in love in his early fifties. In his 1997 biography, *Something of a Rebel*, William Shannon writes about this affair. While in the hospital for back surgery, Merton met a young nurse and the two became deeply attached. It was a time of wild joy and painful anxiety, and Merton experienced the whole gamut. We know, of course, that the relationship eventually ended and that he renewed his commitment to the monastic life. "If only you and I were possible," he wrote for her in *Eighteen Poems,* making one wonder if he willingly embraced celibacy thereafter.

Dag Hammarskjöld, the Swedish Secretary-General of the United Nations who died an untimely death in a plane crash in the Congo while still in office, is someone whose life has always intrigued me. I see him as another model for a single life lived in an intensely focused way. Although he is best known for his life of duty and self-sacrifice in the public interest, he left behind a journal, *Markings,* which added a little-known dimension to his person. In it he revealed his passion for the interior life and his deep faith in God. At the time of his death he was in the process of translating Martin Buber's seminal book on communication, *I and Thou,* into Swedish (a copy was found in the plane wreckage), and he had several times visited Buber in Israel.

While it was speculated in an unkind way that Hammarskjöld was homosexual, his reasons for remaining single were as he said publicly. Having seen his mother suffer from the long absences and preoccupations of his civically committed father, he early on determined that, should he choose public life, he would forgo marriage. Whatever we understand or will come to understand about his sexual orientation does not bear on the force of his life and the work he accomplished during it. What is essential is his courage in the face of depression and a consuming loneliness. Only with the help of God, he said, was he able to put aside persistent thoughts of suicide.

Hammarskjöld's life is a testimony to the powerful effect a single person can exert even without the supportive presence of an intimate relationship. He found his strength in the society of friends, in his love for the mountains of his native Sweden, in his superb athletic prowess, in his work (which he considered mission), and in his deep belief that God was intimately present in his life.

Models from Scripture

In Scripture, too, there are a few excellent models from which to draw our lessons. One of my favorites is Hannah, the mother of Samuel. Although she was not celibate—she was the wife of Elkanah and was to bear many children—she, too, had an invisible moment through which she entered upon a powerful new turning in her life. Her self-esteem at a low ebb because she had not conceived, she went to the altar of God to pray. There she poured out her grief, railing at God in silent agony, only moving her lips. Eli, the priest, observing her behavior, thought she was drunk and admonished her.

"How long will you go on behaving like a drunkard!" he said. "Put away your wine."

Hannah then spoke eloquently and boldly to Eli. "You are no person of authority," she said, "nor is the divine presence or the spirit of holiness with you, since you have presumed me guilty rather than innocent"—an impressive retort from someone who had until then been a silent woman with a victim mentality. When she returned to the synagogue after the birth of Samuel, Hannah spoke with dramatically improved self-assurance in words that became the basis for Mary's "Magnificat" at the time of the Visitation. Through her trials and tribulations, and her humbling, Hannah had emerged as a prophet. (These thoughts are derived in part from Marcia Falk's chapter on Hannah in *Out of the Garden: Women Writers on the Bible.*)

What does Hannah, a wife and a mother of many, have to say to the unwilling celibate? That silence is no virtue, that God always helps, that one's agony can be transforming, that one can emerge from trials with an awakened social consciousness.

And dare we say this, do we blaspheme, when we wonder if even Jesus may have assumed that he would one day return to Nazareth to live in the heart of a family? Many of the apostles and disciples certainly, having put aside their family relationships for a time in order to follow Jesus, eventually returned home to embrace their wives. But these are mere speculations, not entertained by the church.

But who do you say that I am? Jesus asked of his intimate friends. And he got the "right" answer from Peter—that time anyway. I think he must have breathed a sigh of relief; at least one person saw him as he saw himself, at least in that moment.

Did Jesus, I wonder, ever have an invisible moment? If he did, when did it occur? At Nazareth? In the desert? I think it would have occurred early on, sometime around the Wedding at Cana, the event when Mary pointed out to him that he had outgrown the life he was leading. Maybe he was reluctant to move away from that, maybe he knew that the good times were about to end. Somewhere around that time he went to John to get baptized and was publicly affirmed by God. But the moment of glory was brief, and almost immediately he went off into the desert either literally or figuratively, and faced his existential fears. Perhaps that was Jesus' invisible moment.

What intrigues me about this story, among many intriguing elements, is that, of all the stories told about Jesus, this is the only one that could not have been witnessed. It must have been Jesus himself who told it to someone he trusted. It was a part of his story, and he needed to tell it, just as we all have to tell our stories, especially the parts that have terrified us. Perhaps in the telling of it, he rendered himself once again visible.

Like us, Jesus looked for confirmation: from family, friends, the people and institutions of his culture, his religion, and found that it was limited at best. He did have the good fortune of having a loyal and believing mother and a supportive and affirming father. And Jesus' belief that he was fulfilling a mission ordained by the God with whom he had a personal relationship, was sustaining. God was more often in close proximity for him than far away. Despite the differences between us and Jesus, we can nevertheless, look to his life as a model for our own.

So what were his strategies for surviving life as a misunderstood person living on the periphery of his own religion, family, culture? I think there were three. First of all, he was intensely interested in the meaning of his life, eventually focusing on a clear vision of what it was all about. Second, he worked hard to provide himself with community. He had several purposes in this, to teach, of course, to ensure the completion of his mission after he was gone, but also to sustain himself emotionally with the comfort that comes from an intimate group. I don't think we can emphasize too much the place community had in Jesus' life. This aspect of his life, I believe, equals in importance any moral or theological lessons he preached. Because he did not preach it, *per se,* because it was his lifestyle instead, we tend to overlook its significance. But for me, it is a paradigm of the nature of God incarnate, and it demonstrates how God wants us to be in the world. Third, of course, Jesus never ceased to pray whether it was the prayer of quiet or the prayer of action.

We will explore these three strategies: reflective living, prayer, and community in some depth now. They are the foundation of a model for single adults that I call "focused living."

"But who do you say that I am?" Like Jesus, we care about the answer, we want to be known by those we care about as we are known by God. But before we can ask the question of others, we must know the answer ourselves. This then is our starting point.

CHAPTER FIVE

The Focused Life

I love the Scripture story about the cure of the blind man because it is so much closer to reality than most of the miracle stories. Jesus put spittle on the man's eyes then laid hands upon him and gradually the man could see. The telling of the story shows us that these things take time. It takes time for someone who has been blind to see clearly, for someone who has been laid up to walk with strength and confidence, for someone who has been abused or neglected to trust again. And this story also speaks to me in a very real sense about the process of coming to self-definition, of finding a focus for our lives. The process of revisioning oneself, or regaining a clear vision that was lost, is a slow process requiring patience and determination.

"Focused living" is a term used by Teresita Weind, S.N.D. de N., in a 1995 interview with Dick Westley. At the time, Sr. Teresita was running the Sacred Heart House of Prayer in an inner city neighborhood in Saginaw, Michigan. It was an around-the-clock commitment, very active work, and presented a special challenge for her, as she preferred the contemplative life. She had come to an acceptance and, indeed, an enthusiasm for this intensely public lifestyle, however, by embracing it in a "focused and attentive mode, the opposite of which is agitation." This she calls "focused living."

My friend Peter Mark Roget offered me additional insights on the word focus and its meanings. Focus, he says, is "a center of consciousness, a polestar, a center of attraction." These words put me in mind of Carl Jung's and Thomas Merton's vision of the interior life, the absolute "center of attraction." Every human consciousness, they say, is on a quest toward wholeness, a quest

51

that requires us to go deeply within ourselves in search of our center. Merton calls this center the True Self. Here is how he defines it in *Conjectures of a Guilty Bystander*.

> The True Self is the hidden and inner self, the creative and mysterious inmost self, the real self, the deepest most hidden self, the self beyond observation or reflection, the self that can never be an object or a thing but only a "Thou," the self without biography or history, the self that cannot become but simply *is*. That which is deepest, most original and most personal to me. God's "I AM" continued in me.

This self is different from the ego, that part of ourselves developed as a defense mechanism or a strategy for success, that we choose to show the world. We develop the ego in response to the influences of family, culture, education, childhood, and adolescence, all of which contribute to a distortion of the essential person we were at birth, the "original," untampered-with ideal God had in mind at the moment of our creation. In order to move back into our truth we must crush the ego. To put it in milder terms, we must find ways to integrate all that has had an impact on us with our true center. If we choose to enter this process, we will emerge at the end, not as innocent babes, but rather as the mature expression of the "promise" we were at birth.

So, if that is what it is like to be "in focus," what does it mean to be "out of focus"? I think it means to see as the blind man saw. One translation has him saying that the people looked like sticks walking; only with time and more healing was he able to see what they really looked like. Roget places "out of focus" under the heading "Invisibility." (Remember invisibility?) Being "out of focus," he says, renders one "indistinct, unclear, indefinite, faint, pale, feeble, weak, dim, dark, shadowy, vague, obscure, unrecognizable, confused, blurred, fuzzy, hazy, filmy, foggy, not quite visible." The blind man's vision was out of focus, his view of the world around him distorted. He could almost see, but not really, not yet.

This, I believe, is how we are at times in our lives. Our vision, too, is out of focus. We live as if in a haze and mistake distortions, of ourselves and those things and people outside ourselves, for reality. Wouldn't we prefer to be the opposite: "distinct, clear, obvious, evident, well-defined, conspicuous, prominent, pronounced, in bold relief, well marked?" Wouldn't we prefer to be visible?

We single adults, I believe, should plunge into life in a wholehearted and wholesome way and develop a unique style of being in the world. By seizing the opportunity to design ways of being that are consistent with our unique personalities and gifts, and at the same time complementary to religious tradition—in other words, to take on the creative task of sanctifying our lives even if others won't—we can transform our lives. Focused living is a holistic integration of body, mind, and spirit, and I believe it is the solution to the problem of self-definition so common in single adults, whether young or old, never-married, divorced, widowed, gay, or lesbian. If practiced faithfully, I believe it will gift its creator with a self-image strong enough to withstand the wounds inflicted intentionally or unintentionally, by family, friends, society-at-large, the workplace, the church, even one another. It promises the achievement of personal fulfillment, meaning the actualization of the potential God had in mind for each of us at the time of conception. Ultimately, it will reward not only the person, who will have attained true Selfhood, but larger worlds as well, for the self-fulfilled and spiritually evolved person has the power to contribute in a powerful and unique way to the solution of the problems faced by the world today.

Not To Be Taken Lightly
This is a daunting task and not to be taken lightly or without support. Thus, I emphasize the importance of three grounds on which the focused life is based: healthy, guided self-reflection, prayer, and community. For the reflective life we are well advised to collaborate with a spiritual director and, perhaps, at times, a therapist. Prayer, the second base of our three-part

foundation, is any occasion entered into with the express purpose of encountering God. God, our loving parent, is waiting for
us to initiate these opportunities so as to instruct us through
them on how to attain our highest goal (and God's highest goal
for us), our True Self. In addition to being constantly reflective
and prayerful in our lives, serious seekers will want to join a
suitable intentional community or to create one if necessary.
Other aspects of the focused life, as I see it, follow from these.
They are: friendship with silence and solitude: the spirituality of
home; hospitality as a way of life; proper balance in work; stability in commitments; study of sacred and spiritual resources; a
preferential option for the poor; and disciplines in daily living.
All of these culminate in the creation of a personal rule of life
that includes some of the above as well as others which may
have more meaning for the individual. The model is an outgrowth of my own personal spiritual journey, and the parts I
have chosen to include are only suggestions. I offer them in
deep humility, which I understand to be the recognition of one's
own true Self as it puffs and then collapses like a sail at sea.

I have been and continue to be influenced by mentors, who
have guided me in my always-active search. These include
Benedict of Nursia, founder of the Benedictines; Thomas
Merton, the Cistercian monk whose writings have had a profound influence on twentieth-century spiritual and social consciousness; Dorothy Day, founder of the Catholic Worker movement; Dag Hammarskjöld, who lived the single state with grace
and style and a passionate sense of mission; and many others
who write today out of the various viewpoints alive and active
in the church, especially the contemplative tradition, the preferential option for the poor, and the small Christian community
movement.

Many if not most of these elements of the focused life are found
in the ancient monastic rule written in the sixth century by
Benedict of Nursia. Since then it has become the backbone of
communal spiritual life and has been written about, taught, and
discussed for centuries. Primarily, it has been practiced by con-

templatives and other deeply spiritual, mostly celibate, persons, and has not generally been considered relevant for the average layperson. I challenge this assumption.

Benedict, in reaction to the excesses of his time and place in history, invited others to live a communal life of prayer, work, and study, and he wrote his seventy-three item Rule to regulate this vision. Prayer was an all-day experience and so important to Benedict that he called it the *opus Dei,* the work of God. At prescribed hours of the day and night, his monks came together to chant the psalms, a custom still practiced in monastic communities today. Work in Benedict's time meant manual labor. Although today this is less and less the case—some monasteries are now about the business of data entry and creating websites—there is still intrinsic value in work of the hands. Study included the meditative reading of Scripture in a style called *lectio divina,* and also the reading of other holy writings, a body of literature that continues to grow. Benedict also saw to it that time for rest and recreation was built into the daily routine.

What one notices in reading Benedict's Rule is that it is about the stuff of life: when and how much to eat, when to sleep, what to wear, how to care for garden tools and kitchen utensils. Benedict attended to these matters seriously and in so doing honored all that is ordinary and human. He had an intuitive understanding that everyday mortals such as his monks were and are, such as we are, cannot "rise" to things of the soul and spirit unless they have first attended to things of the hearth and home and to the relationships of the people who live there with them. He believed that one cannot be open to the voice of God until the tangibles—the body, the home, the environment—are in harmony.

In her explication of Benedict's Rule, *The Rule of Benedict: Insights for the Ages,* Joan Chittister, herself a Benedictine, contends that it is an especially applicable spirituality for our times. This is because it attends to contemporary issues such as relationships, authority, community, balance, work, simplicity, and psychological health. Anyone who reads her book—which is a good idea because the original is burdened by the language of past times—will quickly realize that the Rule is not an esoteric and rigid formula for asceticism, but a wholesome acknowledgment that all aspects of life, including the relational, should be honored. What we can take from Benedict in our vision of the harmonious life lived in modern times by single people, are the concepts of prayer, work, and study, along with lessons on silence, stability, hospitality, and, of course, community.

The Influence of Dorothy Day

Another influence that has helped me develop my personal vision of focused living is the life of Dorothy Day. Born to intellectual middle-class parents, hers was a relatively stable and happy childhood, much of it spent reading and caring for younger siblings. From her earliest years she was an independent person, curious about her surroundings and willing to explore beyond her known world. While still a student, she began to lead a tumultuous "free" life, mostly in New York, but also in Europe, and was part of an elite circle of intellectuals that included Eugene O'Neill. By the time she met Peter Maurin, the French peasant savant whose ideas ignited with her own, her energies were depleted. Her late-in-life confidant, Eileen Egan, in her biography *Dorothy Day and the Permanent Revolution*, describes her at this time. "Dorothy was in her mid-thirties, a tall handsome woman with an illegitimate child, and behind her a free, bohemian life marked by several unhappy love affairs and a civil marriage before her common-law marriage."

The meeting with Peter, arranged by an editor from the intellectual Catholic publication, *Commonweal*, was a fortuitous one for Dorothy and one that turned her life around, according to Marie Adele Dennis in *A Retreat With Oscar Romero and Dorothy Day*. From that moment on, she said, she came to know her focus and lived out the rest of her life "in what seemed to be a profound integration of heart and soul, faith and good works, commitment to social justice and life in God. Dorothy was mother, sister, companion; worker, journalist, inspiration; radical activist and prophet." And yet, before this meeting, before she sacrificed an intense love because she chose to embrace Catholicism for herself and her daughter Tamar, and in the years following that agonizing decision, Dorothy was not the serene and dedicated person the world came to know. She was often in a state of anxiety and agitation. Like the blind man at Bethsaida, she saw her vision in a fragmented way, and years went by before all aspects of it became clear. In short, she was "out of focus."

Dorothy led a passionate life, and I think that is why she is an example for younger adults especially. Although she is remembered and revered for the accomplishments of her later years, it is the experience of her early years with which many young people today can identify. She was enthusiastically in love with life; she delighted in it and in her friends, her lovers, her family; she was ardent, spirited, eager to learn. Later, when she became the "author" of her life, this enthusiasm turned to zeal. Throughout the rest of her remarkable life, she modeled for us a robust extroverted spirituality.

Like many of us, Dorothy experienced a loneliness which at times throughout her life brought her to depression; she knew the heartbreak of a relationship irredeemably destroyed; she knew what it was like to live on the margins of her beloved church and her society. In these experiences she was like Jesus. And like him, she knew where to turn for comfort and strength. She turned to community, which she herself actualized in the Catholic Worker houses of hospitality; prayer, which included communal worship and liturgy; and study. Her days and evenings were fixed by the responsibilities she assumed, but in the afternoons she retired to her room to read Scripture and the nineteenth-century novels from which she drew so many lessons. From Dorothy I have taken the ingredients of stability, study, prayer, community, hospitality, the preferential option for the poor, and the concept of a daily rule.

The values that Thomas Merton lived and wrote about, too, have influenced my thinking and contributed to my image of the focused life. Like Dorothy, he was pursued all his life by a deep sense of loneliness, the result, in his case, of being orphaned at an early age and subsequently dispatched to an English boarding school. Like Dorothy, he lived an enthusiastically undisciplined life as a student and young man. While in the midst of that dissolute existence, he made a trip to Rome and was profoundly affected by a sense of peace that he never forgot. But at Cambridge and later at Columbia he lost himself in a party life. Then, in the spontaneous style that was uniquely his, he converted to Catholicism and entered the Cistercian order where he remained for the rest of his life.

Called to the Inward Journey

Merton lived the monastic way. It is through his writings about that way and his ability to explain and make accessible the spiritual life to the layperson that he has exerted an extraordinary and continuing influence. His falling in love in mid-life only enhances the authenticity of his humanity and makes it possible for those of us not called to vowed celibacy to embrace him as one of ours.

Merton spoke often about the difference between the False Self, that persona which is the product of ego, and the True Self which is the point in everyone's soul where the individual and God meet, what he called "the deepest ground of our being." All of us are called to this inward journey, and it is from Merton that I have taken the first imperative of the focused life: the commitment to reflective living. Some will argue against it, some will avoid it, some may think it is the way of the weak, damaged, or deranged, but these are signals of resistance. To the extent to which we are able, we are all called to the inner journey. As Merton found while still very young (as Dorothy did as well), there is no escaping it. In addition, Merton's lessons on how to pray contemplatively and on the value of silence and solitude are of great value.

Another call that Merton often wrote about and certainly lived, is the call to community. He makes a point of differentiating between community and collectivity, explaining that the individual in an authentic community is set free by his or her associations, while in the collective setting conformity is imposed. While Merton may have been referring to political Communism when he was speaking of collectivity, the discussion, I believe, is relevant to ours here. Contemporary culture with its demands for conformity, is a form of collectivity, and the pressures it exerts on the unfocused individual can be debilitating. Therefore, Merton's thoughts on this matter are significant. So, the call to authentic community experience is the second contribution Merton has made to my concept of the focused life.

Third, Merton urged involvement with the poor and otherwise marginalized. As the world swirled on beyond the grounds of the monastery at Gethsemani, Merton responded and grew. He professed nonviolence and began to love and honor other religious traditions beyond Western Christianity. At the time of his tragic accidental death, he was still in his intellectual and physical prime and fully engaged in life, a testimony to the inquiring spirit he inspires in all of us.

Dag Hammarsjköld is another great man who died at the height of his powers. He described the value in making a record of the philosophy by which he lived in his journal *Markings*, and the act, the process, of making that record showed how he valued his life—as we should ours. *Markings* is an invaluable model for our own efforts to write about our daily experiences in prayer, at work, within our families and our intentional communities, and in the deepest places of our hearts.

But it is the life of Jesus that is our paramount guide. Much about Jesus' "hidden years" and the events that led him into a life of total commitment is not known to us. Whatever his perspective on celibacy, which he neither fostered nor discouraged, he is an example of what one can bring to fruition even if not affirmed by an intimate partner. We study the actual events and insights of his life so that we may direct ours accordingly. On another level, we identify our own life experiences with his so that we may gain, as Karl Rahner said, "a sense of our own identity and vital impulses, as willed by God." Third, we read the broad messages of his life—

continuous dialogue with God, community, and a preferential option for the poor—as imperatives for our own.

These are my models and from them I have derived my vision of a unique, spiritually based life for single people. Because it is a personal vision, some of it may make sense to you and some of it may not. However, it is my passionate belief that the underlying principles inherent in the specifics that I have chosen for myself can guide others who wish to undertake this journey.

"The path of which I have spoken is beautiful and pleasant and joyful and familiar," said Meister Eckhart of the inner journey. I hope that those of you who have traveled this far with me will enter deeper, and in the following chapters find your path and discover that it is "beautiful and pleasant and joyful and familiar." Here we go.

CHAPTER SIX

Reflective Living

"What does that mean, the inner life?" asked my son-in-law Dean one quiet Sunday afternoon as we waited for Nora, fourteen months old, to wake up from her nap. We were talking about an incident that had happened at his church, a small Protestant fellowship. During a "sharing" about the Transfiguration story, a woman in the congregation stood up and began to tell about a time in her life when she felt herself to be under a cloud, how she emerged from the difficulties, and what her life had been like after that. Her degree of candor had apparently made the gathering uncomfortable and no one was able to respond to her story or to share with her in any meaningful way. Everyone had been embarrassed.

As his retelling of the event unfolded, I wondered to myself how I would work with the event if I were wearing my spiritual director's hat. First, I would want to probe the elements of her story to help her see how God was working in the events. I would also want to ask the other members of the congregation why they had found it so difficult to receive and respond to her sharing. The essence of the inner life, I explained to Dean, consists in the willingness to stay with the uncomfortable or difficult moments in our lives and to explore them for unconscious or spiritual meaning. The opposite would be to pass them off and get involved in a pleasant diversion. Perhaps I was being overly simplistic in my response, but, then again, perhaps not.

Still he persisted—he works with computers—and wanted to know in more concrete language what it really means, this spiritual journey, this inner voyage. What does it mean to become reflective? What does one need to do to "get into it?" How does one begin? These are valid questions, but unfortunately, we can look long and hard before finding adequate guidance. Many suggestions are out there. Bookstores are filled with self-help books and all kinds of "spiritual" assistance is available, from dry commentaries on the Bible, to messages from charismatic tele-vangelists, to tarot card readers. It's important to be cautious here and to consult only with authentic and trustworthy guides.

One such guide is Parker Palmer, the Quaker teacher, writer, and lecturer. He explains the inner journey with a story from real life. In *The Active Life* he talks about an Outward Bound experience in which he found himself, a novice to mountain climbing, rappeling down the side of a steep cliff. Halfway down, he met an impasse and had no alternative but to change his direction, something he had never done before. He froze. The words his instructor yelled to him at that moment became something of a motto for the inward journey (as well as the cliffside one). "If you can't get out of it," she yelled, "get into it." And so he did. "There is no way out of our inner lives," he writes, "so we'd better get into them. In the downward, inward journey, the only way out is in and through."

I also had a mountain climbing experience, and it, too, revealed something about the inner journey. It was a fine summer's day when I agreed to climb Khatadin, the final goal on the Appalachian Trail and the highest peak in the state of Maine. My companion and guide, although strong, was not a good planner, and we ascended with only three apples between us and his memories of a speedy ascent he had made with several college friends forty years earlier. Halfway up we had to choose from among several trails that led to the summit. Looking at the trail map, we decided on the shortest route. Big mistake. It was the shortest, no question, but also the steepest. Higher and higher we went, and steeper and steeper became the trail. Eventually we left all trees behind and also the dirt trail and began to make our way by grabbing onto the roots and branches of the dwarfed junipers that clung to the rocks over which we scrambled. Pausing for a moment, I turned to enjoy the view and realized with a gasp that, not only were we high above the tree line but that there was no visible way down, only a dense mass of gnarled juniper roots on a precipitous slope. Above and below, it was the same. With a sense of the inevitable, I knew that, no matter how tired or hungry I was, no matter how shaky my legs or my arms, I would have to continue to hitch my exhausted and hungry body up the slope assisted only by the roots of miniature trees. I had no other choice. This is like labor, I thought at the time, remembering how I felt as the first contractions announced the onset of the birth process. I was on an inescapable course, and there was no way out but ahead.

I am here to tell the tale, so I can report that arriving at the peak and looking down at hundreds of miles of lakes and rivers and forests was one of the most exhilarating experiences of my life. At that moment a shuddering sob akin to those I released when my children entered the world broke through from the depths of my being. Peak spiritual experiences both.

So, we accept that the journey is difficult, that, once begun, it takes on its own momentum, and that great joy greets us at the end. But still the question remains, Where is the beginning? What is the starting point?

We Are Relational

"Begin with the heart," says Meister Eckhart, "for the spring of life arises from the heart and from there it runs in a circular manner." Matters of the heart lead us into deeper spirituality simply because for us humans there is no other place to begin. Our trinitarian God is relational, and since we are modeled in God's image and likeness, we too are relational. Our human relationships, our matters of the heart, then, are legitimate issues for spiritual speculation. Consider the difficult moments, the disagreeable and even terrible times of our lives, the times when we stood up in front of one other or many others and told about our clouds, the times we sat on our hands. These moments of awareness are the keys that unlock the doors that imprison us. If we open those doors and follow the stairs down into the sometimes dark spiral of self-examination, they will eventually lead us up again out into the light and to our goal, the release from bondage of our True Selves.

The "matter of the heart" that marked the beginning of my spiritual awakening took place when my marriage failed. I was forty years old. Although I was devastated, I was also filled with a new energy and (thanks to the women's movement) sense of adventure. No longer encumbered by an uneasy marriage, I began to explore several avenues at one time. I contacted a young man who was in charge of the religious education program in my parish and asked him about places to worship. He recommended a Benedictine community in a neighboring town. I took the children there for some of the most creative and joyful liturgies I have ever experienced. I went to counseling through Catholic Charities. I participated in a Bible study group and bought my first Bible. I had always kept a journal and now it helped me to process my turbulent emotions.

Then I was sidetracked. Going back to school and caring for my children took up all of my energies. At the same time I found myself falling in love and experiencing heartbreak. In the aftermath of one of those breakups, ten years after my divorce, I found myself once again "attending to the difficult moment," this time with a therapist. In one session I was asked what, besides my family and career, really meant anything to me, and I found myself speaking passionately about my spiritual life and how it had been repressed while I was married and how I was curious about what it was all about. It was a moment of lasting significance. Soon after, I enrolled in a three-year spiritual development program run by my diocese, and my life was changed immediately, powerfully, and forever. At last I was converted. I was fifty years old.

This time I chose not to escape, but to take the ride. Many choose otherwise, prompted to some degree by today's culture that tells us not to pay attention to the difficult moments, advising us rather to "do something to keep your mind off your troubles." The "something" can be as benign as taking a walk or eating an ice cream cone, or as sinister as getting revenge or going on a shopping spree. Yet, even those who are willing may not have the proper tools to begin the journey.

My own spirituality was formed in pre-Vatican II days during the forties and fifties in a typical Irish family and in a typical parish grammar school and all-girls high school. We did not talk about spiritual practice in our family, and we did not even say the rosary as many families did. We talked about religious practice, which meant obeying the rules and regulations set down by the priests and sisters. Both my parents adhered to their own rule, which was to stay clear of pious observances and to keep a healthy distance from the clergy. Notwithstanding, and perhaps because of their neutral stance, I became deeply spiritual as a child and adolescent.

As with so many of us brought up in the forties and fifties, my spirituality centered around the parish church and its elementary school. They were my central focus and I was in that church every day of the week. Monday through Friday my brothers and I would "make a visit to the Blessed Sacrament" as we made our way between home and school in the morning, at lunchtime, and in the afternoon. There in the darkened cavernous church, made warm by the presence of benign statues and the ever-glowing votive candles, I communed with Jesus in the tabernacle, bringing to him whatever problems I had as a child. On Saturday afternoons we lined up for confession. On Sundays we filed by classes into predetermined pews for the 8:30 a.m. I still have the missal my father gave me for confirmation; its elegant thin pages hold all the memories of that time. I know that my love for language and literature, and especially for the scriptural record of Jesus' human experience, is rooted in the acclamation that begins the Last Gospel: "In principio erat Verbum"—In the beginning was the Word. At 5:00 on Sunday afternoons we returned for Benediction to sing the lovely Latin hymns which I can still recite to this day.

All that changed radically when I married in my senior year of college. My spiritual life went underground, curbed in order to make the relationship work. I had no choice, I felt, but to serve two masters. It didn't work, neither the arrangement nor the marriage. As problems piled up over the years, I turned again and again to the habits instilled in my childhood. I went to Mass and hoped for insight and consolation from the homilist. Whenever possible, I slipped away to "make a visit" and sat in darkened churches, often in tears. One Thanksgiving Day, overwhelmed by the preparations, the demands of four young children, and tensions with my husband, I slipped out of the house on the pretense of doing a last-minute errand, and drove to church. I will never forget that day and even now as I write about it, sorrow for the desperate young woman that I was then brings tears to my eyes. When I got to the church, I found the doors locked. I returned to the car and cried. From that moment on until the marriage ended, I floundered, my only spiritual exercises being Sunday Mass with its occasionally meaningful homily and some devotional books of prayers I had kept from my childhood.

The Inner Journey Was Calling

When I finally realized during that therapy session so many years later that the inner journey was calling me, I was fortunate. The diocesan spiritual development program at Our Lady of Peace in Narragansett, Rhode Island in the early '90s was under the guidance of an excellent team of religious and lay women and one priest. As a group, they were well versed in the emerging as well as the traditional spiritualities found within the church, and I began to learn again, from the old and from the new. Our models were the great spiritual masters. These included the prophets of Scripture, the "magisterium" of the church, the gospel record of Jesus' life, Ignatian spirituality, depth psychology as presented in the work of Carl Jung, liberation theology, process theology, Matthew Fox's creation spirituality, the early mystics. These teachings were presented in a careful blend of lecture, experiential methods, small and large group-sharing, reading, ritual, and individual and group spiritual direction.

But first I had to learn the basics. I needed to know that even though I thought I was "going on retreat" by participating in the program, I was not "retreating" from the world and becoming a solitary. "Spirituality," Meister Eckhart said, "is not to be learned by flight from the world, by running away from things, or by turning solitary and going apart from the world. Rather we must learn an inner solitude wherever or with whomever we may be. We must learn to penetrate things and to find God there." Lesson One for the inner journey. I also quickly learned that there is a vast difference between simply being reflective in a daydreaming sort of way and being reflective in a disciplined way. Lesson Two. Lesson Three is that spirituality is a community experience. All our instruction was reinforced in small and large group sharing.

As I intensified my study independently in the years following, I picked up on the writings of St. Benedict, Thomas Merton, Teresa of Avila, Jesuit father Teilhard de Chardin, and Franciscan Richard Rohr, as well as writers who view the preferential option for the poor as an imperative, writers who view small Christian community as an imperative, writers who view personal spirituality as an imperative—a broad spectrum, all held gently within the parameters of a church grand enough to embrace all of it. Much of my own personal spirituality, reflected in what follows, has been influenced by my attraction to the insights of Carl Jung and the spirituality of St. Benedict, which I find to be both profound and practical. These writers assume a close affinity between spiritual and reflective living as do I.

In Benedictine terms, the spiritual life consists of being faithful to living the commandments and the corporal works of mercy, living in a spirit of community, and being committed to personal growth. Kathleen Howard, in her devotional book, *Praying with Benedict,* says that the primary assumptions of the Rule are threefold: that one's relationship with God is primary, that the way to that is through Christ as he is found in Scripture, and that the Holy Spirit continues to shower the spiritual Christian with guidance, inspiration, and enthusiasm. Those who

wish to live by these principles do so best when living a harmonious life, what we here are calling focused living. From
Chittister's explication on the Rule of St. Benedict, *Wisdom
Distilled From the Daily*, I have selected some further aspects of
that unique lifestyle which I think apply particularly to the life
of the single adult who chooses to live a focused life.

She suggests that, initially, we must reduce the amount of
noise and distraction in our lives. In so doing we will be able to
cultivate an ability to "pause" the action and enter into a contemplative posture. We turn distraction to the OFF position and
our attention to God to ON. Second, we can find ways to incorporate ritual into our lives. Chittister speaks primarily of the rituals and customs of Benedictine life and of the liturgy as we see
it in our own churches, but ritual by definition invites and
involves community, also an essential ingredient in Benedictine
spirituality. We practice ritual in our homes and intentional communities, for example, when we share a meal or open and close
our gatherings. With a little forethought and some courage, we
can become more intentional about this.

Benedictines are faithful stewards of the material things they use
for their work and their living, things such as clothes, tools, and
kitchen equipment. Everything is honored with gentle use and careful maintenance, nothing is too humble or too old to be misused or
discarded. Even the obsolete, an old kitchen or workshop tool, for
instance, can be contemplated as a thing of beauty, and carefully
preserved. Stability, discipline, hospitality, prayer, work, study, and
manual labor are all aspects of Benedictine spirituality, and can be
adapted to the lifestyle of the single adult. We will consider them in
later chapters. (Those who wish to deepen their knowledge of
Benedictine spirituality may read more of Joan Chittister, O.S.B., and
of Esther deWaal, and Kathleen Norris, whose books *Dakota* and
Cloister Walk have been widely read and greatly admired.)

Another Spiritual Mentor

Another of my spiritual mentors is Carl Jung, a Swiss depth psy-
chologist who lived well into the twentieth century. He was for

a while a student and colleague of Freud but eventually took exception to the basic premises of Freud's work and disassociated himself from him. Jung's research and personal experience led him to believe that there was a transcendent world and a transcendent being, most often called God, toward which every person strives to unite. The process through which everyone must go in order to reach this union he called individuation. Individuation means returning to wholeness by stripping away the false personality each of us assumes in order to conform to the expectations of the outside world. It is accomplished only by taking the road inward.

Because it is impossible to describe the inward journey in concrete language, Jung uses symbols and sacred geometry, likening the journey to a downward spiral, a labyrinth, a mandala, the nautilus shell, all of which circle around and around until they come to a single focal point. During the inner journey, he said, we meet not only our individual selves but also the selves of all humankind collectively. These he calls archetypes, the images and characters that are found in primitive stories. We also meet the underdeveloped aspects of our personality, those parts we have suppressed in order to please others, what he called the shadow. Integrating the shadow is another important task for personal growth. Another integration necessary for wholeness is the joining of the male and female, both of which reside in us all. Males need to explore the womanly part of themselves, and women their masculine energies.

Dreams are an especially useful tool in the effort to release the imagination, says Jung. We move toward wholeness and union with God when we take time to reflect on the images and symbols that arise in them by writing about our dreams in journals or talking about them in conversation with another person. We also unlock our resistance to wholeness when we get involved in artistic endeavors such as painting, photography, pottery, woodworking, and other creative activities. Reading or rereading the myths of primitive peoples, fairy tales, and folk tales in such a way as to invite our psyches to enter the stories is another way to invigorate the imagination. These stories include the story of Jesus' life. For Jung, Jesus represented Everyman; thus, in Jungian thought, immersion in the stories of Jesus' life is self-revelatory.

During a mid-life crisis, Jung took a year off and spent much of it building a miniature village. Through that experience he came to believe passionately in the therapeutic value of play. Play, he believed, led the soul gracefully into the depths of the inner world. Thus, dreaming, gazing on icons, playing with blocks, listening to music, visiting art galleries and museums, learning how to "throw a pot," taking a trip to an exotic place— all the things that allure us—are keys to our own truth. So are natural objects, such as the leaves, rocks, and shells one slips into a pocket while on a walk, and the little surprises of every-day life: the coincidences, the chance meetings, the face across a crowded room. Pay attention to all of these, he suggests. Immerse yourself in them. Write about your reactions to them. Draw them. Sing them. Dance them. They are all aspects of grace. (Again the brilliant Roget breaks open the amorphous concept of grace, suggesting the terms smiling on, inward monitor, and—surprise, surprise—still, small voice.)

I keep several sets of children's blocks on my coffee table. For some time they have appealed to me and I play with them at odd times when I feel the urge. They are called parquetry blocks and come in the shapes of triangles, squares, and parallelograms in the brightest of primary colors—blue, green, red, yellow, purple, orange. They came with suggestions about how to make designs, and I can place the blocks right on the paper models. I am not very creative about this sort of thing; it is not easy for me to play. I have noticed an amazing thing when I make these designs. As soon as I place the blocks on the paper pattern, they seem to come alive. They present optical illusions that flicker in and out of focus. I consider them for long moments. They are fascinating to me, mysterious. Jung would say that my play is inviting me into another realm.

Another vehicle I take on the journey to wholeness is the

study of icons. There are few traditional icons that appeal to me. Their austere visages and rigid body stances generally put me off. But it was once suggested to me that many things can be icons, snapshots and formal photos, for example. Rummaging through family mementoes one afternoon, I found a picture of myself as a child of seven. Something about its tone and mood struck me. There I am peering solemnly straight ahead at the photographer, my hair tugged severely into two long braids that hang down the front of my dress, their ends curled and beribboned. My mother chose this proof instead of the smiling one because my two front teeth were missing at the time, so it is the solemn me that has survived. In later years I forgot about that solemn child. She was eclipsed by the chipper performer I came to be in order to please my mother. But now that face has become an icon for a facet of myself I am developing; she greets me every morning when I wake from my dreams.

Playing with blocks, attending to dreams, choosing and contemplating icons, indulging in daydreams are all things our culture considers "wasting time." But the purpose of this play is not to have fun; it is serious business, very serious. And sometimes very dark.

"In the deeps are the violence and terror of which psychology has warned us," says Annie Dillard, who has written extensively on matters spiritual, "but if you ride these monsters deeper down, if you drop with them farther over the world's rim, you will find...the matrix which [leads to] the unified field." Teilhard de Chardin, the extraordinary French Jesuit paleontologist and priest whose radical thought continues to influence theological thinkers profoundly, speaks of the Omega Point as a metaphor to explain that core of ourselves which converges with the mysterious transcendent being we call God. In *The Divine Milieu,* reflecting on his own inner journey, he said:

> We must try to penetrate our most secret self, and examine our being from all sides. Let us try, patiently, to perceive the ocean of forces to which we are subjected and in which our growth is, as it were, steeped....For the first time in my

life perhaps…, I took the lamp and, leaving the zone of everyday occupations and relationships where everything seems clear, I went down into my inmost self, to the deep abyss whence I feel dimly that my power of action emanates. But as I moved further and further away from the conventional certainties by which social life is superficially illuminated, I became aware that I was losing contact with myself. At each step of the descent a new person was disclosed within me of whose name I was no longer sure, and who no longer obeyed me. (*The Divine Milieu*, pp. 76-77)

These experiences are not uncommon when we begin to experiment with what Jung calls "shadow play," the identification and transformation of the denied aspects of our personalities. The task is to bring them out of the shadow world by integrating them into our personalities and blessing them. My own shadow side is still elusive. It teases me, hides from me, toys with me, and refuses to name itself, suggesting that perhaps it is playful as well as sinister. To others I am sure it is quite obvious.

All life, whether in the outer world or the inner, is a circuitous journey, sometimes in shadow, sometimes in the light, and everything we experience in it is significant. Some of our experiences are circumstantial, others the result of conscious decision-making, yet each prepares us in some mysterious way for the next. At some point in this process we are called to step back and reflect on the meaning of all this and invited to begin a more intentional and intensive search for meaning in our lives. Those of us who accept the invitation and leave the beaten path, deaden ourselves in a way to real life, and intentionally take off on a meandering route, destination unknown. As W.H. Auden said of it, "The center that I cannot find is known to my unconscious mind." Ultimately, and ironically, this seemingly tangential trip, according to Meister Eckhart, means that we are "coming alive." Once begun, this inner journey beset as it is by terrors, monsters, dark tunnels, fear, resistance, and exhaustion, leads to the secret hiding place of the pot of gold. And the pot of gold is one's own True Self, differentiated forever from the false.

Three Talismans

It would be reckless to start off on such an arduous path without assistance. Like the travelers in myths and fairy tales, we too should take along some talismans. I suggest three: a spiritual director, an intentional community, a spiritual journal. A therapist who is attuned to spirituality may also be helpful during some parts of the journey.

Spiritual direction, an ancient form of soul friendship or companioning, is enjoying a renaissance. Thus the phenomenal growth in recent years of its professional association, Spiritual Directors International. It sponsors an annual conference, publishes a journal, and has formulated a Code of Ethics. Spirituality is as much about human situations as about prayer, so there is much to do with psychology in a spiritual direction session. It is essential, therefore, to make a clear distinction between the two. One should not be mistaken for the other.

The similarities help explain the differences. In both, the client or directee meets with a trained professional for an hour's session on a predetermined schedule, usually once a month. The material of the session is driven by what the person coming for direction or therapy "reports," i.e., the ups and downs of daily living. With professional skill, the director or therapist guides this person to new self-awareness. Here the similarities end. The therapist has probably assessed the "situation" and wants to show the client how to change that situation. The spiritual director, on the other hand, calling on the presence of the Spirit in the encounter, rests in attentive expectation for the movement of God in whatever pain or joy the directee is experiencing. While the director may also have "assessed" the situation and gained insights into the personality of the directee (as directors are informed to some degree in the principles of psychology), he or she is not in the business of changing either the situation or the personality. Change may occur as a result of spiritual direction, but it is not the primary task of the director to see that this occurs. The task is simply to bring to the directee an awareness of God's movement in his or her life. Therefore, the subject matter of the session, unlike that of a therapy or counseling session, will include real talk about God and real talk about prayer.

A Community of Peers

A community of trusted peers is equally invaluable on the spiritual journey inward. A few years ago, having just moved to a new city, I sent out an invitation through our church bulletin for some people who would be interested in coming together to read the Sunday gospels. We agreed that this was not to be a "bible study" and that we would follow good group guidelines, such as active listening and confidentiality, that we would refrain from giving advice, or pontificating, or matching one person's story with our own. And so we began—four single people, three with grown children and one the mother of a five-year-old; two couples, one with a teenaged daughter; and a married woman who has a six-year-old. The children are often with us.

During the two hours we are together every other week, we allow the gospel story to determine the content of the evening. Sometimes one individual's issues are on the table, but most often we share in turn how each of us has been touched by another's story. All of our personal issues eventually surface. Our life stories unfold and continue to do so. Our present challenges and joys, whether they be related to work, family, or church are "everybody's business."

Outside of the group few people with whom we interact know about our tough issues or our prayerful way of going through the day. They see us as teachers, artists, office managers, computer technicians, scientists—everyday people. We go to the shore for vacations, endure families on the holidays, fight with our husbands and children, agonize over decisions and conflicts at work, just like everyone else. But unlike most others, as we maneuver the pitfalls of everyday living and the personal spiritual journey each of us travels, we have one another. Our gratitude for our group grows and deepens. We are comforted in the knowledge of our mutual love.

The habit of keeping a journal is also an important aid for the inner journey, even for those who hate to write. One way to begin is to follow the advice of Julia Cameron in *The Artist's Way*. She recommends starting every day at the computer, or with pen and paper, by writing three pages of reflective thoughts. This work is not structured or organized consciously; rather, it should be like free writing, a form of writing in which all "mechanical" rules—punctuation, spelling, grammar—are put aside for the time so that thoughts can flow unhindered. After the free flow of ideas is recorded, the writer takes some time to reread what he or she has written, circles words, phrases, or concepts that stand out, and continues to write from these new inspirations. Eventually he or she liberates from the glut of the free flow writing the essential material that has been released. The reason this is a good way to begin to keep a journal is that it bends the rules that have hindered many of us from enjoying the process of writing.

At the very least one should try to write every day at some convenient time. For many, this is also their time of prayer, morning or evening or both. Besides "logging in" the events of the day, this is the time to record what happens during prayer, dreams, personal interactions, mood changes, stress points, moments of gratitude or thanksgiving, moments of fear or anger. A good way to start the flow is to ask oneself where God was most present in the day, in other words, where the day seemed brightest and lightest; and the converse, what were the dark moments, where was God's apparent absence most felt? Both will be issues to bring to prayer.

One can get very caught up in keeping a journal and go very far and very deep. When Ira Progoff first presented his Intensive Journal workshops, which were based on the principles of Carl Jung's depth psychology, they were very popular. Because his ideas are so appealing and so easily understood, they were swiftly incorporated into education, spirituality, the arts, etc. The once-popular workshops are now given less frequently. His classic book, *At a Journal Workshop,* however, is still in print and very helpful for those who want to deepen their journaling experience. For example, he suggests a technique called dialogue in which the writer records imagined "conversations" with his or her own work and activities, with significant persons from the past and present, body, dreams, culture, society, and wisdom figures. One especially powerful Intensive Journal technique or exercise is called Time-Stretching. Here one records the most significant periods of the past and then writes about the significant people, circumstances, events, and influences of those formative years. Progoff refers to this work as being in the "life/time dimension."

To begin, the writers literally draw a line across a large sheet of paper and then mark off segments indicating approximate seven-year periods from birth to the present. Within those spaces they list everything they can remember and then begin to pull out the most significant persons, moves, decisions, places, experiences. These are called "Stepping Stones" and are the beginnings of further reflection. To Progoff they are of the utmost importance because they stand forth as indicators of the inner connectedness of each person's existence, a continuity of development that maintains itself despite the vicissitudes and the apparent shifting of directions that occur in the course of a life. The Stepping Stones are indicators that enable persons to recognize the deeper-than-conscious goals toward which the movement of their lives is trying to take them.

Dag Hammarskjöld called these moments in his life "markings." They were not always the best moments; many were painful or spoke of failure as ours do, increasing their value as pointers to wholeness. Hammarskjöld used a powerful metaphor to describe this journey by way of stepping stones. On our spiritual journeys, he says, we are like mountain climbers; we go upward toward the summit and downward into valleys and gulches on the way, leaving our markings along the way. Once when I was hiking in Norway on a rocky passage above the tree line, I noticed such markings. They are called cairns, and are piles of stones placed at strategic turnings on the way toward the huts or as warnings at tricky places on the way. As Hammarskjöld says, both are valuable for the pilgrim, both the highs and the lows, the good and the bad. We need to record our own markings.

There are a number of books on the market that tell how to be creative about keeping a journal, and all of them are helpful. But we do well if we just keep it simple, addressing God or our inner selves in conversational tones, being honest in our writing, and revisiting our journals periodically to look for trends, recurring themes, and hidden messages.

When To Write

A good time to write in a journal is anytime. One can write before or after prayer, a counseling or spiritual direction session, at dawn, at midnight, in the dentist's waiting room, on a plane or a bus, when in crisis, when at peace.

One final point. Intentional and disciplined self-reflection has purposes that far exceed personal fulfillment. While it may be seen by others, and even by ourselves at times, as irrelevant, "out-of-touch" with the realities of the world, or self-indulgent, it most certainly is not. When humans emerge from false living and begin to live out of their True Selves, the consciousness of the entire world is changed and the consciousness of God is made manifest. Thus, when we make the decision to live reflectively and to undertake the difficult tasks involved in self-development, we are making a contribution not only to ourselves as individuals but to the world.

This consciousness of God that we are to make manifest is reflected in the life of Jesus. Jung suggests that we immerse ourselves in the gospel stories and take on Jesus' life experience as our own. In another sense, his life gives us clues about the desires of God, what he himself called "the kingdom of God." And what did his life reveal about the consciousness of God? That it is imperative for us to take on the cares of the world, especially those of the poor. Jesus' words and actions while he lived were directed toward a kingdom in which the Beatitudes were the manifesto, the "constitution" if you will, not a kingdom with royal privileges which the people at the time had come to expect. Our pursuit of wholeness, whether through spiritual practices, following the suggestions of Jung, or committing to a spiritual development program, serve a larger purpose than our own individuation and is only the beginning, a preparation for our "real" work in the kingdom.

"The unexamined life is not worth living," as we have already noted. What is the difference between an examined life and an unexamined one? How does one go about examining his or her own life? Does such an examination change us outwardly, dramatically?

We have looked at some answers to these questions, but there are many others. What is important is that we approach everything in our lives reflectively, examining them, using them to stimulate personal growth and respond to the call to enter Dillard's "unified field." The testimony of Merton, Benedict, Jung, Day, John of the Cross, de Chardin, and others proclaims that, without a doubt, this reflective stance in life is only for the courageous. "Wimps" need not apply. Sadly, some people will never know what could be at the end of the journey that they have "postponed indefinitely."

This is what Teilhard de Chardin found: "And when I had to stop my exploration because the path faded from beneath my steps, I found a bottomless abyss at my feet...and if someone saved me, it was hearing the voice of the Gospel... speaking to me from the depth of the night: *ego sum, noli timere* (It is I, be not afraid)."

CHAPTER SEVEN

Commitment to Prayer

"Prayer is the raising up of the mind and heart to God," said the *Baltimore Catechism* in days of yore. Can we count how many times we have heard that "old chestnut" coming out of the mouth of the homilist or being repeated in our own mental tapes? Another "definition" I read recently in Ochs and Olitsky's *Jewish Spiritual Guidance* is: "an occasion for an encounter with God." Both sound good, and we can't argue with either, but we are still left hanging. What should one actually do in prayer? What does prayer look like and feel like? What are its parameters, its textures, its characteristics? Be more specific, we twentieth-century pragmatists demand. *Tell* us.

In the days when many were actually taught how to pray by their parents or the sisters in elementary school, we learned to pray the rosary and we learned many rote prayers such as the Hail Mary, the Our Father, and many others that were printed up in little booklets or prayer books. Novenas, nine-day cycles of petition to Mary and the saints, were also part of the canon of rote prayers. Small publishing houses still produce these devotions and prayers; they remain unchanged.

The decades since the fifties have introduced us to new ways of looking at prayer and broadened our definition to include acts of social justice. In the sixties the Second Vatican Council (Vatican II) encouraged Catholics to read the Bible, and an interest in sacred Scripture as prayer began to grow. This was followed by a resurgence of interest in the mystics, "benignly ignored" for centuries, and effected the movement toward centering prayer, a form of contemplation. These welcome changes offer more opportunities for laypeople and for religious not living as monastics. Spiritual direction, in which someone who is desirous of deepening his or her experience of God consults with another who is trained to facilitate that process, has also been dusted off and is now offered to laypeople as well as religious.

But many are still unaware of these movements. And why? Because information about prayer practice has not been disseminated from the pulpit. References to prayer and spirituality may be embedded in discourse about the meaning of the gospels, but they are seldom addressed as distinct topics. Consequently, the average person has to scratch around to find any advice or new information about prayer from the official church. In my practice as a spiritual director, I find that many people, even young people, still do not know of options other than rosaries, novenas, and devotional books. They find that their spiritual life lacks energy. "It's boring," responded one young woman when asked how this kind of prayer felt to her.

I learned my lessons in prayer from women religious, people of courage who saw what Vatican II was all about and did not keep the good news to themselves. But even before that, it was the nuns who educated me in elementary school, who addressed the deep issues of prayer and spiritual practice. Sister Benet, S.S.N.D., at Holy Name School taught me how to engage with Jesus in the Passion, station by station, drop of blood by drop of blood, thorn by thorn, groan by groan. To this day, I still look forward to "doing the Stations" once or twice during Lent, although the experience for me now is less visceral. Later on, when I became more sophisticated about prayer, I discovered the scriptural rosary which grounded the practice in the legitimacy of biblical references. In high school in the mid-fifties, Sister Mary Eloise, R.S.M., after Latin class was over, would sit us down at our desks with our feet firmly planted on the floor and instruct us in "mental prayer." "Close your eyes and put yourselves in the presence of God," she would say, drawing us into a long period of silence, which may have been a precursor to centering prayer.

College years followed, and the sixties and seventies for me were filled, not with political and social action, but with the duties of raising a family. My prayer life, what there was of it, stalled. I went to Sunday Mass, but no one talked about prayer. "Prayer is the raising of the heart and mind to God," I was told over and over again, but I was not told how to go about it. That I learned from a book.

I can still see myself, a thirty-year-old mother, sitting up in bed late one night reading the introduction to a textbook my children were to use in religious education class. It told about the covenant God made with humanity in the Genesis story, how it was honored throughout the Old Testament, and how it came to fulfillment in the birth of Jesus. I never knew about this before, this covenant fulfilled. I never knew Scripture. I went out the next day and bought a Bible, my first.

I learned a lot about prayer when I taught religious education classes under the guidance of the sisters who ran the programs. In later years, I was fortunate enough to become associated with other women religious who continued my education. It has been quite a trip. Without the generous guidance of these vowed women, I would never have learned how to delve into the depths of Scripture or about other liberating and powerful ways to pray. Those of us fortunate enough to have been associated with them on retreats or in friendships during these past several decades have been privileged indeed.

Recently, while preparing for a series of evenings designed to prepare people for spiritual direction, I drew up a list of ways of prayer. I started out with some obvious ones: meditating on the gospel stories, finding God in the natural world, centering with the use of a sacred word. But as I began to consider the many varieties of spiritual practices, my list grew—and grew, and grew, and grew. It embraced widely divergent concepts that included hospitality, body prayer and yoga, working with clay and other "art" materials, play, and mindful walking.

The Intention of Prayer
Before I expand on these, we need to set up some guidelines.

As we said previously, it is necessary first of all to have the intention of prayer, in other words, to consciously set aside a time for the sole purpose of preparing a welcome for God's presence just as we would for the imminent arrival of guests. Initially, although we will talk about communal prayer later on, it is best to be alone and in silence. If at home, set aside a special place designed specifically as a place for prayer. This could simply be a chair placed in a quiet corner or in front of a shelf or table top that holds objects representing the divine mystery— a candle, a rock or shell, a favorite image of Jesus.

In their excellent *Take and Receive* series, five book-length guides to the Spiritual Exercises of St. Ignatius, Jacqueline Bergan and S. Marie Schwan make the following suggestions regarding prayer. First, decide on what your prayer will be and on the amount of time you will spend in prayer. They suggest twenty minutes to one hour a day. Quiet yourself with slow deep rhythmic breathing. Then express your desire to be in God's presence and ask for the grace you need at this moment in time. Enter into the prayer experience you have chosen and close it at the appropriate time with the Our Father or the Doxology.

A prayer journal is essential; it constitutes what Bergan and Schwann call "a precious record" of your conversations with God. Write or draw in your journal as you pray, or afterwards as a review. In your journal reflect on the "interior movements" you experience during your time in prayer. What insights did the Scripture passage or other prayer experience reveal to you? Did you feel joyful, anxious, angry? Were you disturbed or at peace? Were you focused, distracted, impatient? What insights and meanings were revealed to you? Record all these feelings, attitudes, and insights. Later on, when you reread your journal or share it with your spiritual director, you will see how it describes your spiritual journey and clarifies the meaning of your life experiences.

I have learned some of the following ways of prayer from books, some from the teachings and retreats given by women religious, some from our splendid tradition. In organizing my list,

I first thought to divide it up into praying with Scripture, praying with "things," such as objects from nature and art, and praying with "nothing," i.e., contemplation. Then I realized that Scripture itself is a "thing," which, just like other forms of prayer we will be considering—nature, creativity, images, the body, books, dreams, ritual, play, the senses, shapes and figures (sacred geometry), manual and intellectual work—can lead the seeker into the place we call contemplation. Scripture holds a primary place in our tradition, however, so that's where we will begin.

Praying With Scripture

The prayerful reading of Scripture—as distinct from the study of Scripture—is a classic way of prayer and much has been written about how to approach it. One of these is meditation. In meditation one reads the passage expecting to find a personal message. Bergan and Schwan suggest reading the passage aloud so as to intensify the impact of the words, and to pause whenever a word or phrase captures the attention. Stay with that word or phrase, repeating it over and over, paying close attention to the feelings that arise. Continue in this way until the effect has diminished. Write down your reactions immediately afterwards.

Entering into a Scripture passage with the imagination is called contemplation. (The word contemplation is used elsewhere to mean the prayer of nothingness, i.e., withdrawing attention from objects or words and focusing instead on creating an emptiness that invites in the presence of God. Here the word is used to mean active involvement in a gospel story or passage.) The passage is read as if it were a story and we are trying to unlock its meaning. We observe the action and the people in the story, attend carefully to the words, take the part of one or all of the characters, ask how their experiences mirror our own. If Jesus is prominent in the story, we may identify with his experience in it and his response to it.

The use of the imagination in prayer, first introduced by Ignatius as "active imagination," has been given a new twist recently with the popularity of "guided meditation." Guided meditation, active imagination facilitated by another, can be a profound experience that should be entered into carefully. In guided meditation one is led by a facilitator, usually a retreat director or spiritual director, into an extension of a Scripture passage. As a spiritual director, I have sometimes used it; more often I have benefitted from it in my own prayer or as a participant during retreats or with my own spiritual directors. I feel it necessary to say that when used by uneducated or wrongly motivated practitioners, the technique can be harmful and even dangerous. In general, however, it is a widely accepted and highly valued practice, a way to deepen one's understanding of Scripture.

Praying with Scripture can be carried into one's daily routine by selecting a word or phrase as a mantra. A mantra is like a breath prayer. If it is a phrase, one part is said on the in breath and the other on the out breath; if it is a single word, it is repeated on both. A mantra is a very handy form of prayer; it can be taken anywhere—into the swimming pool, on the treadmill, waiting in line at the supermarket. Another way of continuing the effect of scriptural prayer is by writing down a significant line or two on a piece of paper and referring to it occasionally throughout the day.

There is no end to the vast spiritual gifts Scripture holds, and we need not restrict our reading to the New Testament. Many of the books of the Old Testament, and of the prophets and psalmists particularly, strike deeply into our hearts. The ancient tradition of praying the psalms throughout the night and day is carried on even now in monasteries all over the world. It is called the *opus Dei,* the work of God. The words of the psalms, which sound so gentle in chant, express the deepest emotions felt by the devoted in ancient times as they alternately railed against God and rejoiced in God. No one has suffered more or hated more or repented more or praised more than the psalmists. As these are the voices of each of us at one time or another, they have been called "corporate prayers," for if not ours at the present time, they surely speak for someone else.

Praying With Nature

Praying with the Word as it appeared in Scripture was for a long time my exclusive way of prayer. Its appeal is powerful. As a source of connection to the transcendent, prayer is vast and like the ocean, ever changing, ever new, ever constant. "Word," to me, means all there is about language and literature and revelation. It also means God's human incarnation in the person of Jesus, and by extension, in the people I encounter in my life. If God, therefore, is manifested in inspired literature and in humanity, it only seems reasonable that the world created by God should also be a way to see and understand the Divine Mystery. In other words, nature is also a way to pray.

In *How to Meditate Without Leaving the World,* Avery Brooke showed me how objects from nature could lead me into a conversation with God. I had always experienced strong connections to the transcendent world in natural environments, especially beaches, but the notion that this could be prayer was "way out" for me until I began to think about it and realized how obvious it is. Brooke begins by instructing the reader first to take a close look at the smallest of things, shafts of meadow grass, for example, in a slow and reverent manner until they eventually reveal insights into the spiritual realm.

I well remember the time when a cross-section of a large nautilus shell was placed in my hand and I was instructed to look at it for twenty minutes, to contemplate its pink pearl colors, its gloss, to remember the animal which had once inhabited it and whose excretions had formed it. And I did. It was that spiral skeleton which led me into an important insight about how and where God resides in me and the circuitous nature of the inward journey to that place. Recently I found a jeweler who makes pins in the shape of the nautilus and I wear one on the lapel of a jacket or on a sweater as my own personal symbol of the inner journey.

Teilhard de Chardin challenged us to look at the natural world, not in the primitive pantheistic sense or as something to be mastered or controlled, but as embodying the energy of God. The implications of his work are enormous; Père Teilhard de Chardin, in fact, has been called the father of environmental spirituality. But our experiences of nature are small and personal ones, too, for we are never far from God's creation; like Scripture, it is an abundant resource, an ever-present occasion for prayer and reflection.

Because it is so present, we must be careful not to let the beauty of nature lead us into an amorphous trance where we wallow pleasantly and endlessly. If the experience of being in nature or meditating on a natural object is to be prayer, it must be entered into by preparing, structuring, and reviewing the time of prayer just as we do with Scripture. That is true as well of the other forms of prayer in the "things" category.

Like nature, our senses and our sense awareness is constantly with us. And so, in order to understand them as prayer, we must follow the same guidelines of preparation, structure, and review. I like to think of the senses as body poetry, for like poetry, they rely on the potent perception. As each word in a well-constructed poem is weighted with meaning, so are our sense impressions. We smell turkey baking and memories flood our minds. We hear birdsong for the first time in a spring dawn and our hearts soar. We touch a baby's cheek and tears mysteriously flood our eyes. We see a church spire and our thoughts rise with it. We bite into the first apple of the fall—as I was once instructed to do during a retreat—and its crisp clean taste declares that some simple things will always be wonderfully with us. Like nature, our senses are God-given and therefore redolent with information about the transcendent world.

In one of her wonderful books—and they are all wonderful— Joyce Rupp suggests that we take a full day to attend to each of our senses in turn: a day for taste, a day for touch, a day for hearing, and see how many observations we can make. This, I would suggest, is a good way to introduce ourselves to the idea of using sense impressions as prayer. Taste every morsel of food for a day, feel the snowflakes on your tongue or the grit in your mouth from the subway ride home, taste the toothpaste. Feel yarn, wood, human skin, cat's fur, garden dirt, finger paints. Hear the

sound of yourself practicing a musical instrument (as you appreciate the struggle it takes to learn), the voices of your neighbors, the crunch of snow, Gregorian chant, your paintbrush on canvas. See dawn. Smell the garbage, the musty cellar, a rose you have just bought from the corner florist, incense that you use for prayer time. Or set aside time at the beach, on the ski slope, walking in the neighborhood, taking in a variety of sense impressions in the expectation that God will break in and reveal something to you. And when you have collected a good sampling, begin to select those that hold meaning for you and devote some prayer time and journaling time reflecting on why this is so.

Creativity is also a way to pray. By releasing our creative drives we identify with God whose creative acts initiated the world in which we live, the universe beyond ourselves, and the universe within. It is part of the Godness at the core of our beings. It may not be the creativity of the great or accomplished artist—although we have much to be thankful for in that regard, and appreciating their work can be a prayerful experience in and of itself—but the humble acts that we ourselves create. Again, like using the senses or objects from nature, we can experiment with many arts until some begin to take hold of us; then we can plan prayer times around them.

On the walls of my house are pictures painted by friends of mine. I love their colors and compositions and subject matter. The one that hangs over my computer is dominated by a bright red croquet set. Off to its side, for no apparent reason, sits a vase with bright yellow daffodils sticking out of it; a green watering can sits before it on the right. The edge of a wonderfully bright blue table is visible in an upper corner. I would like to be able to make something beautiful like that picture, but I can't draw. And I am not alone. Many of us have said "I can't," forgetting our days of glory when everything we brought home from kindergarten was placed for all to see on the refrigerator door. But many of us could learn if we took the time away from "important" things to find out. I bet that if I took a drawing class I could learn ways to make images with lines and colors, even

a croquet set in a garden room.

One thing I do like to do occasionally is play with clay. This is because I had a successful experience once during a retreat when I was given a piece of red clay and instructed to close my eyes and play with it. When I opened my eyes and looked at the thing I had molded, I saw a little wizened old woman with a crooked smile. I decided that she was my wisdom figure. For a long time she sat on my "sacred shelf" to remind me that wisdom lives within, that getting old is an honorable thing, and that wisdom often plays jokes on people.

Now whenever I go on retreat, I take clay with me. I never know what is going to come up, but whatever does carries a spiritual message. One time I ended up making two braids just like the ones my mother had tugged into place every day for the first nine years of my life. At the time I was feeling angry with my mother for trying to mold me into her version of perfection, a version I was struggling to redefine. When I had finished making the braids, I decided to intertwine them into a knot. They looked beautiful that way, two separate things intertwined there. Looking at what I had made helped me see how the interweaving of my mother's vision and my own could together make something unique and lovely.

On my last retreat, I took an icon with me, a face of Jesus that is stern yet soft, penetrating. I studied the icon for long minutes searching its enigmatic features for revelations. None came. On my last night away, I took up the clay. I didn't know what to make, so I played with it for a while. Then I decided to try to make the face of the icon. I carved out the long nose with the tip of a pen and drew two almond eyes, attempted the beard. Nothing. I decided to ball up the clay and start again, but as I began to push it into the palm of my hand it began to look like a bas-relief and the face took on the expression of the picture. I stopped and let it dry there. Now it looks out at me from its place on my sacred shelf. I feel as if I had held that face in my hands, that I know it as a blind person knows a face, by fingering its lines, caressing its contours, loving it with touch. I know

the icon now in a way I could not before.

Writing of any sort can be a creative act. Poetry such as the simple haiku is not difficult to learn and is one way to sum up in a few words time spent in prayer, or some other reflection on the spiritual life. So is writing a letter to God or composing a dialogue in your journal. The act of writing down the events of our lives and our personal philosophies can be revelatory, an indicator of what we need to leave behind, what we need to develop. We know about the lives of renowned women and men, but it seldom occurs to us that the record of our own lives is equally important. It is to God, certainly. Write a short story in which you are the protagonist. Take a favorite fairy tale and rewrite it with yourself as the prince or foundling. We have read enough of them to know how. Who or what are the witches and monsters you encounter? What is your dark journey? Can you draw a picture of the beautiful princess? Is it you?

Appealing to the Senses

Art materials appeal to the senses. Paint and clay smell good. Go into an art supply store—there is too much plastic in most craft shops today—and smell and touch all the media there: clay, paint, chalk, charcoal. Go to craft shows and look at all the possibilities. I bought a wooden train set for my grandson at a Christmas craft show. The unpainted wood is a wonderful contrast to the plastic most of his playthings are made with, and he seems to enjoy the smoothness and contours of the little cars. I know I do. I like the smell of them, too. It reminds me of the wood shavings that used to surround the chair of a favorite uncle who whittled away the evenings in a kitchen warmed by a wood stove. I personally love the smell and feel of yarn slipping through my fingers. Weavers like raw fleece, quilters and sewers like the colors and textures of cloth. Time spent in all these endeavors can be prayerful times, especially in the absence of noise. In silence, the mind is left alone to explore whatever needs to be processed. It is another way to create *temenos*, sacred space unpolluted by the unnecessary clutter of media noise.

The writer writes to make order out of chaos, a famous author once said. The potter shapes and reshapes until she gets it right. I think that is what God did and continues to do with the mess of the embryonic universe. I think that is what I did with the clay when I was on retreat, molding it until the chaos of my thoughts coalesced. I think that is what my brother Ed does when he tells a story or frames a picture in the lens of his camera. All of creation is moving toward perfection and fulfillment, but we need to wrestle with the stuff of it, just as we wrestle with the stuff of our lives. When we are being creative, we learn this in a primary way. When we are being creative we are learning to know what it must be like to be God.

Acting out of our creative side is sometimes called play. The story of a young mother I know shows how play in and of itself can also be prayer. Susan is in the process of writing her dissertation for a doctorate in theology, an intensely intellectual exercise. At the same time she is functioning as a deacon in her Methodist church. Early each morning she gets up to study, write, or exercise before making breakfast for her husband and two little girls. Then she drives the children to daycare. One day a week she travels to Boston to advise graduate students. She ends her day, every day, in a state of near collapse. "Pray," she says laughingly, or despairingly, depending on her mood, "I don't have time for prayer."

In our spiritual direction sessions, we have worked out a few things. Susan decided to set aside one shelf in a bookcase where she places special objects that put her in mind of the spiritual: a feather she picked up on a meditative walk during a retreat, an icon someone gave her, a decorated egg from last year's Easter celebration at church. Sometimes she plays a tape of her favorite hymns while she is doing the dishes.

But what has really brought her into touch with God's energy and taken her out of the place she is most comfortable, her intellect, is spending time in the evenings playing with her children. At one time she entertained them by reading books, and that is still wonderful, but now she is learning how to get involved herself in their imaginative play and simple art projects. As they make a mess with the paste pot and scraps of construction paper, so does she. When the finger paints come out, she makes designs too, watchful of how they touch a deeper place for her. Building with blocks or piecing puzzles together allows her mind to float, to relax, to open, mostly to rest in the present moment. When she decides to call this time prayer, she later records in her journal how the experience has affected her. And it has affected her in surprising ways. She tells me that she sees God more now as a playful presence than the stern taskmaster of her Presbyterian childhood. Tasks that she once took on automatically have lost their meaning, and she is thinking about letting some of them go. Anxieties about finishing her graduate work have lessened. Her interactions at church are more relaxed.

On my coffee table and on bookshelves in my living room are children's blocks, crayons and magic markers, pads of blank paper, puzzles, a coloring book of mandalic designs. These are for the grownups who visit, and for myself on evenings alone, as there are no children in my house. Under my table top tree at Christmas, I arrange toys I have picked up over the years—a singing top, a yo-yo, jacks and a ball, marbles, a "super pinky." It is fun to see creaky grownups on the floor doing "onesies" and "twosies" with the jacks and ball. (I send them outside to play with the super pinky.) I guess I am intrigued by these toys because they take me, as they take the young theology student, out and away from the intellectual spaces in which we usually live. Using them helps me develop emotional and psychological balance.

"Sacred Geometry" is a term I came across in a book I read about the Labyrinth Project begun by Lauren Artress, an Episcopalian priest at Grace Cathedral in San Francisco. Since then I have developed an awareness of the presence and significance of certain shapes and designs as symbols of the spiritual journey. Many of these shapes are found in toys. The singing top, for example, becomes a spinning spiral. The blocks—squares, triangles, and parallelograms—can be worked and reworked into an infinite variety of designs. A game called Tangelos challenges the players to make hundreds of designs out of seven basic shapes.

A few years ago when I was in the process of moving but had not found a space to move into, I saw an oriental rug in a secondhand furniture store and fell in love with it. At the time I had no floor on which to unroll it, but I bought it anyway. Now that the rug and I have found a place to call home, I look at it often and it never ceases to fascinate me. The designs, all geometric, are at times birds, at times llamas, at times dragons or lizards. Others who look closely at the rug see different things, things that speak to their unique imaginations. It is the same kind of inward drawing that we experience when we look into a kaleidoscope or contemplate a prism.

Our churches are designed on principles of sacred geometry. Consider the spires of the Gothic cathedrals, the arches and naves, the crucifix itself. So it can be that contemplating the pleasing shapes of geometry or "playing" with them using blocks or puzzles can lead us into an attitude of prayer.

The appearance of shapes in dreams, some say, points to a developing spirituality. Jung believed that the appearance of mandalas, the perfect arrangement of shapes within a circle, indicated integration of the personality (a merging with the Absolute Perfection perhaps?). An intriguing thought. Similarly, Teresa of Avila's *Interior Castle* is an example of the journey to spiritual perfection expressed in terms of sacred geometry. "I began to think of the soul," she said, "as if it were a castle made of a single diamond or of very clear crystal...." Certainly the image it evokes engages the imagination, not an easy task for practical Teresa. It was the tangible image of the chambered crystal castle which opened her imagination and freed her to express her thoughts about the soul in its journey to union with God, and to write her profound treatise on that journey.

Contemplating an icon, as already mentioned, can be another way into prayer. (And it is of some interest at this point to note that classical iconography is strikingly geometric.) In a 1995 issue of *Praying* Magazine, Dawn Gibeau described icons as "strange, bug-eyed, archaic things." Learning to pray with icons, learning to unlock their mysterious ways, she acknowledged, can be quite a task for the modern person, but with a little education and a little instruction they can become a useful addition to one's backpack on the spiritual journey.

Befriending Your Icons

The following guidelines from iconographer Fr. Peter Wilke appeared in the *Praying* article.

First, select one that appeals to you—they are available from catalogues and religious bookstores as greeting cards or small plaques.

Gaze on your icon in a quiet place for ten minutes. At the end of this time, record your responses. You will note that the effect of this prayerful gazing is similar physiologically to meditation and contemplation. Breathing and heartbeat rates slow down to the alpha state; one comes to a place of peacefulness.

Fr. Wilke says that "befriending" your icon—where it came from, who painted it, what the colors and physical attitudes of the subjects signify—enhances the experience. Then it becomes a familiar place to which to return over and over, "like a quiet, pleasant chapel," our experience of it ever deepening.

Meditative reading is another way to pray with "things." Just as one prays with Scripture by slowly absorbing the message it holds for us in the here and now, so we can approach the reading of spiritual literature. Dorothy Day spent several hours every afternoon reading the novels of Tolstoy and Dostoyevski. She read them over and over; they never ceased to hold meaning for her. Wonderful stirring fiction is still being published, novels and short stories and poetry, too, which distills language into a thick potent soup. Mainstream publishers seem to be capitalizing on a renewed interest in spiritual matters, so there is no lack of books to read; the problem, in fact, is that, with the plethora of available reading, one is tempted to take a smorgasbord approach and dabble or overindulge. Reading, like any passion, needs to be tempered.

I was introduced to the concept of meditative reading by a Quaker woman who was my spiritual advisor for a brief time. The idea startled me, as I had been trained to read as quickly as possible as a student, and as a librarian I had unlimited access to any book I desired. I read volumes. She advised me to slow down the process and to savor what I read instead of gulping it down, burping, and immediately beginning to chew on another. Instead, she suggested that I stop periodically when an idea, a word, or a phrase arrested my attention and think about it, explore its meaning and message, reflect on it, write it down, write a response to it.

Another source of spiritual matter exists in our dreams. They, too, can be honored as prayer if we approach them in an intentional way. Once we begin to understand dreams as a manifestation of a reality just as valid as conscious thought, we can invite their presence. We discover that it is possible to ask for dreams before going to sleep at night, to stay still upon waking from a vivid dream until it has imprinted itself on the conscious mind, to record the dream, and then to "play" with it until its meaning has been revealed. When we begin to be aware of the dream state, we realize that on some level it is more conscious than our waking state. In the waking state we are distracted from our subconscious mind by all the things—people, tasks, jobs—moving around us. In the sleep state on the other hand, we are free from all these distractions and therefore more able to pay attention to our unconscious, the other realm in which we exist, with all its gifts and opportunities.

In times long ago, dreams were honored as direct messages from God. The day on which I am writing this is the feast of the Epiphany, the time of the visit of the Wise Men. During the past two weeks the liturgical readings have been rich with stories of people who allowed themselves to be guided by dreams and intuitions. Joseph in particular comes to mind. It was in a dream that he learned of Mary's pregnancy, in a dream that he was warned to take Jesus away from Herod, in a dream that he was told to return and settle in Nazareth. The Wise Men followed a sign in the heavens; so did the shepherds. What is significant to me, as I reflect on this issue in the present day, is the fact that all of these people took direct action in response to mysterious events. The Eastern scholars dropped whatever it was they were doing to follow a distant star; Joseph removed his family to a foreign land.

More Than Novenas

With the rise of rationalism, this way of being fell into disrepute. Today some consider dream work to be nothing more than New Age nonsense, if not the work of the devil. Respected writers like Louis Savary and Edward Sellner, however, believe that everything is from God. They, and others who explicate dreams from that perspective, agree with Carl Jung that the experience of trust, which is at the core of religious faith, is activated in the dream state. Not only should we "work" with our dream material in order to extract its meaning, they say, but we should extend it into our conscious world in word and action. To sacramentalize our dreams as prayer, we must apply the same process we learned for approaching other forms of prayer. That is, we set aside appropriate time and space to reflect on them, "work" with them, and write down what has been revealed to us.

"The purpose of dreams," said Ursuline sister Pat Brockman (in a dream workshop I attended at the Center for Action and Contemplation in Albuquerque), "is to transform your inner self for the sake of the outer world." As mature Christians, it is our responsibility to move beyond mere reflection and extend the meaning of dreams into our own lives, the lives of those with whom we are in relationship, the life of the world. Like all prayer, dream work should not stop with interior renewal. Here is a process Sr. Pat suggests for praying with our dreams:

First, we should consider the dream as our personal parable; it is first of all about ourselves.

Apply "muscle work" to the dream, writing it down as if it were a story.

Give it a title. Then, retell the story in the first person. "I was on a beach....I saw a wrecked car...., etc."

Think of the dream as play, not portent, and recognize that lightness and darkness coexist.

Also think of the dream as pointing toward personal growth. It is your dream and you can explore it in any way you wish. It is your past, your present, your future; it is you in relationship to all aspects of your personality, and to your friends, family, enemies, acquaintances, and society in general.

Select one figure or image or event in the dream to write about in your journal.

Or otherwise ritualize the dream in movement or gesture, drawing, working with a piece of clay.

Most important, if elements of the dream suggest it, respond through action. Place a phone call, or write a letter, or pray for a person who appeared in your dream. Make an act of charity in your sphere of influence whether it be your home, workplace, community, or nation, even the world.

Bodily Prayer

But now it's time to wake up from our dreams and move the body out of bed and into the day. The poor body, like dreams, has also been relegated to a place of benign neglect, if not disgrace, in modern times. Whether this is because it is identified with "vile sex" or Milton's "nature red and rough in tooth and claw," it seems to frighten socialized cultures that see it as something that needs to be subdued and even dominated. In reality, God made a tangible world which is perceived through the sensate functions of the body, thereby validating both. But the body needs more than validation, it needs to be brought out of the shadows and into the light.

Those fortunate enough to have the gift, have "danced" prayer, but the rest of us can "move" during prayer. We do this already in the postures we assume during liturgy. We do this in prayer when we sit attentively or kneel or make the Sign of the Cross. And we can learn new ways.

Fr. Thomas Ryan, C.S.P., has joined a long list of serious spiritual leaders who have attempted to introduce the practice of yoga to the faithful. Yoga, which is from the Hindu tradition, is essentially a way of readying the body for sitting in contemplative stillness. That its origin lies in an Eastern tradition has been a stumbling block for many, but Fr. Ryan and others like him recognize that, whether from the East or the West, it is the same God with whom we all aspire to connect. Furthermore, if purifying, steadying, strengthening, and balancing the body can prepare us for union with the transcendent presence, then the practice must have value. Western ways, in fact, have dishonored the body by encouraging excessive eating and physical inertia. The image of the rotund nun or monk either at prayer or at table comes to mind. That image is quickly being replaced by another, one of an aware, alert, and lean spiritual practitioner.

Some yoga postures, Fr. Ryan suggests in his book, *Yoga: Prayer of Heart and Body*, are perfect accompaniments to psalm verses and well-known prayers such as the Our Father. He shows drawings of these postures along with the words to familiar prayers or lines from the psalms. While holding the Forward Bend posture, for example, he suggests reciting Line 36 from Ps. 119, "Bend my heart to obey your law, O God." Appropriate for the Child's Pose, in which the torso bends over folded knees and the arms lie by the side, are the words, "At the name of Jesus, every knee should bend in heaven, on earth and under the earth." In the Sun Salutation the body starts in a standing position with arms raised overhead, then bends forward, head to floor, the knees bending to allow the body to lower to a prone position, then straightens again to standing with arms raised. Phrases from the Our Father are recited as the body moves fluidly from one element in this posture to the next.

Kathleen Fischer in *Women at the Well: Feminist Perspectives on Spiritual Direction* makes the following suggestion for a Scripture reflection using the body. First, warm up by taking some deep breaths and moving every part of the body in a flowing sequence, starting with the head and moving to the feet. Then take a piece of Scripture, perhaps a psalm or a story from the gospels that speaks to you, and ask your body to express the feelings that arise. Standing, sitting, kneeling, bowing, walking, or lying down, pray with the passage or psalm for ten minutes or so, letting the arms, hands, legs, upper and lower body move as they will. When the prayer is over, spend a few minutes in quiet reflection on the effect the experience of moving has had on you.

The system of postures we call yoga was specifically designed to prepare the body for contemplation, but many other forms of physical exercise can be undertaken in a spirit of prayer. Swimming, for example, can be a bliss of serene rhythmical movement through the element of water, symbolic of cleansing and transformation. Someone I know repeats a mantra taken from her day's reading of Scripture as she swims her laps. Others take a mantra on their daily walk or jog, or otherwise seek the presence of God during that time. A busy young man reads spiritual literature while on the treadmill at his gym.

Work of the hands is another expression of body prayer and can be creative as well. Teresa of Avila, wise, wise woman that she was, saw to it that all her sisters did some sort of handiwork—knitting, sewing, embroidery. Benedict, that wise, wise man, also mandated that his monks spend as much time doing manual labor as chanting the psalms. Working with the hands steadies the soul and leaves the mind open to spiritual meanderings. Gardeners have always believed this, as have weavers, potters, furniture makers, and cooks. Such work grounds us and reminds us that spirituality is really very ordinary work, not at all elegant or reserved exclusively for the super good.

Praying With Nothing

Contemplation is said to be the "highest form" of prayer, a place of pure union with God. It is that state of being where we disengage from our ego and become aware of the presence of God. The most desired attainment of mystics and monastics, let it also be said that "ordinary people," too, can practice contemplative prayer. Spiritual leaders like Thomas Keating have reintroduced it to thousands as Centering Prayer. Thich Nhat Hahn, the Vietnamese Buddhist monk, describes it as mindfulness.

While one usually enters into the contemplative state by a process of deep rhythmic breathing, receptivity to the presence of God can also be quickened by the prayer forms we have reviewed. At a certain point we stop engaging with them, actively searching for inspiration, and move into a more passive state. This is what happens when Scripture is approached using an ancient four-part process known as *lectio divina,* or divine reading. For years I have had a card in the pages of my Bible that lists the four parts of *lectio divina.*

> *Lectio:* "Listen to the Word of God with the ears of your heart." Part one is an attentive reading of a Scripture passage, a slow, careful reading and rereading of the selected line or passage.

> *Meditatio:* "Ponder God's Word in your heart." Meditatio encourages musing on or analyzing the meaning of the passage, working with it so as to understand it better.

> *Oratio:* "Let your heart speak to God." During the time of oratio, we are invited to respond emotionally to the passage. What is the personal message for me? What feelings or needs does it speak to?

> *Contemplatio:* "Rest in God." Breathe into this step. Release the need to understand, the need to feel, the need to respond. Simply be. Spend as much time there as you can.

Whether it's with the Word or whether it's a walk on the beach, a moving passage from a great symphony, a quiet hour spent in a woodworking shop, or a game of checkers with a six-year-old, the prayerful movement toward contemplation can begin. It looks like doing nothing, but in reality it is a meeting with God, a meeting made possible because all distractions have been eliminated. Paradoxically, it is the intense and intentional immersion into "something" that can lead us into this "nothing."

Other Considerations

Some of the prayer forms we have looked at may seem alien to you, some appealing. Some may work for a while and then be replaced by others. That is fine. What I hope is that you have broadened your understanding of prayer to be "an occasion for an encounter with God," and not a rigid performance of out-moded practices. Still, there are other considerations.

That silence and solitude are the "setups" for a life of prayer is undisputed. All the great spiritual writers and practitioners agree. This is not to say that prayer is impossible amid noise and even during times of chaos. Just look at the riot of expression in the psalms. Nevertheless, there is value in silence and solitude, so highly preserved and respected in the monastery, and so unavailable to those who live "in the world." How often in the gospels do we read that Jesus went off by himself to pray? And on his return he was always empowered to handle the chal-lenges and demands that awaited him. Like him, we need to retreat from time to time.

In his book *Yoga: Prayer of Heart and Body,* Thomas Ryan, who advocates the practice of yoga as preparation for contem-plation, also recommends an occasional "Poustinia Day" for the serious seeker. A Russian word with the literal meaning of "desert," Poustinia was brought into current use by Catherine de Hueck Doherty who founded Madonna House, a lay apostolate training center in Ontario, Canada. She had several small cabins built on the grounds of her retreat center, Madonna House, where her staff and residents of the program could live for short periods of "desert time."

But a poustinia day need not take place in a specific location.

One can move about freely on such a day in a city or country environment. The idea is to put oneself in a situation where it is not necessary to speak with anyone. Various places are appropriate—one's home, a city park, the beach or countryside. Fr. Ryan takes one day a month to go off by himself. From 8:00 a.m until dinnertime he is alone. He takes his Bible and prayer journal and a minimal amount of food and water with him and disappears. It is not a difficult thing to do, and this practice offers an excellent opportunity to try some of the modes of prayer we have been discussing.

Retreat houses, for those who can take more time away, offer weekends, days or evenings of reflection, or "directed" retreats during which one consults daily with a spiritual director but spends most of the time in silent prayer and reflection. My own recent discovery of a Benedictine monastery not far from my home has opened up a whole new world of spiritual practice to me, a world of chant and silence and discipline. And because hospitality is one of the gifts of the Benedictine way, I feel welcomed at the same time, not to mention well fed. I find that I return refreshed and rested from these extended periods of intentional prayer with a new clarity on the life I have chosen to lead.

Intentionality is another aspect of prayer to which we should give consideration. When we set aside a certain amount of time for prayer, we are being intentional. We are saying, "Come and speak to me, God. I am sitting here, kneeling here, standing here, walking here, swimming here, waiting. Tell me you know this. Let me know you are near." Even though we realize that God frequently "breaks in" at unexpected times, we believe equally that the chances of hearing the divine voice are increased when we are being attentive in a special way. To be intentional is to decide on the form of prayer, to set aside a specific amount of time for it, to "set the mood" with music, incense, a candle, or some other clue to ourselves that this is a time of prayer, and to follow up on the prayer time in our journals. When we attend to these details, we avoid the pitfall of moving through our days in a cloud of pious daydreaming.

Interior prayer, such as we have been discussing, reveals and initiates the inward movements of our souls, but is invalid, I believe, unless coupled with an outward expression of some kind. Individual fulfillment is God's wish for each of us, but that fulfillment is part of a yet larger picture. At some point in our own coming into true being, a moment arrives for each of us when we can say, "All right, now I can move ahead. I feel clear about myself, and I have a new sense of personal power. What can I do to help create the future?" Now is the time for each of us to assume the place in God's plan for which we were created. Now is the time to participate in the grand movement toward which the world is inexorably moving, what Teilhard de Chardin calls the Omega Point, the culmination of God's primary creative act.

Many believe that this culminating moment is directly related to the condition of the poor and that working to alleviate their plight is the work of the kingdom. For many of today's thinkers, writers like Albert Nolan, O.P., and William Reiser, S.J., the prayer of action is the most valid form of prayer. They argue that the life of Jesus is sufficient evidence for taking this position, that the primary purpose of his presence among us in human form was to show that God wants us to attend to one another's needs in a very particular way.

"Jesus is the icon of the invisible God," said Gil Bailie in an interview in *Presence*, the journal of Spiritual Directors' International. If we accept that he is indeed a revelation of the nature of God, then these aspects of his life—his activism, connection to community, concern for the needs of the sick, the outcast, the marginalized—cannot be ignored. For many centuries the "spin" on Jesus has been personal redemption, that he came to expiate our "sins." This led to a strong focus on introverted forms of prayer and ways of being. Today we are taking another look at the whole picture and asking ourselves: if I am personally redeemed, what next? What do I do now? And the answer is not: go to more Masses, say more rosaries. The answer is: help your neighbor.

Just as individual sanctity is not enough unless it finds expression in the outer world, so individual prayer is not enough unless balanced by communal prayer. All of the prayer practices we have discussed in this chapter, including contemplation, can be experienced in the company of others or shared with others in a group setting. This is an expression of a broad-based movement toward collaboration in classroom settings, in the workplace, in boardrooms, in social service agencies.

It is a movement grounded in theology. God is three-personned, each one of the persons interacting with the others in an ever-moving circle or cycle. There is a fluidity in the relationships among them that implies change rather than immutability. Therefore, the traditional static image of a God who never changes is suspect and we are drawn toward a more vital belief, that we are in an ever-changing relationship with the divine mystery, a relationship that implies mutual responsibility for ourselves, others, and the world in which we exist.

In a way, we are not finding anything new here, but rather an awareness of things that have been in place for a long time but not looked at, the relational aspect of God, for example, the role of community and collaboration in the life of Jesus. Note how he always questioned his followers in his teaching, challenging them to "consider the options," teasing them to think critically by using irony and paradox in his parables. Seldom did he heal without first asking the sufferer to name the problem and ask for healing in so many words. He wandered, he sat at meals, he went when called, not in an undisciplined way, but out of the realization that the future is fulfilled in the business of every present moment. Fluidity, relationship, collaboration, community. This unrestricted, communal way of being is the subtext of Jesus' life.

A life of prayer, therefore, is not for the reclusive. It is for those who are fully engaged—with the three-personed God, with the world, with humanity, with all aspects of one's self. Its requisites are as they were for Jesus: intentionality, community, and social action. Its ultimate reward, as it was for Jesus, is reunion with God, our loving parent.

CHAPTER EIGHT

Participation in Intentional Community

She sat across the room from me on my first day of class in graduate school, the only other middle-aged person there. A small compactly built woman with grey-blond hair cut in a short bob and large modish glasses sliding down her nose, she exuded an intense anxiety cloaked in a brittle wit. Within minutes she had engaged the professor in a playful banter that would continue throughout the semester. We would be bosom buddies for the next two years.

Her playfulness in the classroom belied a bitter heart; she was crushed by the recent breakup of her twenty-five-year marriage and her husband's swift remarriage to a much younger woman; she was devastated in fact. And desperately lonely. Her four children were grown and living independently. Some of them were loyal to their father and alienated from her because the divorce had been a bitter one with both parents demanding that the children take sides.

But Joan had a plan.

"I'm going to become a nun," she said, and she meant it.

She had a number of friends in religious orders, a life she idealized. They had financial security. (Joan had refused alimony.) They lived in nice places. (She had no home at the present and was living in graduate housing.) Most of all, they had each other, a built-in community. Now that she was unmarried, she would fit in just fine. She would become a nun.

For the next few years, Joan pursued her goal of becoming a nun, but met with no success. The orders were ready for her it seemed, and I was able to figure out after a while that she wasn't the only late-in-life candidate for religious life who came knocking on their doors. Many other women in Joan's circumstances—and, at the time, the early seventies, the numbers were growing exponentially—had the same idea. The life of a religious was the perfect antidote for the broken heart of mid-life divorce: secure, comfortable, holy, and with every need met.

The Realm of Myth

The romantic notion of community life as nirvana has long passed into the realm of myth, and most of us now realize that it is a lifestyle as difficult as any. Security and comfort are no longer the prerogatives of religious women, who have been hit with some harsh realities in recent years. Their every need is not met, and I speak not only of financial needs. My friends in religious life experience loneliness and emotional pain as often and as deeply as anyone. Community living is fraught with trials as much as it is blessed with joys.

Many have written candidly about the challenges it poses. Parker Palmer, a well-known educator and writer from the Quaker tradition is one. He has said, with some humor, that "community is that place where the person you least want to live with always lives," and, to add insult to injury, "when that person moves away, someone else arises immediately to take his or her place." In spite of these complaints, however, he asserts in *A Place Called Community*, a Pendle Hill pamphlet, that, although "community always means the collision of egos," it is what forms us. Thus, the idea of community, the reality of it, and the allure of it, persist in our own distracted times when individual self-sufficiency and the nuclear family system have failed to bring their promised rewards.

Joan's idealistic vision of community met the criteria of this more sober definition from Parker Palmer: "Community [is] a capacity for relatedness within individuals—relatedness not only to people but to events in history, to nature, to the world of ideas, and, yes, to things of the spirit." Religious communities meet the criteria of this definition, but so do others. Joan, although she may not have realized it at the time, belonged to several communities. She shared one with her children. She joined a parish in the town where the university was situated. She formed ties with the other graduate students and the faculty. And she had a strong network of lifelong friends. Later when she became a school librarian, she connected strongly with the students and faculty where she worked. What then was missing? What was the unique element Joan was looking for?

This question has been a leading one for me in the twenty years or so since I suffered the same traumatic loss as Joan, and is a critical one for all single people, I believe. I pondered it without finding a resolution for years. Like Joan, I belonged to various groups, but did not find them sufficient for my needs. I thought long and hard on the question, trying to identify the missing link. Why weren't they sufficient? Why didn't they have the power to assuage my feelings of isolation? Then one blustery March afternoon while I was taking a walk, the answer came to me. What I was looking for was *intentional* community, one in which I and other like-minded people overtly expressed our mutual commitment to one another in a conscious and deliberate way. My question was finally answered, but my quest only just begun; from then on the search for intentional community became the spark for my most intense study and best energies.

As I moved deeper and deeper into my quest, I became aware of something called variously the small church, base church, small Christian community, faith-sharing, or intentional Christian community movement. Dick Westley, a retired Loyola University professor of philosophy, is an articulate and energetic proponent for the small Christian community movement in North America. (See his books, *Redemptive Intimacy* and *Good Things Happen,* both published by Twenty-Third Publications.) As the church has developed throughout history, and especially in North America, he maintains, the spiritual intimacy inherent in the Jewish tradition, the one in which Jesus lived and taught, and in the years of the early Christian church, has been replaced by a culture in which humans operate as individuals rather than as members of close groups. As a result, feelings of isolation and disconnection prevail, feelings that lead inexorably to attitudes of disinterest and a climate in which hostility and violence toward others can be tolerated.

A New Metaphor

In *Dangerous Memories,* their seminal book on the subject of community, Bernard Lee, a Marianist priest who now directs the Institute for Ministry at Loyola University, and Michael Cowan, a professor of pastoral theology at St. John's University, say that Catholics are in need of renewed inspiration, and that it must be framed in a new root metaphor. Metaphors, according to the novelist Milan Kundera whom they quote "contain in a nutshell a basic human possibility." Until the Second Vatican Council (Vatican II), Catholics thought of the church as institution. An institution has strict boundaries of authority. The lines of authority in the church emanate from the clergy to the laity, the clergy leading, the laity following. With Vatican II, a new metaphor, the concept of the "People of God," with its implication of shared or collaborative leadership was introduced. Although we are far from realizing this ideal, this "new metaphor" has forced a number of issues within the church and has been the inspiration for strong undercurrents, the small Christian community movement being one.

Lee and Cowan trace the history of the small Christian community movement from the time of the early church, when it was the normal pattern, to the House Church movement, fundamentally a European phenomenon, to the transformational base ecclesial communities. These last began in Brazil and spread throughout South and Latin America in the late 1950s and '60s. From there the movement found its way to Africa where the groups were called small Christian communities, and, eventually, it came to North America. There were some differences, however. In South and Latin American they emerged from the "base," i.e., from the people, while in Africa the initiative came from the ecclesiastical hierarchy.

In the United States the movement has struggled. Although considerable progress has been made in parts of the country where there are large Hispanic populations, efforts to form small communities of faith have arisen from the white middle class who have not experienced firsthand the economic and social inequalities that cause people to form natural bonds. Perhaps that is why the RENEW project, an attempt to superimpose the Third World experience on the North American one, failed to sustain itself after the initial campaign. (It has also been suggested that a strong emphasis of structure and written materials overwhelmed the participants and stifled their spontaneity and initial enthusiasm.)

Lee and Cowan gave me the definition for intentional community I was looking for.

> "An intentional Christian community," they say, "is a relatively small group of persons committed to ongoing conversation and shared action along four distinguishable but interrelated dimensions:
>
> • They are consistently committed to a high degree of mutuality in their relationships.
>
> • They pursue an informed critical awareness of and an active engagement within the cultural, political, and economic megasystems of their society.
>
> • They cultivate and sustain a network of lively connections with other persons, communities, and movements of similar purpose.
>
> • They attend faithfully to the Christian character of their community's life." (p. 92)

These four characteristics of mutuality, social engagement, networking, and Christian remembrance are complemented by four Greek words used to define church. They are: *koinonia, diakonia, kerygma,* and *leitourgia.* (These words are also used by Buena Vista in Arvada, Colorado, one of the several national organizations in the United States that promotes and supports the small church movement.) *Koinonia* means that all the members of the group are concerned about the welfare of all the other members and that they connect with other like-minded groups. *Diakonia* refers to the commitment to social justice issues both in and beyond the membership. *Kerygma* is the immersion in the Great Story of Jesus' life as found in the gospels; and *Leitourgia* refers to ritual, especially the celebration of the eucharist. Without any one of these characteristics, the group fails as a model of church, a model that intentional Christian communities strive to emulate. Thus, while any number of groups can call themselves community, only those who meet these four criteria constitute true intentional community. That, I decided, was what I would search for, and, like the Three Wise Men, I began to follow the star.

My first stop along the way was a group begun by two Congregation of Notre Dame women, Mary Ann Rossi and Joan Mahoney, chaplains at various times at the University of Rhode Island and Rhode Island College. Joan, who is now at Boston College, and Mary Ann called together a group of women and men who met monthly to share their life work and experiences, to reflect on the gospel, to do simple ritual, and to pray. Eventually, the group made a commitment to an agency that ministered to women in recovery. Thus, it embodied the four marks of church. It was about sharing the gospel, mutual support and networking, service to the poor, and worshiping together at Sunday Mass when possible. Although I have moved away from them, I am still committed in spirit to this ongoing community and thank Mary Ann and Joan for their teachings.

My second stop was the Center for Action and Contemplation, founded by the renowned Franciscan preacher, Richard Rohr. I stumbled on it by chance, through an advertisement in the National Catholic Reporter, and with some trepidation and not much information, signed up for a six-week internship, bought my plane ticket, said goodbye to my mother and children, packed up a briefcase full of research notes (as I was on sabbatical at the time), and set out for the great unknown. What I found was a model for living that affirmed the values I was gradually incorporating into my own life.

The Center is dedicated to creating a seamless blend between social justice activities, including peacemaking, and the contemplative stance. Richard, as everyone calls him, having gone through several passages in his own life, had come to the realization in the 1980s that social activists, if focused too intently on the external world, sometimes lose their ability to reflect on the workings of their own souls, while those who are on a contemplative path often lose sight of the needs of the outer world. The curriculum of the CAC, for us interns and the staff as well, was a carefully designed combination of both.

A typical day for me and the other five people in my internship group began with a half-hour of contemplative prayer. Later in the morning we drove into the inner city of Albuquerque to various social service agencies—a daycare center for children, a shelter for the homeless, a senior center—for a few hours of work. The afternoons were given over to individual and group spiritual direction, lectures on the practice of contemplation, presentations by local social service personnel or peace activists, even lessons in vegetarian cooking and permaculture, the art and practice of creating self-sustaining urban ecosystems. Living communally, a lifestyle I had never experienced outside of ordinary family life, was a new and wonderful experience for me. We took turns with the cooking, cleaning, gardening, and laundry chores. As we lived together for six weeks, we were surprised, and not a little disturbed, by the emotional impact we had on one another. Each of us was tested to our depths; the Spirit works in strange ways.

The Center also served as a focus for the larger Albuquerque community. Wednesday evenings were devoted to a model of gospel reflection based on one used by the base ecclesial communities of Latin America and Africa. When Richard was in town, he gave talks on spirituality that were open to the public.

The Center also ran weekend retreats and sponsored witness activities such as a trip to White Sands, the sight of the testing of the first atomic bomb, a profound and soul-shattering experience for me. Once a month on Sunday morning a large group gathered for an agape, a participatory liturgy followed by a potluck. There we met people from the area who had aligned themselves with the work of the Center. Besides the other interns, the staff, and others from the Albuquerque area, I met people from all over the country and indeed from all over the world. Missionaries and laypeople often stopped by on their way to Latin America, and many Europeans visited and interned at the Center because of Richard's frequent trips there. I will always remember my stay as a time when I lived with others in perfect accordance with the marks of church—mutuality, social engagement, networking, and Christian remembrance. The last, breaking bread and remembering the life of Christ in the company of others during inclusive liturgies, along with Richard's inspired homilies, will always be, for me, "dangerous memories" indeed, happy foreshadowings of the church to come.

I returned to "normal" life from the internship profoundly affected by the experience and reinforced in my determination to find the kind of community the CAC modeled, ruling out communal living. With the support of Fr. Bob Hawkins, the Catholic chaplain at the University of Rhode Island, where I was working at the time, I organized something called "The Contemplative Hour." Approximately eight people joined the group. We met at the end of the work day from 5:30 to 6:30 in a small chapel on campus and spent the first twenty minutes in silent centering prayer. The rest of the time we read and reflected on the gospel using the African base Christian community model I had learned at the CAC.

In this model, the gospel is read three times. The first time everyone in the group simply repeats the one word or phrase that strikes him or her. After the second reading, the group shares reflections on the meanings taken from it. The third reading leads the group into specific social action, both individual

and group. Those who attended (we always kept the membership open) found the silence refreshing (after some early discomfort). Reflecting on the gospel in a way that personalized it,
was radically different from what most of us had experienced,
and this led to deep bonding among the members. We held
together for about two years, during which time I was gradually making plans to leave my position at the university in order
to activate the new life vision I was formulating for myself. The
group helped me through the process.

Throughout our time together we remained a contemplative
prayer and gospel reflection group but did not evolve into a true
intentional community. The marks of mutual concern and
Christian remembrance were strong characteristics of our shared
spirituality, as we cared deeply for one another and participated
in the life of the local church. However, we never moved toward
shared social action or networking, indicating that, as a group,
we were not ready to be small church. The commitment to
social action, I have come to realize, is a process that must be
allowed to evolve gradually as mutuality and commitment grow.
Whether we would have found ourselves there eventually, I do
not know, but I do know that the memories of our shared prayer
and the insights we generated as we sat in our small circle, week
after week, season after season, while day darkened into
evening, will never fade.

When I moved to Maine, I looked for opportunities to join an
intentional community, and, finding none, set about forming
one. These were the people in my parish who accepted the invitation: a married couple without children, a married couple with
a teenager, a married woman with one child, a single mother
with one child, two single divorced women, one divorced man.
We meet without exception every second Monday evening from
seven to nine, and have been together for two years now. We
are still working toward fulfilling the fourth mark of church,
diakonia, shared commitment to a social justice issue, but we
are considering working with the youth ministry on their service
projects in a poor neighborhood within our parish. In addition,

we occasionally meet with another intentional community in the parish for conversation around issues of social justice. On Sundays we sit together at Mass.

I think Joan would like a community such as ours. She did not really want to become a nun, she was just angry with her husband and wanted to show him how much she didn't need him, on many levels. Her desire to join in community, however, was right on. For single people, the presence or absence of a small intentional community may be the single most important factor in their lives, and a critical matter of survival. Let me explain why I feel this to be so.

The Effects of Loneliness

"Loneliness may be hazardous to health," read the heading for an op-ed piece in my local paper recently. The doctor who wrote it cited the statistic that there are five times as many people living alone now as there were 100 years ago. These people are more susceptible to cancers and stress-related illnesses, he said, and "Long term loneliness itself produces chronic stress, a toxin with serious health consequences."

Not all single people are lonely, of course, but the single life is surely a risk factor. Therefore, those who live it, more than those who are married, need the support and affirmation of others. They are the sole mirrors of themselves; no one else is present to them exclusively as a spouse is—or should be—present to the other spouse. All their decisions are made by themselves alone, all their fears are met alone, all their triumphs are celebrated alone, all their failures endured alone, and all their heartbreaks suffered alone. When single people come home from work, they are alone, and when they make weekend plans, they often do it alone.

It is no wonder then that they yearn deeply for the companionship of another, and it is no wonder that they often make disastrous decisions in their attempts to ease that yearning. Furthermore, once having made the uninformed or misguided choice, they may stay with it even when they are being neglected, mistreated, or even abused.

Membership in an intentional community based on right principles is one remedy. It provides not only relief from isolation but also a valid model of healthy proper relational behavior. With such a model before them, they are more inclined to make right decisions. Community also provides a platform for bold action, this because individuals in community see themselves as part of a whole rather than as a vulnerable and unprotected independent agent. During times of insecurity and vulnerability, they can be tempted to take a timid approach to life, avoiding risk and failing to actualize their gifts. If reinforced by the presence of community in their lives, however, the opposite can be true; they can learn to take risks and release their talents for the benefit of themselves and others.

When two of my children were being confirmed, I bought each of them tasteful bronze crucifixes. One of them depicts bread and grapes, the other the figure of Jesus and two others sitting over a loaf of bread. That is my favorite, and my children, disinterested at this time in their religious heritage, have graciously left such artifacts from their past with me. It hangs at the doorway to my room. I love that depiction because, for me, it symbolizes Jesus' firm grounding in the community of believers that he called into being.

What motivated him to do so? Was it a part of his experience as it is ours, I wonder, that feeling of isolation and vulnerability? Did he realize, when he set out into the world, that he would miss the old life in Nazareth and would need to build a new comfort zone? I do not wish to be irreverent here. Clearly, he created a following for the specific intention of propagating his teachings, and in the gospels we see him constantly attempting to educate them around his beliefs. But I cannot believe that that was his only motivation, otherwise he would have spent more of his time alone. Instead, we get a picture of a man who was usually with others. Someone once counted how many times in Luke's gospel he sat down to a meal with others. I don't recall the number but it was significant, a strong indicator, I believe, that identification with a community was an essential ingredient in his life, and that this community was more than a school for disciples. He needed it. He was strengthened by its presence in his life. Because of it, he was emboldened to continue his difficult work.

A Relational Model

In light of this belief, I find that it very reasonable to understand the Trinity as a relational model. Father, Son, and Holy Spirit—initiator, love incarnate, spirit sustaining—move around one another in an eternal renewable cycle. The way process theology interprets the divinity reinforces this interpretation for me. Kathleen Fischer in *The Inner Rainbow*, explains this complex idea in terms a layperson can understand. I paraphrase it here. Process theologians, she says, believe that when we assume that God is supremely independent, controlling, and active, and *only* that, we interpret God inadequately. This interpretation has led us to create a mental and emotional conception of God as stereotypically male, immutable, and lacking in passion, all of which contradicts another belief, that God is full of love. Love does not present itself in these rigid ways. Rather, it involves mutual interaction, the sharing of suffering and joy, and creative activity in relation to another. These characteristics give rise to different images of God, images reflected in the Old Testament themes of constant covenant played out in intimate associations, and in God's incarnation in the person of Jesus. In both these representations of God we find the tender elements of sympathy and love, and we see that God's involvement in human experience is persuasive rather than coercive.

Thus, Alfred North Whitehead, whose thought and writing inspired process theology, conceives of a very different God from the traditional one. Whitehead bases his vision of the attributes of God on what he saw reflected in the life of Jesus. His God is "the poet of the world, with tender patience leading it by his vision of truth, beauty, and goodness." God is the "great companion" and "fellow-sufferer," not someone removed and distant. God does not keep a distance, but rather enters human time and experience with us, hears and responds, shares and suffers, gives and receives, in a constant flow. God's stance toward humankind is subjective rather than objective; God participates in it.

The implications deepen. God, says Whitehead, is the initiator of a cosmos built on mutuality and interdependence, not self-sufficiency and independence. Therefore, every thing and every person in the world is influenced by every thing and every other one. Environmentalism arises from this theology, as well as the movement toward collaborative models of decision making. The usual hierarchies and dualities are replaced by a network of relationships between interdependent beings, an interdependence that requires one to be willing to receive as well as give, to be affected by the other, and to respond to that influence or affect.

We are said to be in a time of convergence, when an immense transformation, inspired by currents of thought that have been bubbling up below the surface for decades, is about to break through. One of the inspirers of this movement is Whitehead; another is Teilhard de Chardin who fell in love with a piece of iron while walking in the countryside one day and spent the rest of his life testifying to the interrelatedness of everything in and under heaven, even the seemingly inanimate. Little by little, thoughtful people are taking up these ideas and applying them to their spheres of influence.

Paulo Freire is one. He has had tremendous impact in the field of education. A Brazilian, he was commissioned by the government to "eradicate" adult illiteracy. The literacy program he developed was effective, not only in raising the reading level of Brazilian peasants, but in raising their political consciousness as well. Not surprisingly, these results proved intimidating to the establishment.

His program sought to displace what he called the "banking system" of education, the method by which a teacher delivers information to passive students. Instead, his learners determined among themselves what it was they needed to know and were encouraged to analyze that new knowledge with a critical consciousness. "We started groups we called 'culture circles,'" he told an interviewer. "Instead of teachers, we had coordinators; instead of lectures, dialogue; instead of pupils, participants." Freire's illiterate students, of course, were also poor and politically and economically oppressed. For them to begin to think realistically and rationally about their situation threatened the established order. Thus Freire was called a revolutionary and deported. Nevertheless, his ideas spread throughout the Americas, including Latin America, and were reflected in the convictions of liberation theology.

The base ecclesial (church) communities, which were also formed at that time, were modeled on a format similar to his "culture circles." Instead of generating their discussions from words about the social and political realities of the communities in which they lived, however, the participants looked at the gospel stories and interpreted their message in light of their contemporary experience, both personal and social. Thus enabled (in the best sense of the word), they became more critical of the political, social, economic, and, yes, ecclesiastical status quo. This, again, led to reaction from the hierarchy, a reaction that sadly continues to this day. In spite of opposition, however, the base community experience has made its way up through the continent and has been welcomed in North America, inspiring the small Christian community movement of which we spoke earlier. Indeed, the movement toward community-building on a small scale is one of the transformative undercurrents of our time.

North American Communities

Middle-class Americans need community as much as the poor do, but their need arises from causes other than material poverty and social and political disenfranchisement. Poverty of spirit is the primary North American experience. Unfortunately, we do not easily minister to one another in these matters. Thus, in many ways, the poor are more fortunate than the well-to-do. Supported as they are by a closely linked community, they may be more spiritually and emotionally "in touch" than their richer sisters and brothers who suffer from spiritual emptiness and social isolation. When awareness and consciousness are raised among the rich and middle class, however, the call to community is clear.

Single adults, even if affluent, may be more grateful than most because in many ways they also are a disenfranchised population with little corporate influence. Unfortunately, communities like those we have been discussing, in spite of their appeal and appropriateness, are scarce. Individual initiative is necessary if they are to come to life. But they will come to life, once begun. The hard part is beginning them. Fortunately, there is a sizeable body of literature on the subject and many excellent guidelines have been published. Dick Westley, in *Redemptive Intimacy*, offers some practical advice:

> In the formation of a small Christian community one person generally takes the role of convener. The convener makes it known that a group is being formed and may take the initiative to "target," or invite people into membership. She takes on the responsibility for scheduling and planning the first few meetings and leads the discussion of guidelines and expectations.
>
> After that initial period is over, the leadership is to be shared.
>
> The optimum time for groups to meet is every other week for a maximum of two hours.
>
> A manageable number of ten to fifteen members is recommended; larger groups can be cumbersome and less likely to bond.
>
> Individuals should commit to at least six meetings and defer their decision to join until that time.
>
> The primary purpose of gathering is to share faith, but after the members get to know one another, the tendency to

spend too much time socializing can be tempting. A "check in" time helps people make necessary connections, but it should be kept brief. Special times can be set aside specifically for socializing.

It is important to differentiate this kind of gathering as faith sharing. It is not about intellectualizing, no one is the "authority." Nor do pontificating, moralizing, or giving advice serve a purpose. All voices are equal, and each has a right to take as much time as needed to express his or her feelings without interruption. Only after each has had a turn to share should dialogue begin, and care should be taken that it does not become debate and that the most powerful or articulate members do not dominate the conversation.

Regardless of the focus a group may choose, the format remains basically the same. Westley suggests that the meetings begin with prayer and move into a twenty to thirty minute reflection on the gospel for the coming Sunday, or some other Scripture passage, perhaps selected by the host for the evening. Everyone should have a chance to express his or her uninterrupted response to the reading; those who don't wish to contribute can simply state that they are "passing" for the moment.

The next part of the meeting is devoted to whatever purpose prompted its formation. Westley's group meets to discuss books; other groups may meet around a common activity in the community or parish or a social action project of some sort. Others may choose to spend their time together in simple faith-sharing around the Sunday gospel.

When it is time to draw the evening to a close, the host may invite prayers of thanksgiving and petition before giving the closing prayer.

The best guide to the nuts and bolts of building and sustaining an intentional Christian community that I have ever come across is the book *Keeping the Conversation Going: A Method of Community Formation and Process* by Marianne Griebler and

Felicia Wolf, O.S.F. Besides giving practical suggestions about how to start a group, Griebler and Wolf have written chapters on leadership, the conventions of faith-sharing, prayer and ritual, the process of theological reflection, and conflict resolution. Buena Vista is also an excellent resource for small communities and has published four pamphlets, one each on the four marks of church: community, Scripture reflection, ritual, and social justice.

One final note. Notwithstanding the reality of spiritual impoverishment and the need to alleviate it, Americans in intentional community do not have license to ignore the more tangible realities of their less fortunate kin. A central focus of community must be social justice. Third World people and the poor in our own country sit right at the center of social justice issues. They step into them every time they set foot outside their doors; they sleep with them, they eat with them. Not so for the middle class. For us, it is a far trip to the world of the poor, and the trip can be an uncomfortable and even threatening one. Nevertheless, it must be made.

First World people need to become proactive in helping to bring about social justice in an economic and political system that is seriously out of balance. Thus, even though spiritual nourishment and fulfillment are valid reasons for membership in a small spiritual community, they cannot be the sole reasons; the fundamental purpose of small church is to further the social message of the gospel. It is the ground in which the community is rooted and out of which it grows. And it is one of the marks of church, *Diakonia*. Without it there is no authentic community of spirit.

In *Dangerous Memories*, Lee and Cowan called for a new inspiring metaphor for the church in our times and found it in "the people of God." The metaphor that can mobilize and transform the experience of the single life, I believe, is "focused living," and community is one of its essential parts. As Dorothy Day said, "We have all known the long loneliness and we have learned that the only solution is love and love comes with community." Why should we expect ourselves to be "rugged individualists"? Why shouldn't the expectation instead be membership in a safe and nurturing group grounded in spirituality? Recall if you will the group of people we imagined in an earlier chapter, all of them living in close proximity to one another and, without knowing it, loosely connected to the same parish. Just imagine if they were called together by their parish to join in a discussion of issues of mutual concern, issues such as these we are touching on here. Imagine them coming out of their shadows and reviving their souls in the warmth of companionship. Imagine them enjoying the company of one another in their mutual pursuit of the focused life, bonding with one another, learning from one another, supporting one another around the issues of their daily lives. Imagine them flourishing in this environment and becoming stronger, fulfilled individuals who have not only come to terms with the realities of their lives but embrace their lives wholeheartedly.

A Daring Image

As I envision this, I recall a moment that stands out as one of my most persistent and pleasant memories. During one meeting of the Contemplative Hour, while we were reflecting on the gospel story in which Jesus called for new wineskins, one of our members spoke up gleefully.

"We are what is in the new wineskins," she said, bubbling over with excitement, "but we're not just wine, we're champagne!" We all burst out laughing at the daring and delightful image. But it is not daring really; it can be true. Gathered in small communities of believers, pursuing common goals, we have the potential to transform not only ourselves, but also the larger "accidental" communities to which we belong—our workplaces, civic and political organizations, educational institutions, and yes, even our church. We are "the people of God," remember; it is our show.

CHAPTER NINE

Friendship With Silence and Solitude

At one time I was frightened by the cold. There was good reason for it. When I was growing up, down parkas did not exist, insulated boots were unheard of, and little girls wore skirts and knee socks throughout the winter. My brothers and I battled snowstorms and heavy rains on our way to school, back home for lunch, and back to school again. In February our parents, hardy souls who seldom left the house, left us for hours at a time at outdoor ponds where we skated in cheap skates and then waited for rescue, our feet frozen blocks of ice. During my high school years, I waited interminable hours in all kinds of weather for city buses to take me across town to school. Misery.

I soon discovered how to avoid most contact with the cold and for many years stayed either indoors or in a heated car during the winter. Then I had to face my demon again. I took a job as a classroom aide at my youngest child's elementary school only to learn the first day that part of my duties included playground supervision. Petrified, I ran to the stores and the then-fledgling L.L. Bean catalog looking for proper bundling-up clothes. It took me nearly ten minutes to put them on. First there were tights, then insulated ski overalls, and over that an ankle length down coat with a fur trimmed hood. Underneath I wore a wool hat that came over the head like a cowl and was knitted with bibs that covered part of the upper chest and back. Gloves inside mittens (in case I needed to lace untied shoelaces) and fleece-lined boots completed my outfit. I was ready for anything.

Then a strange thing happened. Jogging came into vogue and I hopped on the bandwagon and began to slip out of the house early every morning for a three-mile run. Dressed in "proper" running gear, I soon learned that, once I started to move, a little clothing could keep me sufficiently warm. It was a revelation. Icy air became exhilarating, bright cold mornings an invitation to go outside. I rediscovered the beauty and delights of the outdoors in winter. I was liberated from my fear.

At one time I was frightened by silence. It was not always so. Our house, when I was a child, was a quiet one with no television and little radio except during baseball season. I spent hours curled up in a big chair by the front window with my nose in a Dickens novel and my eyes periodically scanning the street for things of passing interest. Then I grew up. I was constantly either in school or at work and then married and the mother of four children. After their father left, it was I, four adolescents, a constantly barking miniature dachshund, and three cats—a very noisy household. I yearned for peace and quiet. Then one day I got my wish. The children left for college, the dog and cats died, and I was all alone. I was working, of course, and my days were full. But when I opened the door in the evening, the silence assaulted me and brought me to my knees in despair and even panic. What was I to do?

First, I did what I had done about the cold. I bundled up against it. I put on layer after layer of "protection." I made phone calls to friends, learned to love certain TV sitcoms, went out to meeting after meeting at church and in the community, volunteered, went to (as well as hosted) parties, rushed out in good weather to run and in bad to the gym.

But still would come that moment every day when I opened the door to the palpable presence of silence and, worse, *what was in the silence.* It was as if a monster lurked behind that door waiting to devour me. I could run away from it, and I did, but the monster never really left the house, and the fleeing was exhausting me. Eventually, I went for some counseling, and this is what I was told to do. "When the feeling of panic overwhelms

you," suggested the therapist, "just sit still and let it. Cry if you
need to, but don't get up until the feeling is over." So I tried it
because I had no other choice really. I would come in the door
and go to a chair and sit for as long as it took. Sometimes I wept,
sometimes I just gripped the chair arms. Sooner or later, I would
get up and wander about the rooms, plan and eat dinner, take
a walk around the neighborhood, and settle in with a book for
the evening. One day I found myself curled up in a big chair
reading Dickens, almost as contented as the happy little girl I
had once been.

T.S. Eliot warns us about being "distracted from distraction by
distraction," a phrase that has always haunted me. It reminds me
of a line written by Blaise Pascal. "All the troubles of life," he
said, "come upon us because we refuse to sit quietly for a while
each day in our rooms." Their voices join with myriad others
who throughout the centuries have retreated from the noise and
mayhem of the marketplace to expose themselves to the whis-
pering wind Elijah recognized as the voice of God, a voice that
can be heard only in silence. Contemplatives in monasteries
around the world, Benedictine to Buddhist, live out their days in
silence, speaking infrequently, praying interiorly or in chant. In
recent years, these traditions have been introduced to a broad
public through hundreds, possibly thousands, of books.
Countless workshops extolling the benefits of "sitting" in the
Zen tradition, centering prayer in the Christian, transcendental
meditation, and similar practices too numerous to count are
offered around the country, indeed, around the world. So what
is it about silence that scares us, considering the fact that it is
universally recognized as the essential ingredient for the spiritual life?

Perhaps it is simply a matter of looking closely at the monster,
as I did, to discover the beautiful prince within. I found that
once I confronted the silence and refused to let it drive me out
of the house, I was beguiled. Little by little I let go of things I
once thought essential—network news, weekend videos, morning radio. One Lent I even "gave up" listening to the car radio

during my forty-minute commute, and found that I did not need it as much as I thought. It is less and less often a companion to me on my journeys, replaced now by blessed quiet. I have come to use silence as a form of "stasis," a Benedictine practice that ritualizes the moments between activities. In between work and chapel or chapel and meals, the monks pause for about five minutes so that the energy of the past activity can subside before engaging the next.

Welcoming the Silence

After I lost my fear of silence, I found new experiences entering my life. Instead of television news, I supported my local paper. Instead of sitcoms, I listened to classical music on public radio or tapes and CDs. I learned to read without background noise. I returned to knitting, which I had learned at my grandmother's knee, and cooking, sometimes only in the company of good music. I returned to the practice of keeping a journal which I had let drop. I began to substitute quieter places for noisy ones, shopping in small independent stores rather than malls, seeking out quiet restaurants over the mega-places with loud piped-in music. In my relationships I found myself easier with breaks in the conversation, less apt to quickly fill in the gap, less driven to maintain a constant flow of talk. At home I was less likely to contrive unnecessary tasks in order to "keep my mind off things." My active listening skills improved and my children remarked that I was easier to be with, a good ear, not so directive.

We are inclined to associate silence with being alone, but silence can be enjoyed in the company of others as well. Just consider our Quaker friends. Parker Palmer, a Quaker and educator, in his book, *To Know As We Are Known,* suggests that teachers encourage moments of silence in the classroom, a practice I have been incorporating into my freshman writing classes. My students, mostly commuters, are just off the interstate when they walk into the room. Others have been on an inter-campus bus, or are still buzzing from dormitory life. For ten minutes or so at the beginning of our time together we write in silence.

Some people find that meditating for twenty minutes in the company of others is more comfortable for them than trying to meditate for twenty minutes by themselves. In a contemplative prayer group I once belonged to we sat for twenty minutes before beginning our reflection on the gospel. Amazingly, we began to look forward to the silence as much as the sharing that followed; it knit us together and prepared us for breaking open the Word. The small church community I currently belong to is learning to sit in silence for five minutes before we start our gospel reflection. I have begun to incorporate moments of silence into my spiritual direction practice as well. When I am with my grandchildren I sometimes suggest that we pause for a few moments of silence. After the initial surprise, they find that it is a relaxing break.

Once one learns that there are treasures revealed only during times of quiet, the desire for deeper silence takes over. Like the layers of clothes I wore for playground duty, even the quiet friends—knitting, reading, music—begin to interfere with an elusive something to which the silence calls us. This is the time to strip off the layers, time to turn off the radio and the music, to put aside the newspapers and books, even the voices of loved ones, the time to search out a place where one can be in uninterrupted silence for a few hours or a few days. It may simply be a "poustinia day," a day spent in one's own home, or on a beach, in the woods, at a quiet bed and breakfast, a house of prayer, a monastery guest house. Or it may be a weekend, a week, or even a month spent at a beach house, retreat center, or monastery that offers hospitality. There, in the comfort of accustomed silence, away from the distractions that distract from the essential distraction, which is the "still, small voice" of God, we find the core of our being.

Solitude is a concept spiritual writers often link with silence. Essays on "Silence and Solitude" pervade the literature. The works of Nouwen and Merton, writers like Annie Dillard and others influenced by Thoreau and Emerson, move gracefully from considering the one to considering the other. But why, we would ask out of our experience of being single, why would I choose solitude, why would I choose to be alone? Aren't I alone enough? Isn't it healthier to be with others, to be doing something? The question is valid, for we have not chosen to be monks or nuns, we do not aspire to live apart from society.

One of the problems we have in coming to an understanding and appreciation of solitude, is its association with the word "seclusion," which carries a negative connotation. Our old friend Roget distinguishes clearly between the two. Solitude, when it means aloneness, he says, implies a peaceful detachment, but when it means seclusion, it connotes loneliness, withdrawal, and isolation, all negative. The first rejoices in the gifts of silence and is a time intentionally set aside to enjoy them and nourish the soul with them. It is chosen freely and deliberately, a serious time, but not sad. The second is an involuntary response to neurosis.

The identification of solitude with neurosis is unfortunate but often true. At one time when I was feeling especially lonely, I read a lot of books on the subject. The discussions ranged far and wide and the viewpoints were as varied as the backgrounds of the individual writers. Many delighted in solitude, but only for a brief time, then turned darkly inward to ruminate on past wounds or fresh ones.

What these writers seemed to lack was spiritual grounding. Few of them mentioned God or soul or spirit in their writing. Before seeking solitude, they had lived exclusively in the outer world; they were poorly prepared for what they encountered in solitude. They had not experienced the journey inward; they had not befriended silence. Their solitude was real seclusion, intolerable after a short while. Reading their experiences was depressing. On the other hand, when I was reading Annie Dillard, Thomas Merton, Henry Thoreau, all occasional solitaries, and so many other spiritually grounded individuals, I was constantly delighted with the joy and sparkling insights which bubbled forth. It was uplifting rather then deflating, for they were not alone; they had invited God to be their companion in solitude.

This morning, the day after Thanksgiving, the sun is streaming in my window, and I am sitting in bed making notes on this chapter. My daughter and her new husband are sleeping in the bedroom across the hall. Knowing that they are here in my house makes me feel happy and contented. Tomorrow they will be gone, and I will once again be living my solitary life, a life I would never have chosen for myself. I accept the will of God in this, but when I reflect on the turn of events that put me into it, I realize the truth of Joan Chittister's words, "The will of God," she says, "is what remains of a situation after we try without stint and pray without ceasing to change it."

The will of God for me has been to teach me that I can be joyful in being alone, that silence and solitude are dear friends whom I would sorely miss if they were denied me. In my heart I know that I will be sad when Julie and Eric leave, but it will be a short-lived sadness. I will welcome the return to silence and the opportunities it brings for study, work, prayer, and other quiet pleasures. In the meantime, I'm glad they are here.

CHAPTER TEN

The Spirituality of Home

When I visited Ireland to hike the Wicklow Way a few years ago, our guide took us to the remains of a pre-Christian rath, a "campground" of a family or tribe of Celts. To get there we had to maneuver our way through tufts of peat moss, ford a stream, and walk across a pebbly beach. The rath was demarcated by a circle of large stones and small gnarled oak trees, which were sacred to the Celts. It was a small space, intimate because of the trees that encircled it and the stones that defined its limits, and when I moved into the inner space of it, I was taken over by an ancient memory. At first I ascribed it to some primal remembrance of my Irish heritage, but then a long-forgotten memory from childhood emerged.

In fifth grade a friend and I carved out a hideaway for ourselves in a wooded vacant lot in our neighborhood in Providence. After school we would roller skate the few blocks to it and go to its center where a large old tree stood. Around the tree were several stumps, and in the middle of the tree was a large hole. We sat on the stumps and drank cokes confiscated from our mothers' refrigerators and left notes for each other in one of my father's cigar boxes, which fit perfectly in the hole in the tree. For a time we were invisible to the rest of the world. A brief time it was—our friendship ended not too long after we had built our secret hideaway—but the magic of that time has always remained with me.

The ancient Greek language gives us a word for these sacred places. It is *temenos*, meaning sacred precinct. Often created in circular form, such places have featured significantly in ancient spiritualities such as the Celtic and Greek. The circle protects, contains, and encloses; it defines boundaries. In the Old Testament and the New we see many examples of sacred enclosures—the garden of paradise, Noah's ark, Jerusalem and its temple, the spaces to which Jesus retreated for prayer. We can easily think of these and other beautiful natural enclosures, ancient ruins, churches, and monasteries, as sacred spaces, but there is something much closer to us that can become the most sacred, our own home.

An Honored Place

While it is easy on one level to conceptualize home as a protective circle, a sanctuary, a place where one is safe from outside pressures, it is often not honored as such. With single people especially, home can be merely a stopping-off place to change clothes and grab a cold snack from the refrigerator before dashing off to some other place. Often our apartments are furnished with bits and pieces left over from college days or the castoffs of relatives and friends. Someday, when we marry, we say, or when we "hook up" with someone else, we will have a "real" home, but not now.

It could be now. The phenomenon of single people buying homes has surprised the real estate industry in recent years. "Single, first-time buyers drove home sales in 1998," said a headline in my local paper not long ago. Non-married men counted for nineteen percent of the market, single women, sixteen percent. This is remarkable, and encouraging for young single people. Why wait for the perfect moment, the perfect partner, marriage? Do it now.

There is no better palette on which to "paint a portrait" of our unique selves than home. Books about the Chinese tradition of Feng Shui, the art of arranging entrances, exits, openings between rooms, furniture, and colors for optimum harmony, are abundantly available. In Japan, gardens are designed with equal care. Without necessarily imitating either, we can nonetheless learn from them about how to pay attention to our own interior spaces, how to make them beautiful in our eyes, how to make them inviting when we come home at the end of a busy and distracting day, how to make them hospitable. And how to make them inviting for the presence of God. There is no better place than one's own home to make peace with silence and enjoy a self-determined solitude.

A spiritual director I know has created a retreat space that will forever exist in my memory as one of the most pleasing interior spaces into which I have ever been invited. Mauve and blue, her favorite colors, predominate, and the furniture, practical inexpensive wicker, brightens the rooms even in the dead of winter. The bedrooms are decorated in different color schemes to please various tastes. Bowls of candy and vases of fresh flowers brighten the tabletops. The kitchen is always stocked with good food and lots of coffees and teas. Classical or spiritual music plays softly in the background. It is always a delight to be there.

My present spiritual director, a man, lives in a different kind of space, a many-windowed house set in the middle of a forest. The window views engage the imagination and we always sit so that I can look out and enjoy the scenery. Inside, all is glowing wood tones, mellow oriental rugs, and faded, overstuffed furniture. Newspapers and magazines overflow from every table and some chairs. It is the space of an active mind, of someone who sees the spiritual in both the natural and the intellectual worlds.

Both these people have put an indelible stamp on their living spaces, each announces boldly who lives there. And we can do the same. But first we need to decide carefully if the space we presently occupy is feeding our souls. If it isn't, and if it is possible, we need to move.

As we have seen, it need not be to yet another rental; if we have the means—and there are a number of federal and local programs designed specifically to encourage first-time buyers—it can be a house or condominium of one's very own. Then we can imprint it with our unique personality. We can carefully choose color schemes for furniture, rugs, window dressings, bedrooms; appoint the rooms with pieces of craft or art, mementoes of our lives, loves, or travels, the seasons of the year; add scent with bowls of fresh fruit or flowers. And don't forget that a house is not a home without a mess. The makings of crafts, tubes of paint, balls of yarn, scraps of cloth for quilting, all attest to the presence of an invigorated spirit.

Board games, colorful blocks, and puzzles come into play again in my own space as they stimulate the imagination and invite me and my guests to play. I have discovered a used bookstore nearby that specializes in children's books. The old classics and some of the wonderful new picture books found in bookstores or libraries today are pleasing to look at and fuel the imagination.

At the core or center of every *temenos,* as at the center of every person, is the place where the sacred is found. It can be so in our homes as well. There, in a place reserved for ourselves alone, we can artfully place objects that draw us toward our spiritual depths—symbols of the holy such as a rock from a beach, a leaf or shell, a picture that evokes something mysterious, a candle to light and extinguish at the beginning and end of prayer time, our Bible. Homes once had such shrines or altars. Today they are for the most part passe, reminiscent of superstitious or overly pious religious practices. That need not be a reason for abandoning the concept altogether; rather, we can transform it and bring it into agreement with our more contemporary spirituality. There, in silence, at the center of our homes we can go to our altars to connect with the center of our beings, the divine mystery we call God.

And when we have created our unique interior, we can look to the outside and our surroundings—our gardens, our neighborhoods, our towns and cities—to beautify, and thus to bring to the minds and hearts of others visions of serenity and peace. In my small city of Portland, Maine, a concerted effort to create urban gardens is growing. In surprising places, which were once empty lots or cracked concrete pavement, sunflowers and stringbeans are shooting up. Some people gather around to work the gardens, others just to give advice and kibitz with those who are working. At harvest time some of the fruits of the gardens are distributed to soup kitchens in the area. Throughout the growing season and even in wintertime, these spaces lend an air of joy and expectation to the city.

The concept of *temenos,* therefore, begins with containment but ends with expansion. The sacred core nurtures the energy for extending peace, harmony, and beauty to others. It fits well with our discussion of silence and solitude, and moves us gracefully into our next discussion, hospitality, as now we have created a place we are proud and happy to share with others.

CHAPTER ELEVEN

Hospitality as a Way of Life

The progression from silence to solitude to hospitality was first suggested to me in something I read by Henri Nouwen. It's an interesting progression. Along the way we have encountered ourselves joyfully in silence, embraced solitude, and created *temenos,* the sacred space of our emerging True Self. We have learned to enjoy the presence of God in comfortable solitude. Now that we are focused, now that we have reached a place of comfort with silence and solitude, now that we have created *temenos,* we open our hearts and our doors to share both ourselves and our beautiful homes with others.

Hospitality, a well-known charism of the Benedictine way, means a generous opening up of one's personal space to others. At another time, in another life, we would have called it partying or entertaining, but social activity, when it is an outgrowth of deepening spirituality, is a transformation of this.

The home I grew up in was not a happy one and my parents never socialized except with family, and then only in other homes, never ours. My brothers and I were fortunate, however, in having other associations that modeled for us healthier and happier ways. As the only girl in the family, I was strongly influenced by a number of single women, my aunts and their friends, all of whom were school teachers. Some were neurotic, but most were wonderful self-accepting hearty women, full of laughter and appreciation for the good things in life.

Several of these women celebrated a weekly ritual. Every Sunday evening they gathered for dinner, each one taking turns to be hostess. Sometimes, if I was in good standing, I was invited to join them. It was quite a treat. Their tables were set with the finest china, and they outdid each other with new recipes. Before dinner they had a sip or two of sherry and maybe enjoyed a sweet cordial afterwards. They laughed and talked. Their subjects were work, politics, the parish, and the larger world. Talk of family was taboo. Loyalty to family was a high virtue.

I remember one home especially. On the second floor of a two-family house, it had two parlors, a dining room, a kitchen, and two bedrooms, maybe three. Bookshelves lined the living room, rich oriental rugs covered the floors. On blustery winter evenings, the heavy damask drapes were drawn to shut out the dark and cold, and sometimes the piano was opened and songbooks taken out. The dining room was windowed on two sides and a pantry where glass cupboards housed stacks of dinnerware led from it into the kitchen. There, a canary always sang from her perch in a green cage, and smells of baking cookies and roasts and casseroles came from the oven. It was my heaven, surely *temenos*.

What I most recall, however, is the companionship among these women. They all lived alone, they all had demanding jobs, they all must have endured loneliness—and, yes, ridicule, as the culture of the times cruelly called them spinsters. But they had established a joyful community of nurture and support. They freely and gladly offered hospitality to one another and to their families as well.

I have been more on the receiving than the giving end of hospitality since my divorce. During my married life, my husband and I entertained a good deal and I loved it. The preparation for dinner parties was exciting and fun. I took great pleasure in poring over my many cookbooks in search of the perfect menu, polishing the furniture, getting out the fine china, crystal, and silverware, tucking the children into bed, and greeting our friends. In retrospect, however, I see that our entertaining was more in the nature of what Esther de Waal calls "fulfilled social expectation" rather than true hospitality. Our guest lists were carefully planned. And I had begun to see, even then, that while a great deal of time and energy was spent on entertaining guests, our children were receiving short shrift, an indication that something was quite wrong, as indeed it was.

Afterwards, as a single person, I tried to continue the tradition of hospitality, but with very little pleasure or reward. I found that I was not entertained as often or as well as I had been while still married. The married folk, whom I now observed from the side-lines, seemed to go all out when entertaining other couples, but were either uncomfortable or wary of single people and included them only occasionally, usually at events planned around the children's activities. When the singles gave parties, it was often a frenetic event designed specifically to make connections.

But I have experienced authentic hospitality as a single adult. One place I receive it is in the home of my brother Ed and his wife Diana. Shortly after my husband left, I decided to visit them, all the way on the other side of the country in Seattle. I was feeling shaky, as the idea of being on my own was still fresh and strange, more intimidating than stimulating, so it was with a mixed sense of fear and boldness that I, with my then sixteen-year-old son Mark in tow, boarded an airplane and flew off to the unknown. We arrived late at night, time for bed.

"You can have Elissa's room," said Diana, leading me up the stairs and showing me to her daughter's room. Elissa was a for-tunate child, she had a feather bed. A thick fluffy down com-forter covered the mattress and soon a thick fluffy down com-forter covered me. I sank into a deep peaceful sleep, my first in months, and awoke to the cloudy Seattle morning, feeling warm, safe, and nurtured. These feelings continue to be a constant whenever I visit because Diana and Ed are invariably welcom-ing, warm, and genuinely interested in the events of my life.

Now they have built a wonderful retirement home in the northwest woods. With its cozy furniture and windowed views of towering cedars, it invites me to afternoons of quiet reading. Their kitchen is usually busy with the wonderful mess of cook-ing as they both enjoy good food and good company. I have talked long and deeply around their dining room table, with one or the other of them, or all three of us; with other family mem-bers. Each of my four children is always welcome there as well.

At the end of the day the bed is always soft and warm, and I always wake up feeling safe and nurtured.

A Place of Hospitality

A Benedictine monastery I have been visiting lately is another place where I have experienced genuine hospitality. Along with work, prayer, and study, the hospitality of Benedictine guest houses is well known. As Esther de Waal points out in *Seeking the Way of God*, Benedict's love for humanity extended well beyond his own brothers and monks. In Section 66 of the Rule, he says, "Great care and concern are to be shown in receiving poor people and pilgrims, because in them more particularly Christ is received." He instructed his porters specifically on how to greet the stranger. "As soon as anyone knocks, or a poor man calls out, [reply] 'Thanks be to God' or 'Your blessing, please.' Then, with the gentleness that comes from the fear of God, [provide] a prompt answer with the warmth of love."

When I visit the Benedictine monastery at Petersham in western Massachusetts, I become a sort of "poor man" or "pilgrim" as I, too, am seeking asylum from the distractions of the outside world for a time. Before I go, I first call Brother Jerome, the guest master—or, more likely, his answering machine—to tell him the date and time I plan to arrive and how long I expect to stay. When I last visited during Advent I arrived at dusk to find the outside light on and electric Christmas candles burning in the front windows of the guest house. Brother Jerome greeted me as if I were an old friend and showed me to a room "on the sunset side" as I had requested. As I was settling in and unpacking my bag, I heard the noises that meant one of the brothers was delivering dinner, brought up from the monastery. I joined the three other guests in the dining room for a hot meal of mashed potatoes, roast pork, broccoli, bread, salad, and warm-from-the-oven brownies. We chatted quietly as we ate and then dispersed to our own preferred activities—reading in the comfortable library, praying or resting in our rooms, or attending the chanted "Hours" in the chapel. During the day, but not in hunting season, we can walk on the trails of a nearby forest preserve. When I am there, I feel as I do when visiting Ed and Diana: loved, safe, warm, well-fed. And in that place of peace I am able to recognize the constant presence of God, which can so easily be obscured by the confusion of modern living.

These experiences point to another important aspect of hospitality, a willingness to accept the hospitality of others. This may seem like a frivolous or even silly statement, but it is not meant to be. Many of us know how difficult it can be, especially during times of stress, and when our self-esteem is at a low ebb, to accept kindness from others. For single people especially, the temptation to isolate oneself can be strong. I think of the term "unavailable," which has come into common use these days. We often remark that someone is unavailable, meaning that she doesn't have time to talk on the phone, go to a movie or dinner, sit for a while over a cup of tea.

I have responded this way myself at times, and I know why. It is because I did not have sufficient confidence in my own self-worth to accept the invitation to relationship. I felt that I had nothing to give, and that the person who was showing interest in me would quickly discover that I was a fraud. My busyness said, in effect, why would you want to have anything to do with me? So I fended off the invitation.

When we invite people into our homes, we are still "in charge," but when we go into spaces occupied by others we risk more. We are more vulnerable, and that can be an uncomfortable experience. Once we have strengthened our sense of self-esteem through the practice of self-reflection and prayer, however, we are free of the need to create protective boundaries. We are fully aware that we have something to bring to the party, and that it is not a "covered dish," it is the offering of our renewed selves.

My aunts and their friends opened their houses to others and went willingly when invited out. They also modeled another aspect of hospitality, giving our selves and our resources to those in need. They were conscientious about caring for the sick and elderly, and visited nursing homes often. They attended the wakes and went to the funerals. They often took care of their nieces and nephews, and sometimes helped their families out financially, paying dentist bills, high school tuitions, and department store bills for Easter outfits, always without any fanfare. Because they were teachers, they knew poor families and sometimes gave to them. In other words, they were generous, and not only with their resources, but with their persons as well.

Hospitality may seem like a strange topic to be discussing in a book about the spirituality of single adults, and for good reason. Either we see it in a romantic light, especially during holiday time when television and movies bombard us with visions of "over the river and through the woods to Grandmother's house"—or we may associate it with party time and high pressure social events which tax our souls and psyches. In addition, it may seem to be contradicting our determination to learn to be silent and enjoy solitude.

Actually, it is a graceful and natural extension of the two, for silence and solitude when experienced intentionally prepare us for our meetings with God, and in the same way, prepare us for our meetings with others. In learning how to be comfortable with silence and solitude, we have to overcome our fear of being alone; in fact, we have found new strength and self-confidence in that once strange and uncomfortable place. We have re-visioned our homes as sacred places, "sacramentals," and created that special corner where we pray. We have made the rooms in our houses or apartments into reflections of our personalities. Our inner journey is active, and little by little we have become more confident in our own truth and come to a place in our lives where we know we have something important to share with others. Having created our internal and external *temenos,* we can now open ourselves and our front—and back—doors to others.

The Demands of Hospitality

But hospitality asks more of us than that. As one of the basic

Christian virtues, it calls us to share not only who we are, but what we have. Both impulses drove the life of one of our mentors, Dorothy Day, so much so that she called the shelters she created, Houses of Hospitality. These places were managed as if they were true homes, never becoming institutionalized; at Dorothy's insistence they remained small. "Our houses grew up around us," she wrote in the Catholic Worker. "Our bread lines came about by accident; our roundtable discussions are unplanned, spontaneous affairs. The smaller the house, the better." Smallness was a concept very dear to her, and she called herself a "personalist," meaning that the involvement needs to be an intimate one, that helping is not a matter of writing checks or even of pressuring legislators, but of putting ourselves in close proximity with those we hope to serve. In this spirit, Joan Chittister's community of Benedictine women runs a soup kitchen and food pantry in an industrial neighborhood near their house in Erie. "Hospitality," she says, requires us "to give ourselves away, to provide the staples of life, both material and spiritual, for one another."

While she, like Dorothy Day, is concerned about how "caring for the stranger" can become overly organized and sterile, she is also aware of how the realities of today's world require us to be careful about our own personal safety, and smart about what helps others and what disables them. While hospitality requires us to tolerate interruptions and inconvenience, she says, it never asks us to give ourselves away; we are no good to ourselves or to anyone else when we allow others to drag us with them into lives of disarray. Neither should we make it easy or comfortable for those caught in self-destructive behaviors to remain there. Somewhere in between is a place of balance. A story close to home illustrates this.

One bitterly cold winter night when our small Christian community was meeting in the apartment of one of our members, two drunk people who lived in her building came banging on the door. Apparently the couple had been drinking at a local bar with two homeless people and invited them to stay the night. The four of them came back to the apartment together, but the conviviality did not last, and soon they began to fight among themselves. We could hear the foul words and the sounds of physical violence below us and in the stairwell before one of them stumbled up the stairs and started banging on the door of our friend's apartment. It was a disturbing incident, especially since the police arrived soon after.

She often helped them, she then told us, by giving them small amounts of money, driving them to appointments, or letting one or the other sleep in her home when they had been fighting. This had set up a complicated and uncomfortable pattern for her, one that she felt powerless to change, and on this night she was obviously confused about what her response should be. On the one hand, she wanted to be a "good Christian" in the model of Thérèse of Lisieux, her favorite saint (and one of Dorothy's, too); on the other hand, she was clearly getting drowned in the situation. Fortunately, some of our group were professional social workers and others had had intimate experience with the sickness of alcoholism. They pointed out to her that she would be vulnerable to theft, and even violence, if she housed them, and that her good works would have been forgotten by the time her guests sobered up, when the cycle would start all over again. She received good counseling that night, and her neighbors received a warm bed and a hot meal in the local jail.

Still, it is true that some of us can go deeper and farther than others without jeopardizing our own freedom or stability. Dorothy and her brother and sister-in-law, for example, took the homeless and indigent into their apartment before they found a suitable space to serve meals and provide beds. Not many of us have the capacity to carry off something as heroic as that; we need to know our own limits.

So Much To Do

And yet, we know that there is much to do. Runaway teens roam the streets and give birth, refugees come off planes and boats daily, women run from homes where they are not safe, drifters sleep in doorways. At the same time, new luxury resorts and gated communities come into being every day. And this is only in our country. Television brings the rest of the world right into our faces, challenging us to consider how our ways of life affect people in less developed countries and whether or not the public policies our elected officials write and legislate into law are just. How and to what degree we involve ourselves is an individual decision.

Joan Chittister says there are four levels of the hospitality of social action: the personal, the local, the governmental, and the financial. Volunteering in a soup kitchen is one way to be involved in a personal way. We contribute on the local level when we join an activist or advocacy group. We can influence the government by putting pressure on legislators. We can donate money as we are able. Hospitality of time, energy, money, self. It is up to each of us to know which of these is possible for us.

If we think we can give on the personal level, we need to be aware that being with the poor or marginalized is not always nice work. Someone who had spent many years volunteering in a shelter once said, "The poor smell, and they are also rude and selfish and greedy, just like the rest of us." Being poor does not make one saintly; being mentally ill does not make one endearing; having been violently abused does not make one peaceful. But the word nice does not appear in the New Testament, not even once. If we want to do the work—and there is much to do—we need to go in with our eyes open.

Interestingly, as single people we have more potential to get involved than those who are married or who have other commitments. We alone determine how we spend our time and energy.

What a joy-filled life ours can be. Free to encourage friendship between God and ourselves through prayer, free to create a beautiful space in which to live, free to cultivate new friends, free to go out and intersect with the worlds and lives of others, free to move further out into our communities, both near and far, free to help others. We have much to do, much to be, much to be thankful for. So, invite the neighbors in, the family, the friends you have, the friends you hope to have. See what connections can happen and what ideas can flow.

CHAPTER TWELVE

Proper Balance in Work

I am fascinated by what the monastics teach us about work which, besides prayer, study, rest, and worship, constitutes their day. Theirs ranges from the lofty to the mundane. Besides manual labor—the mundane—monks sing the psalms, morning, noon, and night, day in, day out, season after season after season, year after year after year. This they call the *opus Dei,* the work of God—the lofty. But times are changing, even for monks. The Electronic Scriptorium, an agency in Pennsylvania, oversees a massive project of converting library card catalogs, including those of the Pierpont Morgan Library and the Frick Collection, both in New York, to computer-readable files. I can tell you as a librarian that this work is labor intensive, but it is not the kind of labor we think of as manual. The earth is not felt, bread is not kneaded, cloth is not woven; only the fingers tap on the keyboard. And yet, these projects are being done by Benedictines and Carmelites, and other monastic orders. In some monasteries, the workday has been extended to eight and even ten hours, a situation that raises important questions and causes some concern.

"You have the option of being shaped by the culture or trying to follow your call," said one participant at a recent gathering of the American Benedictine Academy. "Our call is not to be tossed about by the storms of culture. Monastics have become workaholics, always rushing around. I don't think our life is different from anyone else's life." Obviously, no one escapes the challenge; the speaker speaks for all of us.

Our work, more than any other aspect of our lives, defines us.

We work all of our lives until we retire, and then we generally find other activities that become work for us. It seems as if we need work, and, in fact, having work is one of the most basic human needs, even a right. Since the dawn of time humans have worked. We are highly sensitive to the hierarchies of work. At the pinnacle there is the work of the influential or unusually creative or spiritual; on the low end, mundane work, manual labor, what housewives, maintenance crews, and field laborers do. And monks. In between lies a wide range—work that engages the intellect, work that engages the heart, work that is about making money or making war or running an institution or a business successfully.

Some kinds of work have an archetypal dimension. Manual labor, for instance, of all the kinds of work done by humans, whether monks or not, will always have a unique character and value. Not only is it necessary, but also, in certain aspects, spiritually enriching. Teresa of Avila saw the truth in this. Of her Carmelite sisters she said, "Their earnings must not come from work requiring careful attention to fine details but from spinning and sewing or other unrefined labor that does not so occupy the mind as to keep it from the Lord." That, to me is the intrinsic meaning of manual work, that it engages the body rather than the intellect, allowing the mind to relax and be receptive to an inner dialogue with God. Thus, manual labor can be approached both as a job and an invitation to prayer. I also find it a necessary corrective for too much intellectual activity. Knitting in the evening after a day of teaching or writing soothes me. In the summer, being out in the garden pulling weeds has the same effect.

The repetitive nature of manual work is often denigrated, and it can indeed become drudgery if the Spirit is missing or if it is harshly imposed by others. Certainly, workers on an assembly line do not find their labor edifying. For those of us fortunate enough to be able to choose, however, repetition has real rewards. Kathleen Norris in her Magdalena lecture, "The Quotidian Mysteries," tells us that the word quotidian means

daily, also regularly, recurring, constantly, methodically, system-
atically. There is boredom buried in these words, but also a
sense of peace and a certain kind of freedom. At the Preble
Street Resource Center in Portland where I help with breakfast
one morning a week, the same tasks are repeated over and over.
Day after day we set out the USDA butter and cream cheese, the
peanut butter and jelly. Seven mornings a week someone mixes
and pours the orange juice, sets up the coffee pots and keeps
them filled, cleans up spilled sugar, dishes out oatmeal, and
washes the pots. The same is true in family life. In every home,
breakfast must be made, laundry must be done, dishes must be
washed, floors must be dusted, meals must be prepared, over
and over and over again.

Norris recalls noticing this domestic activity while attending
her first Mass. Closely observing, as poets will do, she suddenly
realized that the celebrant, after Communion had been distributed, began to wipe out the vessels with a cloth. "Look," she
whispered to her husband, "the priest is doing the dishes." Her
insight was perfect. The ritual of cleaning the sacred vessels after
sharing the bread and wine, like the ritual of doing the dishes
after any meal, like washing the oatmeal pots after breakfast at
Preble Street, is a "quotidian mystery," mundane work sacramentalized by the spirit in which it is done. When I realized this,
my attitude toward keeping house changed. This is like monks'
work, I realized; it is my manual labor. Now, going to the recy-
cling center with my boxes and bags of papers, cans, and bot-
tles, dusting the floors, folding the laundry, has taken on a new
meaning. I see it as part of my own "daily rule" along with
prayer, study, rest, and my own "real" work.

But it is usually this "real" work, the work we have chosen to
do, which gives us the most pride. And the most anguish. We
are all invested to one degree or another in workplace issues—
the workplace itself, the workers, supervision and management,
organization and administration, personnel decisions about who
works and who doesn't. These take up an immense amount of
our time and attention and generate intense emotional respons-

es and reactions in us. It has been said, in fact, that work is a peculiarly American obsession. Americans, it seems, either work too much or not at all; there is no middle ground.

Working Too Much

For single people, the scale is often tipped toward the "too much" side. Work becomes some place to be when home is an empty place, an opportunity to socialize when life is not shared with another. It is a way to become defined when society ignores us, a way to be named when one is not mother or father or husband or wife. The challenge for us then is to consider how work fits in with our unique spirituality and to find a proper balance between work and the other essential elements of our lives.

Work is a constant in an otherwise shifting world. It is the one thing we can rely on when a long uneventful weekend is over, when we are suffering pain in relationships, when we seem to have no other purpose in life. In the face of this reality we need to challenge ourselves with some important questions. Is the work we are doing nourishing our souls? Does it have intrinsic value? Do we spend too much time there? Do we tolerate superficial or divisive relationships there? Just as we did in the chapter on *temenos,* home, deciding if we are content in the place we are currently living, so should we, as part of our movement toward wholeness, evaluate our work situation and consider whether or not we should leave it.

Matthew Fox in *The Reinvention of Work* has developed a thirty-item questionnaire that is useful in this initial evaluation. I will paraphrase some of the questions. Are you joyful at work? Does your work bring joy to others? Are you emotionally connected in a positive way? Does your work connect positively to solving larger problems of the community, society, the environment? Are global issues being resolved? Are you being educated, or are you stifled? Does your work enable or frustrate your inner work? Can you let go of your work on weekends or do you show signs of workaholism? Do you know how to enjoy your time off? Is there a sacred quality to the work you are doing? If these questions are significant ones for you, the questionnaire will help put your present work into perspective.

The big question remains: is this a job, a career, or a vocation? If it is a job, then you are probably not invested; you are doing something simply to keep going. If it is a career, your investment will be significant, you will have goals and plans for the future, satisfying professional associations, autonomy, perhaps power. But when your work is a vocation, the whole picture changes. Then you see your work as something that not only satisfies you but also makes a significant contribution to the larger world. Albert Schweitzer said it well. "At that point in life where your talent meets the needs of the world, that is where God wants you to be." Frederick Buechner restated it in these words: "The place God calls you to is that place where your deep gladness and the world's hunger meet." In this, the best of all worlds, our work is our vocation, and because it is, it stimulates us and satisfies our desire to further the ultimate work, bringing into being the just world Jesus called the Kingdom of God.

Even so, using the word vocation, for me, is troublesome as it is most often used to mean either marriage, the priesthood, or vowed religious life. A recruiter for a religious order once asked me to participate in a panel discussion on vocations. She had a priest on the panel, a member of her order, a married couple, and she wanted to include someone who was single. The dilemma was that I had not chosen to be single and, therefore, did not identify with or advocate that state in life. I had been married, a choice, and a parent, also a choice; I had been a librarian, a choice but not a vocation. And now I was a freelance writer and volunteer. But vocation? Hmmm. We had a problem.

We could have avoided our dilemma if we were talking about mission rather than vocation, for I certainly had a mission. It was the loaded word vocation that tripped me up. The real question is not what is our vocation, but what is our mission in life? What is it that we are called by God and our deepest self to do? Why are we here?

The Answer Evolves

The answer to this question slowly evolves as we evolve and deepen intellectually, emotionally, and spiritually. It can come in our youth in a flash as it did with St. Paul. It can present itself in mid-life. Or it can take a lifetime, as it pretty much did with me.

My first work experiences were jobs. As a young girl, I worked in stores, I took care of children, I was a library page. After college, I joined the many women of my generation who were fortunate enough to be financially supported in their roles as wife and mother. It was hard work, but mostly satisfying. Later on, I prepared for and took up a career as an academic librarian. For a while I found that field of work intensely engaging. I made my contributions to the profession and enjoyed many pleasant collegial associations. But somewhere along the way, the excitement dimmed and I felt myself called to writing and to working with the disadvantaged, especially abused women, the homeless, and refugees. Had I been younger, I would have changed careers. Instead, I retired early, simplified my lifestyle, and became heavily involved in volunteer work, writing, and teaching. Bliss.

For me, the need to "get out" came at a good time. I had built up equity in a retirement fund and could draw on that to sustain myself financially. For younger people or those who do not have equity through their work, the risk is greater—but not prohibitive. It can be done. Several books on the market advise those who are determined to break away to "pay up now," in other words, to build up a solid nest egg through hard work in a job or career in order to make it possible to embrace their mission in the future. One book that comes to mind is *Your Money or Your Life* by Dominguez and Robin. They point out how many of us spend time in work that has no personal meaning and drains us of our "life energy." In their book (which belongs to a large body of literature on simple living), they plot out a practical process of first naming our dream and then saving and planning for it. To again use the words of Schweitzer, without a vision nothing happens. Theirs is an excellent plan for bringing one's own vision into reality.

Unfortunately, we are not always able to be doing our "vocational" work, our mission, the work we really want to be doing, the work of our souls. Either the time has not come, or we do not know at this time what it will be. For whatever reason, we are stuck. The job or the career track has become burdensome, or we realize that it is a place without soul, where power is misused, where dominance prevails. Even worse, we may be doing our "soul work" and something has gone wrong. The ideal we had envisioned for so long, the goal toward which we strived and for which we sacrificed so much, has soured. There is conflict and strife, discouragement, disappointment. These are the facts of work life.

Again, we can look to our models for consolation and hope. Dorothy Day went through hard times at the Catholic Worker. Her beloved coworkers rebelled against her autocratic management style and threatened to leave. Thomas Merton was often in conflict with his superiors; the vocational choice he made with so much delight and passion as a youth presented constant challenges. Dag Hammarskjöld met crisis after crisis as United Nations Secretary General, and he suffered personal struggles and public humiliations as well. In these cases, it was the virtue of stability that gave them, our "saints," their underpinnings and the courage to persevere. They stayed, and they stayed with vigor and passion, to transform the difficult situations in which they were enmeshed.

Dorothy humbled herself, apologized, and refined her management style. Merton wrote through his pain and shared his reflections with the rest of us. Hammarskjöld never faltered in his hard work for the UN, sustaining himself by hiking in the mountains of his homeland, Sweden, and by keeping a record of his spiritual journey in his private journal, *Markings*.

Their model was the person of Jesus himself. In spite of the fact that he was doing the work he chose intentionally, that he was fully engaged in his vocation, a work of love, he experienced the bitter disappointment of misunderstanding and direct confrontation, of betrayal and abuse. And yet, he endured, as we must. Finding the work is just the beginning.

Our task, it seems, is threefold. First we need to evaluate where we are right now. Is our present work our true mission? If it is not, we must then decide what it is we really want to be doing. Can we leave where we are and move toward our goal? Or must we stay awhile to build up our equity, while making the effort to transform this workplace in the interim? Third, having left, having begun anew, we must muster up the courage to endure, to stay, and to continue to work toward our goals. The challenges are large and difficult. For those who choose to lead intentionally focused lives, however, they must be confronted. But this I know to be true: when we reach that time in our lives when we feel the work we are doing serves a cause larger than ourselves, we have found our true vocation. In that moment, we will experience deep satisfaction. All aspects of our lives will be harmoniously blended, our vision clear. Best of all, we will know at last who we are.

CHAPTER THIRTEEN

Stability

I have always been a restless person. Not for me, the tried and true. I did not marry a hometown boy, but rather someone quite different. Moving to California with him was a thrill as was moving into three different homes while we lived there. Back East again, I loved the excitement of buying and selling and decorating houses, three of them, in the Connecticut suburb in which we settled. When I accepted the reality of divorce, I quickly made the decision to move myself and the children to another state so that I could go to graduate school. After graduate school, I took an entry-level position, and then a professional one, and two years later, another. I stayed there for seven years but found it boring after a while and managed a transfer to another location. There I found things not as I had expected, and after another seven years, I retired. In just those fifteen years I had lived in four different houses or apartments. As I write this now, it exhausts me just to record this history.

The years during which I was married were years when corporations transferred their executives with cruel indifference to the needs of their families. IBM was especially famous for this. We and all our friends "expected" to be transferred. Not a few people I met in Connecticut in the 1970s moved into new homes only to be told within a few months, or even weeks, that they were to leave again. One woman I met in a newcomers group told me, tears welling in her eyes, that she had moved thirteen times in fifteen years.

I never thought much about this pattern until recently when I came across reference to the monastic virtue of stability. At first, I was wary. Why would that be a virtue, I wondered. It sounded like something only a boring, unimaginative person, a "stick-in-the-mud," would value, out of the question for anyone "in the world," anyone who wanted to "get things done." Ours, after all, is a mobile society. But my reaction and my defensiveness are giveaways that I, like many others today, live on the compulsive edge. And something else. While some of my many moves were not that unusual, others were clearly a response to difficulties experienced during the marriage and in the years after.

In sharp contrast is the practice of stability in Benedictine monasticism. When Benedictine monks take vows, they pledge themselves to one monastery and promise to stay there. Regardless of conflicts or difficulties they may experience in their relationships with the abbot or other monks, regardless of whether or not they feel unfulfilled in their work or come down with a bad case of mid-life crisis, regardless of anything, they stay. The monastic pledge to geographical stability is not negotiable; as Joan Chittister says, "Stability is not a subtle virtue." To Esther de Waal, another of our "experts" on Benedictine spirituality, it means that one "commits to situations and to persons," and actually enters into the Paschal Mystery of life, death, and resurrection. Jesus, of course, went "unto death" in the literal sense, as do martyrs even to this day, something most of us need not expect to face. The Paschal cycle, nonetheless, is played out in all our lives if we remain committed to our relationships. If we stay in them, we also will experience the rhythm of fulfillment, diminishment, and renewal over and over and over again.

Those of us who live outside the walls and the cloisters, of course, are challenged with a much different complexity of roles and choices than monastics. We exist in a tangle of situations and relationships. We engage in personal relationships involving friends, lovers, neighbors, and family members. We have jobs and careers and relationships with our coworkers, employers, employees, those we manage, those who manage us, relationships that can be exceedingly taxing. To one degree or another, we are connected to the church. In addition, we may belong to a support group or small Christian community. We live somewhere and are connected in a physical sense to a neighborhood, city or town, state or region, and the larger world. In all these relationships, we are challenged daily. Given this set of circumstances, it is no wonder that moving on is a tempting option. Stability frustrates and opposes the temptation.

What "Staying" Means

The concept of staying or stability has some lovely nuances. In one of her novels—*Animal Dreams,* I believe—Barbara Kingsolver has one of her characters say that love means simply "staying in the same room with me." Those words struck me with great force the first time I read them, and they continue to stay with me. They speak, I think, of the terrible and intimate connection love demands. So often, when trouble enters a relationship, we go away to think things over when what we really need to do is stay and talk things over. This applies in whatever setting we freely find ourselves, whether it is a job, a friendship, a task, or a love relationship. I also associate stability with the lovely word abide. "Abide with me," goes a line in an old hymn, intimating both married love and love for God, who is ever abiding. The concept of abiding is comforting, especially when compared with its terrible opposite, "leaving," when someone we love has decided not to abide with us.

And stability also means permanence, those things that remain constant. Something nostalgic rises in me when I think about stability is this context, and the memory of my bachelor Uncle Tom surfaces. Uncle Tom lived with my grandmother and another brother and two sisters in a house my grandfather built for his sizeable family in the year 1904. My parents, three brothers, and I lived around the corner. Uncle Tom was not a daily presence in my life—strict boundaries were observed between the two houses—but I often met him by chance, I on my roller skates, he on his many walks and strolls around the neighborhood. Uncle Tom walked everywhere: to work and back, downtown on a Saturday afternoon to meet some city hall cronies, to Sunday Mass. He called me "Princess."

Once every year in the spring, he and I had a "date." My mother would dress me up in my new Easter outfit—I remember two, one a navy checked coat and a straw skimmer hat with a row of daisies around the rim, and another, a grey flannel suit with a box-pleated skirt, short bolero jacket and matching bowler. Uncle Tom would come to the house to pick me up and we would walk to the bus stop just a block away and wait patiently there for the ride downtown. Our destination was the Biltmore Hotel. In those days, the Biltmore was a landmark in Providence—and still is, I think—an elegant establishment. We ate in the Falstaff Room, an intimate leathery dining room, the epitome of grandeur and decorum. Uncle Tom had a Manhattan and I had a Shirley Temple and we both had filet mignon. It was a grand time.

That tradition continued for years and stopped, not because Uncle Tom grew tired of it, but because I outgrew Uncle Tom. When news of his death reached me in California years later, I realized that he had remained fixed in my mind as an icon of whatever is unchanging, reliable, safe, and loving. As I read that letter, my childhood faded away forever. No one would ever call me "Princess" again.

For many of us, grammar school is another icon of permanence. Recently, my brother had lunch with six of our grammar school classmates. How many are divorced, I asked. None, he replied. Not one? And their jobs? Still the ones they took after college or high school. I was taken aback. A few years ago this information would not have been of any particular interest to me, but today I wonder not so much why they have lived as they have, but why I have lived as I have. And I call into question all that I had assumed to be true about myself and myriad others like me, the ones who spread our wings and left town, had adventures, became sophisticated, sat in strategic places in the boardrooms of corporations. Are we really the successful ones, or are the successful ones really those who remained behind to transform the old into something new?

There is no sure answer, for stability demands more than remaining in "the old neighborhood." It is not a question of sentimentality or nostalgia; it is really a matter of guts. If we choose to stay in the old neighborhoods, in the old jobs, in the old marriages, in the old church, we may become dull and lackluster. Or we can develop new skills that can be transformative. In the workplace, for example, these may be communication, collaboration, group dynamics, and other innovative practices of organizational behavior. We may need to take assertiveness training in order to improve our personal relationships. We may need to confront our friends or listen well when our friends confront us. We may need to take initiative in our parishes in order to keep our love for the church alive. In other words, we may need to be proactive rather than passive.

Moving from place to place, the literal opposite of stability, can also be disturbing to the soul. "Mobility tempts interior stillness to the breaking point," says Joan Chittister. I have realized this in a small way since retiring. At the time I moved—yes, again—to another city a three-hour drive from my mother who is in her nineties. I fully realized when I made the decision that I would need to travel frequently to fulfill my obligations to her, and I do, but it takes a toll on me, a considerable one. Before I leave for the visit, I must wrap up the work I am involved in, whether this is preparing for the classes I teach, or the committees I serve on, or my current writing task. I clear my calendar, if I haven't done so before, of any previously made appointments, cultural or social activities I enjoy, volunteer commitments. I pack. I arrange for someone to feed the cats. I go. I stay. I come back. I unpack. I open my calendar and reenter my world.

It is not an open and shut process. After every trip, which is approximately once a month, I have difficulty recapturing the energy I had for all my activities, especially writing. My concentration has dissipated, my motivation evaporated in the wake of the time away, the time preparing to go away, and the time spent "reentering." Longer trips are even more disruptive. "Those who frequently take trips," said Thomas à Kempis, "rarely become saints." (Or writers, I would add.)

I asked my students recently to interview someone who was

retired in order to discover what had been gained, what lost. One of the interviews affected me deeply. The woman in question had enjoyed a successful career as an operating room nurse. During those years, she and her husband planned carefully for their retirement, but shortly before she was to leave her job, her husband fell ill and within a short time died. She confided in the student interviewer, her granddaughter as it turned out, how devastated she was by his death and how for months afterward she frequently found herself in tears and deeply lonely. Then she hit upon a solution. She would fill all the waking hours of her days with volunteer activities. And on weekends, every weekend, she would get in her car and visit one or another of her children. In this way, she managed to outwit her loneliness, she is never by herself. This is a solution in a way, but an act of cowardice in another. What, I wonder, is she missing out on while engaged in this ceaseless activity, what knowledge of herself will she never have, what undiscovered gift will go ungiven?

In reflecting on the patterns I have identified in my own behavior, I now realize that I have been very much like that woman. Much of me was lost in all those moves I made from house to house and job to job. I will never know what or how much was lost, or what could have been accomplished with the time and energy and anxiety I poured out in those efforts. It is gone forever. At the time, I misinterpreted my restless activity as creative energy and prided myself on learning to adjust quickly to new situations. The opposite may have been truer; staying put might have activated real creative imagination.

I have heard it said that alcoholics retard their emotional development because, whenever they are up against something difficult, they take a drink to ease themselves through it; thus they never actually experience the emotion or face the difficult situation. Constant movement, I now believe, has a similar effect. By moving away from something, whether it is an unpleasant or overly challenging job, relationship, or geographical location, one is never stretched to the growing point, one never really finds out how he or she could have effected change, one never learns how to live deeply instead of superficially.

A Common Temptation

The temptation to restless activity is especially compelling for single people. When an opportunity to shift gears, change location, or get a new job arises, we have no encumbrances to hold us back or cause us to reconsider our decisions. The flip side of that "freedom" is the absence of a supportive relationship to question the judgment or offer guidance. What can look to others like the ascent up the corporate ladder or the delicious freedom of a "free bird," may really be the unhappy reaction of an unhappy person. The practice of stability for the single person must be entirely self-imposed.

This is not to say that we should stay in abusive relationships. Sometimes, Joan Chittister cautions, it is necessary to move on in order to be "in stability with God." At times we may be called on to make a heart-wrenching choice that involves leaving a person or a situation. And even though it may be right and necessary, pain, deep pain, will be the immediate result.

It is for this reason that the presence of a committed community is helpful, if not essential, for the single adult. Those who live in monasteries live among others who agree with their same principles. Ideally, they help each other out during times of difficulty and decision-making. Regardless of our best intentions, however, we sometimes are opposed by others—in the workplace, in our families, even in our intimate relationships—who do not share our goals for establishing, maintaining, or healing relationships. Furthermore, as individuals who live autonomously whether we want to or not, we are the sole authors of our lives; we do not have the constant concerned input of another who loves us in a special way. The presence of an intentional community in our lives can ease us through these difficult times. For single adults, this kind of support makes staying more possible. Fortunately, we have models, proud ones, of "unwilling celibacy" who stayed in spite of severe challenge. Notice the importance of community in their lives.

The story of Thomas Merton's troubles with an abbot at Gethsemani, by now well known, is a case in point. Merton, having dedicated himself to the monastic life, perhaps the rash act of a desperately unhappy young man, before long found himself at odds with authority, and a struggle ensued. Fortunately, he was able to win approval for his writing and extensive correspondence and stayed where he was. He poured his considerable energies into these labors of love, for which we are all grateful. Who can imagine the losses to him—and to us— if he had chosen instead to leave? Later in his life, he became infatuated with a young woman and considered again the possibility of leaving. What awful anguish he must have experienced, what strength of purpose he must have called upon when he decided instead to stay.

Dorothy Day stayed put in New York after she began the Catholic Worker houses of hospitality, refining the ways in which St. Joseph's House and Maryhouse and Peter Maurin Farm operated, producing the Catholic Worker newspaper. It was not a smooth ride. Like Merton, she was directly opposed by the church; once, the bishop of New York reprimanded her for the radical nature of her work and suggested that her chances for acceptance would be better if she were married. This was the event that prompted her impassioned words about forever yearning to be married. No "willing celibate," Dorothy. And there were internal struggles as well. I cannot find the source now, but I read somewhere about a time of great stress when, as already mentioned, her autocratic management style was challenged by the Catholic Worker staff and volunteers. A crisis ensued during which Dorothy experienced deep feelings of rejection, pain, and mortification, but she recovered and returned to work diligently and with a new humility to renew the damaged relationships.

The prophets, those giants of Scripture who still point us away from trouble and toward concurrence with God's benevolent plan, stayed right in the midst of their people. They did not go to distant lands with their messages but remained where the mess was, irritating and cajoling anyone within earshot night and day, day and night.

The Paramount Prophet

Jesus, of course, is the paramount prophet. Even when his own people misunderstood him over and over and over again, he did not move on. Except once. The story as told in Mark says that he went home to Nazareth right after he had chosen the twelve apostles. There, crowds of people who had heard about his curing and preaching flocked to him. His family had a different take. They thought he was crazy and "set out to take charge of him." On hearing about this and being told that they were waiting for him, he declared that from then on others would take their place in his mind as his sisters and brothers. While this turning away seems to be in direct opposition to the attribute of stability, I prefer to see it as a refusal to "get stuck" among people who would stifle his talents and thwart his mission. When he made the commitment to a larger world, it was for keeps.

This moment at Nazareth is closely linked for me with the stories of the Wedding at Cana, the Temptation in the Desert, and the Transfiguration. The Cana story tells me that Jesus was comfortable at home in Nazareth. It was Mary who saw that he needed to move on. The desert experience represents the time he spent figuring out who he was, what his gifts were, and how he wanted to use them. Satan, remember, had his own ideas about that. And who knows how long the struggle lasted. Three days? Maybe a lot longer. Whatever the duration of the process or the location in which it took place, there in the "desert" Jesus came to manhood. At the Transfiguration, God the Father affirmed his decisions and bestowed on him the deposit of grace.

So it is with us. At some time in our lives we "come of age." It may be in late adolescence or early maturity, during a mid-life crisis, after a divorce, or as the result of an upset in our career plan. It may happen in "three days" or over the course of many years. At that point, and only then, are we really capable of making right decisions. Only then do we have sufficient information to make right judgments about where to put our energies and talents. Like Jesus, we may be called on at that time to move away from the people and places to which we once belonged, and declare loyalty to other people in another place. We put the past into perspective and dedicate ourselves to our real purpose. We are ready to take the vow of stability.

CHAPTER FOURTEEN

Study of Sacred and Spiritual Resources

When I travel, it seems as if I am always going all the way across the country, as a beloved daughter and brother live in Oregon and Washington state, respectively. The trip involves ten to twelve hours of tedious travel time. Needless to say, I go prepared with enough reading material to set up a small library.

On a recent trip I managed to get through Thomas Moore's *Re-Enchantment of Everyday Life,* which had been sitting in my pile of "books to read" for several years. When I reached my daughter's house, I discovered an old book, *Yoga in Ten Lessons,* by J.M. Dechanet, O.S.B., left there on a previous trip. I had found it in a musty secondhand bookstore in Corvallis, and, although I had read it before, it held new meaning for me and I devoured it again one afternoon as I waited for Baby Nora to wake up from a long nap.

The two books complemented each other around certain themes. Moore wrote of the monastic practice of spiritual reading, an aspect of daily life St. Benedict required of his monks. Dechanet wrote about reading aloud as a preparation for meditation. On my return home, I finished reading a book I had started before I left, this one on dreams, a topic also touched on by Moore, and discovered a bibliographical reference that piqued my interest. It was a book by John Welch called *Spiritual Pilgrims: Carl Jung and Teresa of Avila.* Hmmm. Jung and Teresa. Who would have guessed? It is now on order from my local bookstore.

And so it goes. That all these books seemed to link up

intrigued me on one level, yet did not surprise me at all on another. That is how my study goes these days, guided by serendipity in the Jungian sense, coincidence by coincidence, one thing leading to another, not rigidly prescribed by a course syllabus as it once was, but more like a freewheeling spin in seemingly different directions, all of which eventually converge. The book of one author leads me to others by her. A reference from a television interview suggests the work of another. I see an interesting bibliographical reference and get the book from the library. I read a review and buy another. Where it goes nobody knows; the important thing is that it does happen. I do spend time every day in study of some sort.

This is one of the requisite practices of the monastic and of the serious seeker as well. Those who write about the spiritual life invariably recommend a path of reading. That I have been an avid reader since childhood, a lifelong student type, and a librarian, suits this purpose perfectly. I am well aware, however, that for some people book reading is not a delightful pursuit, and that the thought of studying anything after the school years are over can be an appalling and even abhorrent idea. When spirituality becomes an important pursuit in one's life, however, these attitudes often give way to an enthusiasm for spiritual reading. Still, we may feel at a loss as to how and where to begin.

For starters, ask your spiritual director or the members of your small intentional community. Or simply just begin. Go to a good bookstore and browse. You will discover that there are any number of well-written and attractively packaged books about spirituality on the market today, and even on the bestseller lists. The phenomenal popularity of Thomas Moore's *Care of the Soul* comes to mind, and Kathleen Norris' *Dakota* and *Cloister Walk*. There is a lot of silly "New Age" fluff out there, too, but one quickly learns to separate the wheat from the chaff. The best will surface; serendipity takes over.

Spiritual study exists in many formats. I once read a newspaper interview of a woman contemplative who lived in a monastery near my home. When asked about the rhythm of her day, she mentioned reading novels in the afternoons. At the time I was shocked. What is going on here, I wondered. This seemed utterly frivolous. But later on, I read that Dorothy Day did the same thing. A spiritual director of my acquaintance told me that she had been advised during her training to read novels, as they would give her insights into life experiences unknown to her and thus enable her to be a more insightful director. According to authorities I would not dispute, Andrew Greeley's exuberant bouncing novels are theologically accurate and bring to light significant spiritual issues. You can decide that for yourself.

Movies and plays are other genres that open up the inner life. A group called "Values and Vision" based in New York, publishes lists, reviews, and study materials for mainstream movies that are available as videos. They are a link on the Spiritualityhealth.com website. Marcia Sinetar also advocates film as a way of posing questions about the spiritual aspects of life. In an article she wrote with Rich Heffern for *Praying* Magazine, she says that "movies mirror us and invite us to go beyond the obvious." As a way to do this she suggests the following:

Follow the "love" movements in the movie and the values, such as compassion, generosity, and courage, that are treated in the characters, direction, and plot.

Trace these initial observations or insights as you watch the movie, becoming aware of those that speak specifically to your present spiritual experience or "condition."

Develop an internal watchfulness as you take in what appeals and repels you, attending to your breath as in meditation.

Heffern suggests extending this type of meditation by making a list of those films that have affected you intensely and reflecting on what qualities in them speak to your own spiritual experience.

Certain television shows and series also provide appropriate subject matter for reflection. I think of the work Sister Wendy Beckett has done for PBS and how it has led people to a deeper understanding of art and its spiritual dimensions. Now I visit art galleries and museums, another form of "study," with a new perspective. Audiotapes available from Sounds True, the public library, or Books-on-Tape are sources of substantive material. I have lately discovered recorded books, both fiction and non-fiction, rich sources again for the spiritual life. They are great companions for long trips by car, plane, train, bus, treadmills, or city walking paths, and quiet times at home while cooking, doing chores around the house, knitting, or woodworking. Some people prefer study groups—and now, Internet chatrooms—that focus on a line of interest or a particular book, movie, author, artist, or theme. And do not overlook the exponentially expanding opportunities on the Internet. These groups have the additional advantage of being communal in spirit. So are workshops and lectures that may come to one's local area.

A caveat. One experience can lead to another, one book to another, one Internet site to another. Before you know it, you are overwhelmed. I have long been an observer of people I call "workshop junkies," those who travel to the ends of the earth to hear yet another purveyor of the answer to life's ultimate questions. That can be valuable for a while, and we all do it in times of crisis or growth. But there invariably comes a time when enough information has been poured into one's head and the time for action is at hand. This is a necessary reminder for me because I suffer from a surfeit of reading material and become dizzy in the effort to read and digest it all. Someone once told me that after reading five books on a subject, it is time to put down the books and start doing.

Apropos of this "addiction," it has always been amusing for me to see the reaction of other avid readers when I suggest that we "give it up for Lent." I explain that anything one does excessively or anything that substitutes for real living and real prayer can be considered a distraction from authentic spiritual experience. They always greet this recommendation with a nervous laugh, and wonder out loud how anything with such inherent value can also be "an occasion of sin." But it gives them pause.

Balance and moderation are always best. Here again, a spiritual director and an intentional community can be helpful guides.

Wisdom from Storytellers

Myths, stories, fairy tales, tall tales, and epic tales from primitive times, while stimulating the imagination and enhancing our inner journey, also give us insights into our own traditional beliefs. My brother Ed has become a storyteller in his sage years. When I visit him and his wife Diana, I am immersed in stories. While sitting over a prolonged lunch one rainy afternoon, he told me a long tale from Morocco, a story of deceit and forgiveness. At breakfast one morning we three took turns reading aloud a story by a contemporary Irish writer, a magical story that incorporated long-ago tales of leprechauns and will-o-the-wisps. Fascinating. Scary. And one night as I sat knitting in the loft guest room, I listened to the stories of three tellers who had gathered below for their monthly meeting. All their stories, which dealt with universal themes, touched tender cores of my own inner being. I felt as if I were breathing in air from time immemorial as I listened to them.

I also learned something else. As it was their role to critique one another in their storytelling techniques, I overheard one of them comment on Ed's low-key style. She described it as "gentle telling." Before then I was unaware that different schools of presentation existed. Bombastic, colorful, flamboyant storytellers abound; others like Ed who "tell it straight" and let the audience fill in the blanks with their own imaginations are fewer.

In Ireland, I am told, there is a style of telling that takes the tradition of "gentle telling" even further. It is called *sean-nos* which means "old style." Usually a convention for singing, it has also been used by storytellers. In this ancient tradition the singer or storyteller is anonymous and sits behind a curtain or screen unseen by the audience, or may turn toward the wall with his hand cupped around his ear. Thus physical appearance does not interfere with the story or influence the way the listeners receive it. The manner of presentation is quiet and straightforward. After the story or song is finished, another is "cajoled" from someone in the audience, reinforcing the notion that storytelling is not a performance but an expression of shared experience. I wonder if this convention is a way to recapture the way it was in olden times when electricity was a thing of the future and night closed in as the sun set, when village people gathered around hearths fired by peat and listened in the dark to the mysterious and soul-stirring tales from even earlier times.

There is a contemplative, even mystical, quality to this form of rendition that reminds me of *lectio divina* (the meditative reading of sacred Scripture). This, too, is an ancient tradition first practiced by hermits and monks and now being taught to modern seekers. One form of *lectio divina* was described in the chapter on prayer; another is found in *Song of the Seed*. There Macrina Wiederkehr, a Benedictine, describes a method she has found useful.

First, quiet the mind and relax the body with several minutes of deep breathing.

Then read the chosen Scripture passage slowly and reverently, listening carefully to every word and nuance.

In continued stillness, try to put all thought aside and enter into a state of emptiness or contemplation.

Return to the passage and reread it, selecting a word or phrase to return to at times throughout the day as a reminder of the message.

In the evening, return once again to the passage, reflecting on how it has been reflected in the events of the day. Record this in your journal.

Take the passage into sleep.

As we have interpreted it, the concept of study has been broadened beyond the traditional meaning, which emphasizes primarily reading and lecture. Going to movies and plays, art galleries and musical performances can be study. Being with others in workshops or study groups can deepen the meaning of the study material. The method of *lectio divina* is a deep form of study that can be used with spiritual as well as sacred literature. All can be experienced with others in a group setting or in the solitude of one's home.

When we embark on an intentional pursuit of study, single lines of thought or interest become important and are amplified and integrated into other aspects of our lives. We become more selective when using television, radio, the internet, newspapers, magazines, and other reading matter. Ultimately, a commitment to study intensifies the focus we are adding to our lives.

CHAPTER FIFTEEN

Preferential Option for the Poor

A bent-over grizzly figure in a beat-up jacket and black wool toque came in at the tail end of breakfast. Bypassing the oatmeal and sweet stale donuts, he headed right for the coffee urn. I was there making a new pot.

"Good morning," I said, "how are you today?"

"Oh, I have a terrible headache, dear," he replied, "I woke up confessing my sins."

That hit home. I was doing the same thing myself, especially since it was near the end of Lent, and all my good intentions had been washed away in the press of daily living.

"Oh, don't do that," I quickly said to him, suddenly seeing the absurdity of it all. "Wake up and celebrate yourself." He beamed.

"Now that's a better idea," he said. "Thank you, dear, I'll try that." We both left the coffee station feeling a little better.

It was my morning at the Preble Street Resource Center in Portland, Maine, where once a week I help out during breakfast. As I told someone who was quizzing me about my motives, suspecting martyrdom if not masochism, it is the easiest thing in my life. All I have to do is show up. There are no decisions to make because I am told what to do, and I leave when I have cleaned up the spilled orange juice and put away the peanut butter. Only when it is absolutely unavoidable do I wash out the oatmeal pans. It's like any household, I figure; we make the breakfast and do the dishes and the next day we do it all over again. Family life. I like it there.

I don't know when I found out how comforting it was to be in the company of people we call the "less fortunate," but I do know that for me at least this is true. When I am with them, I feel the way I did when I was a young mother. My reason for being is clear. I keep the coffee urns filled or help a refugee from Afghanistan learn the names of the days of the week, just as I once made four school lunches every weekday and drove carpools around the suburbs of Connecticut. Then I felt no need to justify my existence. I was busy and happily tired and doing something necessary.

As time went on, those responsibilities dissolved and "professional" duties took their place. For a time I found them exciting and stimulating, but eventually I was beset by feelings of ennui and isolation that intensified as one by one my children left home. The times when I felt fully engaged and lighthearted were those times when I was involved in volunteer work as a tutor for Literacy Volunteers and at a local women's shelter. Eventually I realized that my professional life had ceased to give me the satisfaction I needed, and I began to make plans to withdraw from it. It was a tough period in my life. Few people in my circle of friends, and even fewer relatives, supported my decision. Some openly criticized it. My level of self-confidence slipped badly. Until one morning.

The ringing phone startled me. Odd to be getting a call midmorning on a weekday when everyone I knew thought I was at work. Exhausted after a sleepless night plagued by anxious thoughts, I had called in sick and was sitting in bed with a late cup of tea making a list of the "positives and negatives" that attended this momentous decision, all the while knowing deep in my heart that however the balance ended up, and against all advice from my more practical confidants, I was going to do it.

"Hello, Jean?" said the soft Southern voice on the other end of the line, and I was transported back several years to a small room on the second floor of a neighborhood center in Providence.

"Jolie?" I answered back. "Is that you?" Then a rush of irritation washed over me as I recalled that the director of the literacy program from which Jolie had recently graduated told me to expect a call from her asking for a letter of recommendation.

Now was not the time. "Damn," I thought, "she wants that let-ter."

But she didn't.

"I'm calling from work," she said. "I'm on a break. I just want-ed to say thank you for helping me and Kenny."

Kenny. The name of her little boy and her voice on the phone brought it all back—the hours and hours we had spent togeth-er over the course of three years, poring over phonics patterns and grammar rules, Jolie making little but some progress, while under the table at our feet Kenny played with toy trucks and col-oring books.

We made tapes of her reading, and she loved to hear her voice. Kenny did too. How many times did I say to her, "No, Jolie, don't say mens, say men," trying to break her away from the Southern Black colloquialisms of her heritage.

Her voice reminded me of the anxiety I experienced trying to find time to put in volunteer hours with her, the frustration when she didn't show because Kenny was ill or because her ride had failed, the anger I felt when she got her driver's license by way of an oral exam instead of a written one.

In our time together we had shared much about our person-al lives. I learned that she had been a basketball star in junior high school, but had moved too often to make close friends as her family made the slow trek from job to job up the East coast from Georgia to Rhode Island; that she had dropped out of school when she was fifteen to give birth to Kenny; that she lived with her mother and an aunt while she worked toward her GED; that on weekends she and Kenny and "Kenny's father"— I never heard his name—took bus rides to the zoo and other recreational spots in the city or watched television together.

Sometimes I would imagine the three of them—Jolie, tall and gawky and probably smiling, happy to be on an outing; Kenny, talkative and restless; and a young man, "Kenny's father," per-haps a little nervous to be in charge of the others, responsible for getting them to the park and back without mishap. Maybe it was quite different. I never knew.

A television ad for literacy programs had brought her to me in the first place, but I admonished her nonetheless. "Don't watch so much TV, Jolie," I would say, "read instead. Read to Kenny." And she did. That's how she finally picked up a sufficient vocabulary to pass the high school equivalency exam (GED). Since that time she had received her certificate from the literacy program, learned to type, and was holding down a steady job. She was living on her own and supporting herself and Kenny comfortably. How was I, she wanted to know, how were my children?

She had called to see how I was and to say thank you, it was as simple as that. And I was touched to the core of my being, especially on this morning when I was feeling all alone and vulnerable. When she hung up I relaxed into the sadness I was feeling and let the tears flow, but they were gentle tears, tears of gratitude—for her, for the memories she stirred in me, for the grace working in me to go back to where I had first encountered her and others like her. From that moment on, I turned myself squarely toward the uncertain future that I could not help but enter.

I spent the rest of that long slow morning in a sort of reverie, recalling other friends like Jolie. One was Pete who lived in a trailer in a rural community. His bright high-school-educated wife discovered after they were married that he could not read and sent him to me. We sat in a small room in our local library on Tuesday nights for three years. He was a truck driver for the local electric company and often came to our meetings exhausted from long night-to-dawn hours in sleet and snow. But he never missed a meeting.

One evening well into our study together, I asked him to tell me a word he especially wanted to learn. "Crystal Ann," he responded unhesitatingly, naming his little girl. I printed it out on a card and showed it to him. "So that's how it looks," he beamed, and his eyes filled with tears. Mine too.

There was Joe, retired from years working on road crews with the department of transportation. He wanted to drive a school bus, but did not read well enough to pass the required written test. To mask his deficiency, he had clowned his way through school. Sad to say, he clowned his way through our sessions, too.

Rosa lived with her two children in temporary housing, having recently escaped from an abusive husband and a life of terror in Guatemala. I helped her get through a textbook on how to become a nurse's aide. "What Rosa needs," said a sister who had worked with her when she was in a shelter, "is a nice young man." No, not now. What Rosa needed was time, time to garner skills, time to learn English, time to find out who she was.

I asked Sister Mary Reilly, R.S.M., head of Dorcas Place, a model literacy program in Providence, if I could go into classes there to show the women how to keep journals. She agreed. It would be a profound experience for me and for them. They wrote about their deepest thoughts and dreams. Sometimes the dreams were literal.

"In my dream," said Deanna, "I left my baby alone in a house and she woke up and cried when she found out she was all alone." Deanna began to cry. "I would never do that to my baby," she said. "Why would I dream that?"

"What about you, Deanna, did anyone ever leave you alone in a house? Were you ever abandoned?" And so she told her story. Her mother, a drug addict, had put her in a foster home for a year while she was in a recovery program. Deanna had never told anyone before, but she was telling now. She wept hard as her classmates surrounded her and hugged hers.

I met them first, these women and men, because I felt a sense of duty, a need to share some of the skills I had learned and some of my particular gifts. Later I began to look forward to the times we were together. When I found myself so tied up in my job that I did not have time for them, I also found that I missed them. I missed their laughter, their chatter, their tears. I missed their directness and blunt honesty and the gentleness with which they comforted one another, and me, the way they celebrated every small accomplishment. Somehow when I was with them, it was I who felt safe and comforted.

Now, I was choosing to turn my back on my career at a time when my powers were at their peak so that I could make more time to be with these people again, this community of strangers. Some would call me a fool. What did they know?

Being With the Poor

In one way or another, mostly economic, all these people were poor and belonged to that large segment of the population that is marginalized. Our society, for the most part, spends little time, energy, and money solving their problems, which are immense. Others do make their issues a priority. Such people are said to operate out of a "preferential option for the poor." This term was first introduced to me through the books of Albert Nolan, O.P., and William Reiser, S.J. Their perspective in a nutshell is that Jesus was all about being with the poor in their struggles within repressive economic, political, and religious systems. Therefore, so must we be. In taking this position, these writers ally themselves with advocates of liberation theology, which flourished in the 1970s in Latin America, went out of favor with Rome, and has recently been cautiously reaffirmed by John Paul II.

That Jesus was for the poor is no surprise, because he moved among them, and we have the Beatitudes and countless gospel passages to remind us of this. What is different about the position taken by Nolan and Reiser and others is that they repudiate the traditional interpretation of Jesus' life as being primarily about personal redemption. While he undoubtedly ensured our salvation through his dying, official church doctrine narrowed the focus throughout the centuries until it was almost exclusively fixated on this aspect. Consequently, personal interior prayer and good behavior in pursuit of individual salvation have been held in the highest regard and considered, like celibacy, to be the "best way" to holiness.

According to Thomas Ryan, C.S.P., in *Disciplines for Christian Living,* the preference for personal interior prayer peaked in the

1950s. The sixties and seventies saw the pendulum shift toward concern for social action; in the eighties, a renewed interest in the mystical tradition, long out of favor, arose. Now, Ryan believes, we are reaching a balanced synthesis and what he calls "holistic spirituality." Many, however, are still content with using devotional practices—silent prayer after Communion, visits to the Blessed Sacrament, saying the Rosary, and "being good"—to ensure eternal salvation.

Nolan, Reiser, and others challenge us to break out of this narrow spirituality. They promote a spirituality based on social action. Like Alfred North Whitehead and the process theologians, they base their view of God on the life of Jesus. For too long, they say, we overlaid the Jesus of the gospels with our ideas of what we thought God "should" be like, and focused our thinking on the event of his death. What we need to do is refocus, this time on his active life. "By his words and his praxis," says Nolan in *Jesus Before Christianity,* "Jesus himself changed the context of the word 'God'." This began soon after he was baptized by John. While some expected him to continue in John's path by "baptizing for repentance," he instead took a radical swing and became embroiled in the daily lives of the poor. Nolan made a list of the kinds of people with whom Jesus engaged. They were:

> the poor, the lame, the crippled, the lepers, the hungry, the miserable, (those who weep), sinners, prostitutes, tax collectors, demoniacs (those possessed by unclean spirits), the persecuted, the downtrodden, the captives, all who labor and are overburdened, the rabble who know nothing of the law, the crowds,...

These are the people the Pharisees called sinners and we, today, call the lower or marginalized classes; these are the people that Jesus, whom Nolan sees as middle-class, moved among in solidarity.

In light of the assumptions promulgated by the Second Vatican Council, asserts William Reiser in *Looking for a God to*

Pray To, "the piety and devotional practices of our youth are hopelessly outdated." A fresh approach to gospel study has revealed a Jesus whose sole purpose was not to found a church but to companion the poor. The cross, the central metaphor of our faith, is more than a symbol of personal redemption. Christ's bloody sacrifice also represents "a permanent sacramental reminder of the history of human oppression, the suffering endured by the poor and exploited peoples of the earth at the hands of the wealthy and powerful." Prayer, then, for Reiser, is much more a matter of visiting a poor family than of making a visit to the Blessed Sacrament.

In this regard, he reminds us of the evolving thought of Thomas Merton whose writings on the contemplative life have been widely influential. In 1955 he wrote about the necessary unity between action and contemplation in *No Man is an Island:*

> Action and contemplation now grow together into one life and one unity. They become two aspects of the same thing. Action is charity looking outward to others, and contemplation is charity drawn to its own divine source. Action is the stream, and contemplation is the spring. The spring remains more important than the stream, for the only thing that really matters is for love to spring up inexhaustibly from the infinite abyss of Christ and of God.

Eleven years later, in *Conjectures of a Guilty Bystander,* he reported a shattering and enduring experience that connected the personal with the theoretical:

> In Louisville, at the corner of Fourth and Walnut, in the center of the shopping district, I was suddenly overwhelmed with the realization that I loved all those people, that they were mine and I was theirs, that we could not be alien to one another even though we were total strangers. It was like walking from a dream of separateness, of spurious self-isolation in a special world...the whole illusion of a separate holy existence is a dream.

"The whole illusion of a separate holy existence is a dream."
I grew up under the influence of numerous relatives who lived
with that illusion. In the oral archives of my family is the story
of an uncle and aunt who, for some unknown reason, lived celi-
bately throughout their fifty-year marriage. During her lifetime,
it was said, the aunt wore out three leather-bound prayer books.
She was presented as a model of piety. Another aunt, with
whom we vacationed in the summer, retired to her room every
morning after breakfast to pray for her boyfriend who had
inconveniently died, after a courtship of twelve years, before
they could marry. We had to keep our voices down while she
sat for her hour of solitary prayer. She was a rather nasty
woman, I recall, who didn't care much for us children, but she
and God, according to family myth, enjoyed a very nice relationship. Another friend of the family went to daily Mass but
often spoke disparagingly about the black families who were
moving to the outskirts of her neighborhood and whose children went to the elementary school where she taught third
grade. No wonder my brothers rejected the faith that produced
such paradoxical spiritualities—and bigots. "The whole illusion
of a separate holy existence is a dream."

These attitudes resulted directly from the theory that Jesus' life
was about the salvation of individual souls through prayer and
adherence to high moral principles; and that religion and spiritual practice are private affairs that have little or nothing to do
with the world. The spirituality of the desert fathers and the
monastics was the preferred model; celibacy and retreat from
the world were the highest measures of virtue. Today, many dif-
fer from this point of view.

Spirituality is not an escape, and those who stand aside only
make things worse in the final analysis, says William Reiser.
"Peace of mind, equanimity, mystical oneness with the universe,
inner bliss, moral perfection, or the heights of contemplation"
are all appropriate spiritual goals, but not in and of themselves.
We cannot in conscience ignore the mandate bequeathed to us
by Jesus—to risk all, to be vulnerable in the outer world, and to

accompany those who may be more so than oneself. "The option for the poor," he continues, "comes from the heart of the gospel itself." Ultimately, it introduces us to a new concept of sin, the absence of a concern for social justice issues. Solitude must be matched with solidarity.

That is not to say that interior personal prayer has no value, but simply that it must be combined with action based on the belief that, to use Reiser's words again, "the salvation of the few is going to depend on the liberation of the many." New ways of prayer will arise and take their place beside the traditional ones, but they will not be taught from devotionals or through the tomes scribed by intellectuals. Instead they will arise from the example and simple faith that exists within poor families and communities. It is the poor themselves who will show us the way, not we, the empowered, who will guide them. It is we who will be liberated through our solidarity with them, not they who will be liberated by us. This has been demonstrated in the powerful liberation theology movement of Latin America. Recently reaffirmed by the papacy, it gives the rest of the world new hope that, by emulating its practices and attitudes, we may, in some distant future toward which we deliberately move, be able to actualize the kingdom of God that Christ envisioned.

The base ecclesial communities, which model the small Christian community movement we considered in the chapters on community and prayer, grew out of liberation theology. These communities also model the way the poor live with one another. In those close-knit relationships, they are present to each other in real ways, freely integrate their lives, share food and child care, and deepen their faith. Their need for privacy is less developed than ours, freeing them from the existential "fear of intimacy" so prevalent in Western culture. When we become members of small Christian communities, we appropriate this experience of the poor even though our own experience is North American and middle-class. In this way, we are "evangelized" by them.

Art Kubick in *A Preferential Option for the Poor: Prayer,* suggests that the poor will teach us in many ways. He refers to an essay by Monika Hellwig, "Good News to the Poor: Do They Understand it Better?" in *Tracing the Spirit: Communities, Social Action, and Theological Reflection*. According to her, the poor show us how to live in healthy interdependence in many ways:

a) The poor know that they are in urgent need of redemption.

b) The poor know not only their dependence on God and on powerful people but also their interdependence with one another.

c) The poor rest their security not on things but on people.

d) The poor have no exaggerated sense of their own importance.

e) The poor expect little from competition and much from cooperation.

f) The poor have no exaggerated need of privacy.

h) The poor can wait because they have acquired a kind of dogged patience born of acknowledged dependence.

i) When the poor are exposed to the gospel, they interpret it very concretely, and readily see it as having historical, practical import. An example of this is the ease with which Martin Luther King could invite his followers to identify with the exodus theme and with the nonviolent protest of Jesus.

j) When the poor have the gospel preached to them, it sounds like good news and not like a threat or a scolding.

k) The promise of future salvation is truly present joy and therefore present incipient salvation to the poor.

l) The really (desperate) poor can respond to the call of the gospel with a certain abandonment and uncomplicated totality because they have so little to lose and are ready for anything.

m) The fears of the poor are more realistic and less exaggerated because they already know that one can survive very great suffering and want.

Thus, the poor help us in our pursuit of wholeness. We, in turn, wish to help them. However, we must be aware that this "conversion" to the option for the poor may very well require us to reorder our priorities, and sometimes even change the way we live our lives. At the very least, it calls us to enter into a relationship with them, which Reiser, in his *Praying* magazine article, "With the Poor, with Jesus," calls "realized solidarity," by which he means an active engagement with the poor.

Actualizing this "gospel spirituality," this solidarity, can be an enormous challenge for those of us who live middle-class lives, says Kubick. A first step, he suggests, is consciously acquiring an attitude of "mindfulness." This follows Paul, who, in Galatians 2:10, said in reference to the Jerusalem Council, "The only stipulation was that we should be mindful of the poor." Kubick suggests that this mindfulness reflects the way Jesus himself was present to the plight of the poor. Like him we need to see them, hear them, and touch them. In seeing, we learn to take the viewpoint of the poor, imitating what the liberation theologians call *desde los probos,* seeing from the side of the poor. Thus, we begin to interpret news events and political issues as if we were the poor, and see that broad systemic changes must take place in our political, economic, and social systems.

Next, if we are to hear the poor, we must attune ourselves to their voices, whether spoken or unspoken. The voices of the poor were heard loud and clear in my small New England city last year when a large allocation of HUD (Housing and Urban Development) funds, which had been forthcoming in recent years, was not renewed. The city was appalled as were the nonprofit agencies and programs that served the needs of the poor. Rather than speaking for them and simply issuing statements to the media, the agencies helped individuals who would be impacted by the cuts give voice to their concerns by helping them set up a press conference. Anyone in sympathy with the issue was invited to "stand behind the poor" by actually taking a place behind the panel of speakers to face the cameras and microphones with them. It was a very effective media event, covered by all the local television stations. If I remember correctly, there was some national coverage as well. The next day representatives of people served by the programs and agencies involved boarded a bus to Boston where they picketed and conferenced with HUD officials. The grants were refunded.

Finally, we must "touch" them as Jesus did and be present in a real way. This we do when we volunteer at shelters and soup kitchens and refugee resettlement agencies; participate in projects that help people in the Third World; and actively seek out other ways to be involved on a gut level.

But "touch" can be unpleasant. "We tend to romanticize helping the poor," said Albert Nolan his article "Four Stages of Spiritual Growth in Helping the Poor" in *Praying* magazine, "when, in actual fact, it is hard, messy work." If we want to go ahead with our intention to serve them, and to serve them well, we must journey through four stages.

During the first phase, we need to develop a real sense of compassion reinforced by exposure, for "nothing can replace immediate contact with pain and hunger, seeing people in the cold and rain after their houses have been bulldozed, experiencing the unbearable, intolerable smells in a slum, seeing what children look like when they are suffering from malnutrition." Charitable acts such as volunteering in a soup kitchen, distributing clothing to refugees, or working in a community garden are ways of getting involved in a primary fashion. While in this first stage, some may also make financial contributions if they are able, or make lifestyle changes that reflect their heightened awareness.

During the second phase we begin to realize that poverty exists because of the political and economic policies perpetuated by the powers of government, big business, and, yes, even the church. Poverty does not exist because people are uneducated or lazy or morally reprehensible, but because the rich and powerful exploit them. Here we begin to know anger. But we need to ameliorate this anger by realizing that God loves individuals who are rich as much as anyone else; the call is to hate the systems and not the individuals in them who may fervently and religiously believe that their way is the right way. In this second stage, we get involved politically.

The third stage in our development is about humility. It begins with the discovery that it is not our job to "save" the poor; it is theirs. We should give our time, effort, and money to bring them relief and we should work to change the political structures that imprison them, but we need to realize that it is they who will have the intuitive insights about what needs to be done. This is the time when we learn that it is we who are to learn from them and that is it in their struggles that God is most present. Spiritually, we come to realize that, because they are "God's chosen instruments for transforming the world," they are the ones leading us to liberation, and not the other way around.

The fourth stage demands that we accept another harsh reality, that the poor are not heroes and heroines but blighted with faults, weaknesses, and perversities, just as the rich are, just as we all are. In other words, we must outgrow our romantic Dickensian notions. The poor are sinned against and suffering, but that does not make them saints, any more than being born into a rich family makes one a villain. All individuals, whether rich or poor, have faults, fail, sin, and sometimes by their own selfish or stupid actions, they defeat their own purposes. Many times, the poor who finally achieve middle-class status will, in turn, exploit those now less fortunate than they. These are harsh and unpleasant realities; nevertheless, they do not excuse us from embracing their cause.

"God's peace prompts service among brothers and sisters. In that way one creature sustains another," said Meister Eckhart. If we go about this service in good faith and free of romantic notions, he is saying, mutuality may develop. This is a particularly appealing incentive for single people as we may experience poverty of spirit more than many. As I discovered in the time I spent with Jolie and her sisters and brothers in shelters, literacy programs, and soup kitchens, a camaraderie indeed develops between the helper and the helped, and the lines blur. The grizzled old man at the coffee urn gave me a gentler perspective on my own self-flagellating habits. Jolie's phone call out of the blue was like the message of an affirming angel. I have never felt a surge of joy quite like the one I felt the day Pete tearfully read his daughter's name for the first time. These are all elements of the community experience that enriches our lives in mysterious ways. If denial of the preferential option for the poor has introduced a new concept of sin, as Reiser suggests, so does its converse introduce another new concept, that lasting joy is the reward for those who involve themselves with the poor. Along with that joy, we also gain a new perspective on our own lives and heighten the focus still further.

CHAPTER SIXTEEN

Disciplines in Daily Life

American culture is marked by pendulum swings. We swing out as far as we can into excess, and then as far back as we can into reaction. During the late 1990s, we have seen extremes at both ends, such as fundamentalism exercising covert and overt political power, and children gunning down children in fits of self-indulgent hatred. Many middle-aged people are recovering from the sometimes excessive parental and educational disciplinary practices they experienced as children, using them to excuse profligate behavior. As a culture, we are pretty easy on ourselves, preferring pleasure and instant gratification to the tough stuff.

In preparation for my occasional trip to the confessional, I recently revisited the seven deadly sins and was surprised at how right on they were, for me and for my times in general. In fact, they make an interesting mantra for a nightly examen, the prayer practice of reviewing one's day for its spiritual ups and downs. After I reflect on what went well during the day—where God's presence was felt most strongly, where the empty spots were—I also go through a checklist of these cardinal sins. For those of you who missed the catechism lesson, they are: pride, avarice, lust, anger, gluttony, envy, and sloth. All bases covered.

I do not recommend a return to ancient practices, but a revisionist approach to some of them may well be productive in righting our souls, which are being pushed around in all directions by the chaos of modern life. The times call for a swing of the pendulum back to center and a tempering of the excesses, both the ultra-moralistic and the hedonistic, that we are witnessing in these times with disbelief bordering on despair.

For single adults, there are other considerations. Without the structure imposed on us by family duties, we may tend to drift along in an aimless manner. And since we are the sole providers of what makes us feel good, feeling good may become overvalued. On the other hand, we may exert extreme discipline in some areas of our lives, exercise for one, work for another, while leaving others unattended.

I am indebted to Fr. Thomas Ryan, C.S.P. for the ideas and insights in his book, *Disciplines for Christian Living*. His enlightened treatment took the sting out of the word. Discipline, he says, liberates us from those things that hold us back from realizing our full potential. Instead, they are the "basic tools" we use to constructively meet the challenges of life. Teresa of Avila agreed, stressing in the formation of her Carmelite sisters that discipline is the foundation of the spiritual life and especially important for beginners on the journey. Since we are certainly beginners, let us take a fresh unprejudiced look at the concept of discipline.

Some of the practices Ryan includes—service, prayer, hospitality—have been treated elsewhere here. Other chapter topics—for instance, reflective living, friendship with silence and solitude, stability, and study—can also be considered disciplines. Again from Ryan, I add keeping the Sabbath, exercise and recreation, fasting, and otherwise using food properly. One more, simple living, completes my list, at least for the time being. This list represents my own preferences, taken from specific influences and reading that have come my way. Take them with a grain of salt and substitute or add your own. These are choices everyone must make for herself or himself.

I had never thought of Sabbath-keeping as a discipline until I read Ryan's book, but then I began to appreciate it as a pleasant and appealing practice that could free us from the compulsive pace of weekday life. In our culture, we "do" leisure, dashing from one activity to the next in a mad desire to escape from the work week. He calls this the "Exodus complex," as we appear to be always in the act of escaping. Why do we need to escape? Quite simply because we have spent too much time and too much of ourselves at work. Sixty-hour work weeks are becoming commonplace in some professions and ministries, and in other areas overtime has become the norm. The result of this behavior is that, while we may be filling up the bank accounts, our relationships and our own souls are being drained. By stopping or slowing down significantly during a Sabbath period, we bring these obsessive behaviors into perspective. Ryan suggests that we forgo having a weekend agenda, at least on Sunday, and that we put the projects aside and become temporarily "useless," as is the custom for observing Jews. For them, the Sabbath is an invitation to cease work, to rest, and to worship with their communities of faith. It is a day to be prayerful yet playful, to walk on a beach or in a park with family and friends, to invite the neighbors in for bread and soup made the day before.

Drawing on Jewish spiritual tradition, Ryan relates a story in which God makes this promise. "My children, if you accept the Torah and observe my laws, I will give you for eternity a thing most precious that I have in my possession." "What is that most precious thing?" the people asked, and he answered, "The world to come." And what is that like, the people asked him again, "the world to come?" And God answered, "The Sabbath is an example of the world to come." The Sabbath, in other words, is a model of Paradise. How wonderful.

Ryan describes the way one family he knows has returned to this ancient practice. They spend Saturday getting chores done, bills paid, groceries bought, "clearing the decks" as it were. On Saturday evening, they light a candle, read Sunday's gospel and psalm in preparation for the next day's liturgy, and say a blessing over a simple meal. On Sunday morning they keep the house free of extraneous noise before they go to church, and after celebrating the liturgy, they spend the remainder of the day in such activities as reading, going to the beach or pool, playing or listening to music, visiting a museum, or taking a walk.

The quality of a Sunday Sabbath kept in this or some other similar manner is dramatically different from our weekday experience. There is an entirely different energy to it. I have often noticed that, by Sunday, people have begun to be themselves. They move more slowly, are more lighthearted, more open to the inspiration of the moment, more inclined to laugh or have a leisurely conversation. In a word, they are mellow. Sunday is a cocoon of serenity, an opportunity during moments of reverie to reflect on just what made the work week overwhelming. A microcosm of eternal life? Quite possibly.

Just as we can become workaholics, so can we overdo it when it comes to exercise. There is an obsessive quality to the way many of us approach physical activity. We set up impossible goals and reach them or fail at them; we work out in noisy gyms; we spend too much money on chic exercise outfits. Some of us, on the other hand, do none of these things and belong to the "couch potato" club, or can't seem to find time to make exercise a part of our daily routines. This may be because we were not encouraged as children; after all, immigrant people, as all of our forebearers were, did not have the time for such "frivolity." Only the rich were trained in sports. Tennis, sailing, and golf were for the affluent. In some cultures a sedentary lifestyle free from manual labor indicated the favor of God.

Times, of course, have changed and we have become educated about the value of a lifestyle that includes exercise and good nutrition; there is no lack of information out there. But attitudes are hard to change. In addition, the spirituality we have been taught fits only too well with a sedentary lifestyle; it is too much of a stretch to think of exercise as spiritual practice. How frivolous, how silly to think that God wants us to be fit. But remember, we have been taught that our bodies are the houses of our souls; it is important for us to do our housework.

Exercise needs to be regulated to some extent just like everything else in our lives. In other words, it needs to become a discipline. Any activity we like, if it uses the body sufficiently— swimming, running, aerobic dancing—is fine. It can be fast and aerobic at times, slow and relaxing at others, even meditative and prayerful. Meditating while walking is a Buddhist practice that we can learn and incorporate into our scrapbook of prayer practices. Mantras selected from a Scripture passage or psalm can assist the runner or swimmer or biker to center the soul as well as the body during the cool down period. We can slow down even more with yoga, a Hindu practice, much admired and promoted by Fr. Ryan, among others. Yoga prepares the mind for prayer by putting the body through a set of breathing and warm-up exercises, postures, and relaxation techniques. Many have found that the blend of these Eastern practices and Christian spirituality can be the prelude to intense interior prayer. It is also possible to coordinate some yoga postures with known prayers such as the Our Father, the doxology, or a line from a psalm.

Like the body, our attitudes toward food are also, for the most part, culturally imposed. I read once that Hannibal was highly praised partly because he never ate unless he was hungry. For some reason that remark has stuck with me and made me consider the reasons I put food into my mouth. I also reconsidered the sin of gluttony when I rediscovered the seven deadly sins. I am a small person and do not have a problem maintaining my weight, but I am often gluttonous, eating three Oreos instead of two, choosing cheese and crackers over a substantial meal. I often eat for comfort or diversion. I am not like Hannibal.

Fasting is in disfavor in our times; perhaps it reminds us of harsh ascetic practices long out of style. On the other hand, we are a society that has overdosed on food for too long. When I go to the grocery store, I never cease to be amazed at the aisles and aisles of cereals and crackers and soft drinks. It is overwhelming. This display of overabundance insidiously invades our consciousness no matter how hard we try not to be influenced by it. A while ago I realized that my mother, then in her seventies, was doing what I called "recreational grocery shopping." With too much time on her hands, she would wander the supermarket aisles in the middle of lazy afternoons searching for something to make her feel good, to make her loneliness go away. Then, one day shortly after I retired, I found myself one slow, rainy, Saturday afternoon doing the same thing.

Being single may have something to do with it. As a group, we have infamously bad eating habits. We do not prepare balanced meals for ourselves. Our cupboards hold only a few cans of soup, our refrigerators, one bottle of milk, a carton of orange juice. We eat out a lot, spending unnecessary money; we shove fast food into our mouths driving between appointments or to and from work. Nevertheless, we are generally overindulgent and eat more than we need to. Eating, for some, especially gourmet eating or dining in elegant restaurants can be something of a hobby.

The spiritual practice of fasting, then, when we are authentically called to it, and not for purposes of losing weight or making a show for others, can be a valid form of prayer. It helps us put our dependence on food into perspective. Besides that, it is not easy; it is a real sacrifice, perhaps the most tangible one we as Americans can voluntarily practice.

There are certain appropriate times when God may suggest that we pray by fasting. One is when we are feeling contrite; we did something wrong and we know it; we want to make amends. We can fast during certain liturgical seasons that call for deepened spirituality—Lent, Advent, the vigils of feasts. When we are busy and distracted or on overload, fasting can be a tangible way to sweep away the clutter and help us return to our center. This is true for me when I am traveling too much or when my calendar is full of unrelated errands. Fasting can be a form of intercessory prayer. When we are asked to pray for someone or when a newspaper item or major news event is on our minds, we can cut down on certain foods we like or eliminate a meal. Another appropriate time to fast is when we are feeling unusually fatigued or burned out and feel the need to take a day off from work, a "mental health day" some call it. On a day like this, fasting can remove us even from the imperative of preparing a meal. While traveling, we can consider ourselves as pilgrims and forgo the dreadful meals the airlines offer, choosing our own diet of fruit and vegetable juices instead. In this way, we turn a frustrating experience into something positive. There is a clarity that results from praying a fast as a necessary corrective to the clutter we experience in so many aspects of modern life.

Fasting need not be a Gandhi-esque event; we are not all heroes. All most of us want to do is raise our level of consciousness so we are gently aware that we are depriving ourselves for a serious reason, that we are experiencing to some degree what the poor and refugees experience daily. Ryan suggests we begin by skipping one meal and then two, going from after dinner one day to dinner time the next. During those periods, he suggests that we drink eight glasses of water or clear juice, diluting it to keep the blood sugar level up and the sugar intake low. It is best to avoid caffeine drinks as they oppose the sense of serenity we are seeking. Fasting cleanses the body by regenerating the blood and eliminating toxins; therefore, it is best to eat a salad to break the fast as this continues the process.

Fasting shows us how to honor food and the ways in which we grow, prepare, present, and share it. In an article she wrote for *Radical Grace,* the publication of the Center for Action and Contemplation, Rebecca Woods, a well-known food writer, suggests that we take a contemplative approach to the preparation of meals. She calls it the "laying-on of hands." First, plan a simple meal that will use only unprocessed foods. At the grocery store or, even better, the farmers' market, admire the beauty of the vegetables displayed, then select each item carefully, using your hands to evaluate its texture and ripeness. If you buy in bulk, let the rice, the lentils, the beans run through your hands as you bag them. Back in your kitchen, be attentive to the way in which you prepare the food. Slowly and in silence, or with gentle background music, peel and slice the carrots, cut the potatoes, trim the broccoli. And raise your meal to a sacramental level by serving it attractively. Light a candle, say a prayer, eat slowly and reverently, honoring both yourself and the food you are enjoying.

Simple living or voluntary simplicity, a form of fasting from all the other excesses of modern life, is embraced by a growing number of people for many reasons, said Jorgen Lissner in "Reasons for Choosing a Simpler Lifestyle," also written for *Radical Grace*. They may wish to make a statement about global inequities in the distribution of material goods, push back the overemphasis on materialism in our culture, reduce their need to be competitive, share more freely with others, be in solidarity with the poor, focus on the spiritual side of their lives, put pressure on those who incite the desire for more and more things. Generally, they want to loosen the grip materialism has on all of us and open up more space for the fundamentals.

On the daily, practical level, this means eliminating those things that clutter up our lives, and making a conscious decision not to bring them in again. We can begin by evaluating how we are living now. Are our possessions becoming burdensome? Are we taking care of what we own? Is the care and maintenance of our possessions overwhelming us? Are we spending too much on recreation and vacations? On work? Are we on information overload with newspapers, magazines, the Internet? Is our pursuit of the latest technology necessary? Do we have too many books, clothes, social activities? Is our use of food moderate and wholesome or excessive and indulgent? Do we need to fast from television, shopping, the car radio? What else is glutting our soul?

As you start to become aware of the small but persistent movement toward voluntary simplicity, you will soon discover that some have elected to go very far. They choose to live among the disadvantaged in poor neighborhoods and participate in community action, to take only public transportation, to use no credit cards, to buy only previously used household items, to eat only what they grow, to work below the minimum income tax level. For most of us, however, simple living means making a gentle but persistent shift in perspective, a shift that will sharpen the focus of our lives. Added to the other practices we have discussed, it rounds out the vision of a positively disciplined life.

None of these is suggested with the intention of making our lives more difficult, but to free us from self-imposed obsessions and demands. Unhealthy lifestyles are the norm these days. Sundays are destroyed by soccer leagues and demented trips to the mall. Weekdays are long workdays, and weekday evenings are filled with further commitments. As a culture, we are over-burdened with things to do and things to buy and things to take care of and more things to want. It is exhausting us. To turn away from these influences and substitute positive habits requires determination and courage, but the rewards are real. They are a heightened energy, clear vision, a sense of purpose, and above all, a focus on the meaning of our lives.

CHAPTER SEVENTEEN

Living a Personal Rule

Monastics such as the Benedictines and members of other religious orders live by guidelines set down by their founders. The Benedictine Rule is a famous one and we have referred to it often here. The word "rule," Joan Chittister points out, does not mean rigid routine, but rather, as suggested by its etymology, something regular. Something regular in our lives is not a bad thing; it fits well into our present goal, that is, to create a harmonious life, a life in focus. Indeed, it is in our best interests to seek regularity in our lives—not routine, not rigid order, but a steady grace-filled rhythm.

Grace, says Esther deWaal, in *Seeking God: The Way of St. Benedict*, is "spiritual energy." That, certainly, is what we are seeking, a *joie de vivre* that inhabits us in a deep authentic way. We can attain this happy state of being, I believe, when we adhere to our own set of life principles. This may be an outgrowth of what I have called focused living, or it may be something entirely different; it is for each of us to decide. Our "rule" will be ours alone, a unique compendium of spiritual values and practices that have meaning for us.

On our way to creating this personal rule, it might be helpful to take a look at the Benedictine Rule itself to see what parts of it inspire us. www.osb.org takes you to the website for the Benedictine order. From there you can connect to the guidelines for oblates, laypeople who wish to align themselves in a special way with the order while, at the same time, maintaining their life and work in the outside world. The guidelines look to be modifications of the Rule as lived by vowed members of the order. Some of them are already familiar to us as they are similar to the topics we have been discussing. For instance, oblates are expected to be serious about spiritual, intellectual, cultural, and social self-improvement. They will be attentive to God in both prayer and work, active in their concern for the poor, and live in a spirit of poverty, detached from material things. Much of their prayer will be focused on the psalms, since the *opus Dei* (the work of God), and the Liturgy of the Hours, along with the celebration of the Eucharist, is the central liturgical practice of the order. They will join with the community to which they are attached on retreat days and otherwise learn from them. In addition to maintaining these strong connections, they will foster a sense of community in their spheres of influence. They will be peacemakers.

The ultimate goal of a monastic, or of anyone who lives reflectively, is harmony, a life lived in a regular rhythm, all things mundane and sublime blending with all others, no thing that jars. Those things that promote harmony, according to Joan Chittister, are being in community, listening to the gospel in one another and the world around us, prayer, sacred and spiritual reading *(lectio divina)*, work, recreation, keeping the Sabbath, hospitality, stability, peacefulness, and obedience (understood as being mindful of the good of the whole). Manual labor, such as cooking, gardening, tending animals, and building things, is the mortar that holds together the bricks of the spiritual life. To demonstrate solidarity with the poor, many monasteries ally themselves with a Catholic Worker house. And hospitality, of course, is always at the core of monasticism.

It takes no great stretch of the imagination to see that these elements of monastic living can easily be incorporated into everyday life as we know it and find their place in a personal rule of our own design. They prompt us to consider ways in which we too can create harmony in ourselves and in the world in our average day. Would we wake at dawn to pray for those who have suffered during the night? Do a yoga practice to prepare our bodies for a period of *lectio divina?* Eat a wholesome breakfast while still enjoying the silence of contemplation? Walk to work or take a bus instead of driving our car? Spend some time after work exercising? Turn off television and read or listen to music in the evening? Write some reflections in our journal? End our day with a psalm?

And what about the week? Will we find some time in it to be with our intentional community, volunteer at a local social service agency, share a meal with friends, work in a community garden? Will we set aside one day a month to spend reflectively by ourselves, to visit an older relative, to attend a workshop given by a peacemaking organization? Are there large projects which have been building in our imagination but not yet released? Something extraordinary we want to do, something that constitutes mission? What steps can we put into our rule to actualize this vision? The options are endless.

After selecting those things to which we know we can be faithful and thinking about what our rule will look like, it is a good idea to write it down. There is no better way to concretize something that could become simply an amorphous daydream. There is also the question of monitoring, as we do not live in a monastery where everyone else is living by the same rule. On those days when we go away for prayer and reflection, we can take our written rule with us, review it, and see if we are being faithful to it. Perhaps it needs revising, with something added that is beginning to have an appeal for us, something deleted that has lost its value for us. Perhaps we need to renew our commitment to an aspect of the rule we have been ignoring. But we should not be overly scrupulous about adhering to our rule. Perfection as Jesus spoke of it does not mean being perfect with all the t's crossed and all the i's dotted; it means fulfillment of our potential as agents for change in God's beloved world. That will take us a lifetime.

In *Lessons From the Monastery That Touch Your Life,* Basil Pennington, O.S.B., a Cistercian monk, writes about the monastic life. The monk's day, he says, is divided into three parts: labor, lectio, and liturgy. The balance of the three eliminates stress and disorder and results in what he calls "the tranquility of order." Happiness, he says, is what God wants for each us, and monastics, he says, because of harmonious living, are happy.

We have not been called to be monks. Our vocations are in and of the crazy, fast-paced world of the twenty-first century, which we love. Given this reality, can we, too, be as happy? I believe so. Our personal rule is the deciding factor. Through it, we too can live in a grace-filled rhythm, a rhythm that releases spiritual energy, an energy that spills over into the world we love. This happy state of being is called harmony.

CHAPTER EIGHTEEN

New Wineskins

The radical revisioning of the lives of single people, which we are calling focused living, represents yet another turning in the church today. Here individuals are taking responsibility for their own unique spiritual lives while, at the same time, remaining within the great tradition. Those of us who take on this responsibility have the potential to become agents of transformation both within and beyond the institutional churches, and a positive and dynamic influence among those with whom we work and play—our friends, our associates in community activities, our families of origin, our children, our former or future spouses. As a former prayer partner once said, "We are not just wine, we are champagne!"

But becoming champagne takes a long time. I once visited the Mumm winery in Sonoma County, California, and saw the process. Every few days for many months, each individual bottle of champagne is slowly and painstakingly rotated by hand. Making something so uniquely delightful and delicious takes time and effort. As serious travelers on the spiritual journey, we know this to be true of ourselves. The life we have chosen is rewarding, but in no way painless. Now we find ourselves at a transition point in our "fermentation." We have proven that we are serious about developing ourselves spiritually; perhaps we belong to an intentional community that we have found or established ourselves; we have been faithful to prayer and to our inner and outer worlds. It has been, and continues to be, an arduous trip.

Clearly, a celebration is called for; this effort we have undertaken should not go unrecognized. But how to go about it? We look to the church in vain. There are no sacraments for single unvowed people. The five sacraments that celebrate the great turnings in human experience—baptism, eucharist, reconciliation, confirmation, the anointing of the sick—are shared by all the faithful. The other two are reserved for special groups—marriage for couples making lifelong commitments, and Holy Orders for men who become priests. Religious women and religious men who are not called to be priests are honored in their ceremonies of profession that, although not official sacraments, are sacramentalized by the holy attitude in which they are undertaken. But there is no sacrament to honor unique passages in the lives of single adults.

I suggest that we take the matter into our own hands. Although others may not, we can celebrate the sacramental quality of our lives. We can create our own ceremony and in the presence of our trusted communities of faith, our small intentional communities, be consecrated in our determination to live the unique and holy life we have designed for ourselves. We have given serious consideration to the formation of a personal rule, our particular version of the focused life. We have ended a time of undefined living and entered a new phase of intentional living. This is a momentous event and needs to be formalized and properly recognized.

The rites of marriage, ordination, and profession into a religious community include the taking of vows. In our rite of commitment to the focused life, we can also make promises—not the old ones of poverty, chastity, and obedience, as they are irrelevant to our station in life, but new ones, serious commitments we wish to make publicly before God and our small communities of faith. And just as the vow-taking sacraments are surrounded and framed by ritual, so can we incorporate ritual into our own ceremony.

This event, this "profession," should not be taken lightly. Postulants in religious orders, we remember, must wait years before taking vows. Therefore, I suggest that those of us who wish to make a similar profession enter into a period of reflection, a sabbatical. During that time we will contemplate with serious attentiveness what direction we wish our lives to take, what aspects of the focused life we wish to appropriate, what disciplines. From that deliberation will emerge the covenant we wish to make and how we plan to ritualize its celebration.

Our church at this time in history has not created opportunities that honor the lives of single adults. Thus, we must do it ourselves. In the following chapters we will plan our own sacramental initiation. We will consider how to take sabbatical time in order to prepare for it. We will decide what promises we want to make, promises that, for us, will be as binding as canonical vows. We will create a ritual for this new sacrament. New wine will burst the seams of old wineskins. We are the new wine, long unrecognized and undefined, now a powerful intoxicating spirit at work among the people of God.

As I noted in my introduction, the seed for this book was planted as I was reading Dorothy Day's autobiography, *The Long Loneliness*. In this book she talks about her life before she met Peter Maurin and started, first the Catholic Worker newspaper and then the CW houses of hospitality. Dorothy was born into an interesting family that allowed her to be unusually independent in adolescence. As a young woman she further separated herself from them and lived an extraordinary existence in the midst of the "bohemian" intellectual world of the times, her interests mirroring theirs. But then something happened. She moved out of New York to Staten Island and began to live a simpler and quieter life, first with her lover, Forster Batterham, and then alone as a single parent with her daughter Tamar. When she returned to New York, she was a changed woman, ready for the remarkable mission that was to define her life thereafter.

So it is with us, I believe, if we let it be. We begin our lives under the influences of a certain family and education, and then set out into the world. That larger world gives us many choices and challenges. We spend some time there, often buffeted about in it. Then, at a later stage in our lives, we step back and take a long backward look. At that time, we may, like Dorothy, be inspired to make radical changes in our way of being. These changes, of course, are not lightly taken. Such a turning point calls for a time of reflection, such as the time Dorothy spent on Staten Island after the birth of Tamar and before she returned to New York and the amazing future that awaited her there. I suggest that we, too, need a time of reflection, especially at this juncture in our spiritual passage.

Why? For several reasons. First, we may want to absorb some of the thoughts and ideas that have been raised here to see if they apply to our life vision. The first section of the book asked the question, "Who do *you* say that I am?" We need to address this question and in that process consider some of the hard facts about our lives. How are we perceived by our friends and family, our coworkers, our church? Have these associations hurt our self-image in ways large and small? While we need not dwell for an unnecessarily long time on these questions, we cannot "rise above" them either. It is important to acknowledge that they are a part of our life experience, and face them.

Then we must ask ourselves the question, "Who do *I* say that I am?" Do we have an answer? Is the answer the one we want to stay with for the rest of our lives? Or do we want to move into a new vision of ourselves? Is it time to consider some of the topics addressed in Chapter 5, "The Focused Life"? Are there any parts in the following chapters that speak to us, that hit home, that we would like to incorporate into our lifestyle? If the answer to any of these questions is yes, then we clearly need time to step back and consider how we intend to bring this transformation about. Albert Schweitzer once said, "Without a vision, nothing happens," and I add, "Without a plan, nothing happens."

Planning time, how do we get it? Academics and members of religious orders are given time off just for this purpose. In the Jewish tradition, one of the extensions of the Sabbath concept is the jubilee year, every seventh year devoted to rejuvenation and the chance to begin anew with a clean slate. But most of us don't have that option. We can't quit our jobs and go merrily off into the woods. We need to put food in our mouths and pay the rent. Does this mean that we must deny ourselves of a sabbatical time? Perhaps not.

I propose that there are a number of creative ways in which we can treat ourselves to a sabbatical. One way is to take "poustinia days," as Ryan has suggested in *Disciplines for Christian Living*. We can use our sick days or personal days if we have that option, or we can take them on weekends. On these set-aside days, we choose to be alone with our thoughts and issues—and a notebook. Another way is to use our vacation time as a conscious and organized time of reflection.

The best-selling book, *Six Months Off,* is well worth reading if this idea appeals to you. Not only does it offer some concrete ideas about how to grab some time, but it presents a step-by-step plan for first stepping back from what you are now doing and then stepping off into a future of your own making. Fascinating. One somewhat radical but possible suggestion the authors make is to leave your present job and become a "temp." Actors and artists often live this way. It gives them control over their time; they work when they need to fill up the bank account, and they stop work when they need to act or write or paint or think.

What we all need, if we are going to make changes in our lives, is thinking time. Like Dorothy, we need to leave the busy life and drift, ever so deliberately, into the slow lane. We need to move into a new rhythm, a rhythm that lets us wake from sleep without an agenda before us, and enter a day without any lists, any demands—something like the summers of childhood. This is a time to let the imagination flourish, to meander, to take a walk around the neighborhood at eleven o'clock in the morning, to see the children on the playgrounds, the old people waiting for buses. Take a bus yourself, go to the beach on a weekday. Find out if God is waiting there for you. When you have established this new rhythm, you will be ready to take up the business of your sabbatical.

If you need to talk yourself into the idea, think of it as an extended Sabbath. In the Bible, the seventh day is described as holy, the first time that word, *qadosh,* was used in Scripture, a reminder that leisure is a spiritual exercise. Even the prescribed prayers during the Sabbath are prayers of praise rather than of petition or grief. There is no fasting on the Sabbath. And, blessings on us all, lovemaking is one of the favored Sabbath "commands."

In Jewish culture, the Sabbath has several traditional meanings. One is related to work. Religious Jews understand work as something that prepares us for the Sabbath, not the other way around. Quite a revolutionary thought for those of us programmed by the Protestant ethic. Sabbath rest is intended to provide a time to experience a sense of rhythm that matches the rhythm of the universe. It gives us license to "float" for a day, to experience personal freedom. Thus, it puts us in mind of those who are never so free and raises our consciousness about issues of social justice.

Nevertheless, we have some work to do on our sabbatical. There are five tasks. First of all, if we haven't already, now is the time to start keeping a journal. Here we keep our thoughts, prayers, dreams, and other written reflections that have to do with our lives. I suggest that another part of that process, especially beneficial when we begin a journal, is to write an autobiography. This will help us see how the present and the past converge and will also point to the future we want for ourselves. The third task is to create one's own personal rule. Out of that exercise will emerge the promises or vows we will make in the presence of our intentional community, our fourth task. And finally, we will plan the ritual for celebrating our commitment to this newly focused life. We have a lot to do during our sabbatical time.

In the chapter on reflective living we described in some detail how to keep a journal, so I won't discuss it here. An extension of that practice, though, becomes our second task, writing an autobiography. This is not a dive into narcissism, although, for some, it surely would be. For anyone who is on an intentional path of spiritual exploration, however, who is seeking self-understanding for a higher purpose than self-actualization, who wants to discover his or her God-inspired sacred energies and release them into the world, it is another way to explore the inner life.

Writing autobiography has become fashionable these days, and memoirs fill the shelves of bookstores. Our society seems to be in a self-reflective mood. There are some excellent guides for those who would write a memoir or autobiography. Some are intended to spur the writer on and give him or her some ideas for how to proceed. I think of Sam Keen and Anne Valley-Fox's stimulating *Your Mythic Journey,* Edward O'Heron's *Your Life Story.* Others are helpful for those who wish to make literature or true art out of their recollections. Thomas Merton's *Seven Storey Mountain* is one, Hammarsjköld's *Markings,* Jill Ker Conway's *The Road from Coorain* and her own most recent work on how women have written about themselves throughout history. Dorothy Day's *The Long Loneliness* will be inspiration for this important work of the soul. By making a record of one's life, we honor ourselves and are drawn into a process through which we define what it is we are about, what our mission in life is or will be, what contributions to self, family, friends, community, the world, and the kingdom will be forthcoming.

A third task for the sabbatical is the design of one's unique personal or daily rule. A daily rule provides the shape for a typical day in the life of someone who is turned toward perfection, an outline that incorporates all the elements of one's vision of the focused life. It delineates a harmonious life, a life in which work, learning, prayer, and rest are consciously balanced. It can be open or tightly prescribed, depending on the personality of the author. Within its framework, one can pledge oneself to silence, spiritual disciplines, hospitality, and additional spiritual practices such as keeping the Sabbath or setting aside one day a month for fasting or silent reflection.

The personal rule each of us creates should be looked on as a guide, and a standard to which we aspire, not one that must be met scrupulously. If it is written down, it can be shared with one's spiritual director and one's intentional community, reflected on, and frequently revised. Simply by existing, it encourages and sustains those who wish to lead balanced and harmonious lives.

The last two tasks for our sabbatical will be discussed in the following chapters. One is deciding on a set of promises, our own vows, that encompasses all the elements of our personal rule, the focused life toward which we have been journeying. Lastly, we will plan the ritual by which we will consecrate this new covenant.

Thus, there are five tasks to complete during our sabbatical. Every one of them is important and none should be neglected for another; making a covenant is serious business. Allow yourself as much time as it takes, even a year or more. The covenant God made with Adam and Eve was constant throughout history, but not perfected before that great moment when Jesus arrived on earth. So think of your covenant as an evolving thing. Like God, you and you alone will know the moment when it has become a perfect true thing, that the time for its annunciation has come.

CHAPTER NINETEEN

New Vows

I believe that we single adults elevate our lives to the status of vocation when we set aside our preoccupation with past losses and unmet expectations and find a central and compelling focus. One way of doing this has been plotted out in the preceding chapters. We will not enter a seminary or a formation program; we will not participate in a pre-Cana program, but we will take sabbatical time to create a personal rule of life. And we will, if we choose, prepare ourselves to make a public statement that expresses our intention to follow the way we have chosen. In this we are like would-be postulants who are told in the "Vocationer's Guide" on the OSB (Order of St. Benedict) website, "You are not a monk at this point, but a pilgrim seeking the feel and taste of this lifelong journey of faith."

And so we, too, will be pilgrims, preparing ourselves for our moment of profession. Our preparation need not be the five and a half years required of the Benedictine novice, but it will last at least for the duration of our sabbatical time, and beyond that, as we begin to practice the personal rule we have devised for ourselves and consider what commitments we are prepared to make. These promises will be unique and in no way a temporary or stopgap exercise. Just as with the ordained or married, it will be binding, a lifelong commitment. We may make additional commitments and take additional vows should we marry or enter religious life, but these will only complement and in no way abrogate what we are choosing to do in this portentous moment.

Joan Chittister, who wrote the article on vows in *The New Dictionary of Catholic Spirituality*, defines a vow as "a public commitment to do a specified good for the sake of religious dedication or 'divine service,' the giving of the self to God. It is both a public contract and a public witness, the value of which does not lie in choosing good over bad in life but in choosing good above good." Vows made in Old Testament times, she explains, were understood to be promises made to God. Some groups, especially the Nazarites, took vows of service for a specific time frame and were rigidly held to them. Paul himself took such a temporary vow. Later on we came to identify the taking of vows with the monastics who promised poverty, virginity, obedience, and adherence to the rule of their community.

Some members of Pax Christi, the international Catholic peace movement, take a vow of nonviolence. Similarly, those who participate fully in the Catholic Worker movement make firm commitments to the following tenets: working for justice in the areas of economics, labor, politics, morals, and the arms race; and practicing the spiritualities of nonviolence, the corporal works of mercy, manual labor, and voluntary poverty.

The traditional canonical vows of poverty, chastity, and obedience, it should be said, are essentially misunderstood in our times. Poverty, for instance, implies dependence on the beneficence of God and awareness of global economic inequities; chastity makes a statement about control and deprivation and does not—at least intentionally—condemn sexuality; obedience requires that one be cognizant of laws higher than personal preferences, not blindly submissive. Be that as it may, these traditional vows, while having much to emulate even for those not contemplating religious life, are largely irrelevant for single people who are not members of a defining institution. We can adhere to our own versions of poverty, chastity, and obedience, of course, but there are other promises we can make that are more suitable to the nature of the way we are in the world.

What might our own new vows be? We can look to models within Pax Christi and the Catholic Worker movement; we can revision the traditional canonical vows taken by religious. And we can look at the aspects of the focused life, considering self-reflection, prayer, silence, home, hospitality, community, work, stability, study, advocacy for the poor, for instance. Disciplines such as keeping the Sabbath, keeping our bodies properly exercised, using food respectfully, being involved with issues surrounding the distribution of food, and living simply may also inspire our decisions.

The challenge is to select those elements that have particular significance for us and to frame them within several broader categories that unify our personal vision. Consider, for instance, the following: living consciously, fidelity, simplicity, temperance, community, preferential option for the poor, self-respect. Living consciously suggests that we will live deliberately and with mindfulness, paying close attention to our inner journey and encouraging the emergence of our true self through silence, prayer, and the process of self-reflection. Fidelity implies loyalty to that true self, and the refusal to allow ourselves to be exploited by other people or institutions. It also encompasses faithfulness, and stability in our communities and in other relationships and groups to which we belong. Simplicity indicates our willingness to put aside our material desires for a larger good, to be consciously aware of the condition of the poor, to honor the earth and its natural gifts. Temperance suggests that we will be respectful in all our desires and relationships, intimate and otherwise, and disciplined in our approach to life. A commitment to community means that we will be active in fostering communal and collaborative ways of being in our personal, work, family, church, and civic relationships; and that we will foster the growth of our own intentional communities. The preferential option for the poor implies active engagement in the affairs of the poor or otherwise disenfranchised, both locally and globally. Other vows that suggest themselves are vows of mindfulness, integrity, and hospitality.

When we dedicate ourselves to these high ideals, we make an act of faith, faith in the constant influence of a God who is intimately involved in our lives, in the positive influence of our intentional communities, in our now-focused selves. They will ground us as we pursue our vision of the focused life; with and through them we raise ourselves to the status of those whose vocations have names.

CHAPTER TWENTY

New Rituals

For many summers now our family has gathered on Block Island, Rhode Island for vacation. We do not have the resources to own a home there so we rent other people's houses. Nevertheless, it has become our sacred space, our *temenos*. These gatherings hold great significance for us, especially since we have spread our wings and nobody lives in Rhode Island anymore. Some of us live in New York, some in Maine, and some all the way out in Oregon. To have everyone together now is a momentous occasion.

Such an occasion came to pass a few years ago. It had been some time since my four children and I had been together. Liz, the West Coast child, had come in from Oregon; I had driven from Maine with Sue and her two little daughters, Eliza and Sasha; Julie had journeyed from Greenwich Village to Montauk and taken the ferry from there. Only Mark, working back in Maine, was missing, so I represented him. The occasion clearly called for a ritual. This is what we did.

On a fine, slightly misty morning—earlier we had seen deer in the dense thicket of shadbushes that surrounded the house—we gathered around the picnic table on the deck. Each of us had brought earth from our gardens north, south, east, and west. Liz had dug from her farm plots in Corvallis; Sue, Eliza, and Sasha from their garden in Scarborough; Julie from her terrace pots on 14th Street; and mine from a Maine beach. My brother Ed had sent earth from his new location on Bainbridge Island, Washington.

In the center of the table we placed a red plastic bowl taken from the house, a long-handled spoon, and five small jars with cork stoppers that I had bought at a gift shop in town. We opened with a prayer of thanksgiving for our time together and then each of us in turn poured our earth into the bowl. As we did, we spoke about what these places meant to us and what it meant to be together again. Then we mixed the soils together and held our hands over the bowl in a blessing. Our acolytes, Eliza and Sasha, had the pleasant job of scooping some of the newly mixed earth into the little jars which we all took home in remembrance. Then we went to the beach.

According to the *New Dictionary of Catholic Spirituality,* the Latin word *ritus,* from which the word ritual is derived, means, "a structured activity that facilitates personal and social transactions, and serves to unify a community." In the *New Catholic Encyclopedia,* Patricia De Ferrari says that the "social, symbolic process [of ritual] develops within a community and uses gestures, objects, words, and sounds as symbols to create, criticize, and transform meaning." One definition I particularly like comes from Malidoma Somé, a West African shaman who speaks about the rituals that attend every significant life event his tribal people and other indigenous peoples celebrate. According to him, a ritual is "a series of gestures, steps, and movements which, when put together, make a sentence heard in the spiritual world." It is his belief that Western culture has lost its sense of ritual or has surrendered its practice to clerical hierarchies. He proposes that laypeople relearn how to ritualize the small and large events in their lives, and I agree wholeheartedly with him.

Our most familiar rituals are tied to family experiences— Thanksgiving dinners, Fourth of July cookouts, the opening of Christmas presents; for Jews, Friday night and Passover Seders and other holy celebrations in the Jewish calendar; births, deaths, graduations, weddings, leave-takings—experiences so familiar to us that we do not recognize them as ritual. In my mind, ritual is closely linked to liturgy, which is defined by Joan Chittister as "the symbolic celebration of the work of God." (Certainly, the ritual we shared that quiet summer morning on Block Island was a celebration of the work of God—the love my children and I share, and the beautiful island that has become sacred to us.) The Mass, we can easily see, is a family ritual as it brings us together to reenact a communal meal with holy remembrance. Indeed, many of our rituals are church-based and beautiful. We can learn a great deal about creating our own from them.

In my work with small groups I find that simple ritual enhances the message of the gospel. One Pentecost, for instance, when my intentional community met, we lit a red candle for each one present as a sign of our impassioned spirits. Then we distributed red flames cut from construction paper. After a short period of silence, during which we reflected on the gifts of the Holy Spirit, we wrote on one side what we thought was our greatest gift, and on the other the gift we most needed to pray for. Taking turns, we shared our thoughts with the group. The experience became truly profound when we decided to go around the circle and tell each one what we thought his or her gifts were. There were tears of gratitude and recognition. At Christmas time we contemplated the figures of the three Wise Men, took up candles, and walked meditatively around the room as if on a journey. After a time of reflection, we named the star we were following and where we were at this point in our journey toward it.

This last ritual was modified from *Taste and See: Prayer Services for Gatherings of Faith,* a book of prayer rituals by Jacqueline Syrup Bergan and S. Marie Schwan. According to the authors, rituals are most successful when certain essential elements are present. First there should be a call to prayer, a brief invitation to a time of silence so that the group can become centered and focused on the theme. This is followed by a longer opening prayer recited by the group as a whole. A Scripture passage is read and followed by more time for personal reflection and sharing. The central ritual or rite follows, then another reading and a closing prayer, also recited by everyone.

In fashioning ritual, I find the books of Kathleen Fischer and Joyce Rupp especially useful. Their use of ritual is creative and accessible. Schraffran and Kozak, in their equally helpful *More than Words: Prayer and Ritual for Inclusive Communities*, offer simple guidelines for preparing a prayer service. Buena Vista, an organization dedicated to the formation and support of small Christian communities, has also published a pamphlet on ritual, one in a series of four on the marks of church in SCCs.

All strongly advise that one be sure about what is being celebrated, and then consider who will be there and how to create experiences that will involve all present. Perhaps the group can tell stories, play a song from a tape or CD, or share a poem or reading. The use of symbolic objects such as flowers, candles, rocks, shells, icons, or sculpture, is extremely important as a way of concretizing the meaning of the gathering. (Think of the symbols used in the sacrament of baptism, for instance.) Invoke a positive image of God in the prayers and readings, the God of compassion, perhaps, or of constancy, friendship, courage, or companionship. Other useful additions to prayer services or rituals are art materials such as paints, crayons, clay, and paper and pencil for journaling activities. Catechetical resources are full of suggestions. My Pentecost ritual was modified from one in *The Best of Holy Days and Holidays: Prayer Celebrations with Children*, a delightful book.

And so we have come to the point in our reflection on the focused life when it is time to prepare our own initiation celebration with promises, ritual, song, movement, and food. The time is yours. You have prepared by creating, refining, and living out your unique personal rule of life. It is time to consecrate that life in the presence of your intentional community. What will you do? Here are some suggestions:

You and the members of your small intentional community sit in an arrangement as closely resembling a circle as is possible. In the center, place a celebration table set with candles, a colored cloth, a vessel of special oil, and symbols that represent the promises you will be making. Also there will be a copy of your promises.

You or someone you have chosen welcomes the group,

expresses the reason for the gathering, and calls upon God to be present.

A favorite hymn, song, or piece of music is sung or played from a tape or CD player. (Do you, or does a friend, play a musical instrument?)

You read a significant passage from the life of Jesus, the Psalms, or the Old Testament and share your reasons for choosing it. If you wish, the other members of the group may share their feelings and responses to the passage.

If you wish, you can declare your intentions by taking up each item on the celebration table and explaining how it represents the meaning of each commitment. Then you can make your formal declaration and have the group sign the written document you have prepared.

The group can then stand in a circle to bless the oil with which you will be anointed, and then each one in turn will anoint you while speaking words of blessing and affirmation.

Reflections, readings, and affirmations are shared from the circle.

Now it is your turn to bless each one present. You may also wish to name your mentors, past and present, alive or dead, at this time.

A hymn or music is sung or played.

Offer a closing prayer.

Celebrate with food and drink.

Your own celebration will be uniquely created by you, of course. You will choose the music, the colors, the decorations, the symbols, the prayers. Most of all, you will choose the promises. It will be a time of abundant joy, as you have made a difficult passage and your life now has unique and important value. Whatever the future brings, there is no turning back. Your focus will never change. You know what your mission is. You are on your way to fulfilling the promise that was there in the eyes of God at the moment of your conception. You are new wine. More than that, you are champagne. Pop the cork!

Conclusion

When day had already broken, Jesus was standing on the shore, but the disciples did not know that it was Jesus. Jesus called to them, "Children, have you anything to eat?" They answered, "Nothing." "Throw the net on the right side of the boat and you will find some." When they had lowered the net, they were not able to pull it in because of the great number of fish....When they landed, they saw a charcoal fire with fish on it, and some bread. Jesus said to them, "Bring some of the fish you've just caught....Come and have breakfast."

Of all the gospel scenes, this is my favorite. I can just see the beach, a curve of sand, shells, and pebbles, and Jesus standing there watching his beloved friends, not too far away, struggling with their empty nets. Then he calls out to them. In this version, he calls them children, in others, friends. Either word suggests a sweet intimacy and reveals Jesus' tender feelings toward his companions. He prepares for their return by making a fire on the beach. Then they all sit around and have a fish fry and talk about the future.

I too have met Jesus on the beach. He is always there in the rhythm and sound of the waves and the steady heave of the swells further out. On several occasions I have felt his presence profoundly. One time, for some reason I no longer remember— we may have been going to a court appearance having to do with my pending divorce—I was driving with a younger brother with whom I have a sometimes troubled relationship. It was a weather-perfect day in late May, one of those days when the sky is so blue it defies description and the clouds so white and pretty that you think you are living in the pages of a picture book. On a whim, Bob decided to take a detour and visit a the beach at Matunuck, Rhode Island, a favorite of his that he wanted to show me. We reached it after driving for several miles on a gravelly road.

I remember that I got out of the car and walked directly to the shoreline which stretched, as Rhode Island beaches do, without boundaries, for miles to either side, and where landfall is Ireland or Portugal. All along the endless stretch for as long as I could see, little waves curled one upon the next in gentle play upon the shore. One after another they came, harmless on this benign day, making the most lovely susurrus.

"This is God," I remember thinking; "God is always here on this beach, I can come to visit whenever I want. My husband went away, but God and this ocean are constant, they will never go away." I turned to share my delight with Bob; I knew he would be loving the moment too. But I was unprepared to see the look of kind concern on his face as he watched me splashing barefoot in the warm waves. For a moment, his face was God's face, his look, God's look. I held his steady gaze for as long as I could before dropping my own and turning back to the ocean, but in that sacred moment and in Bob's look, I had seen the face of God and heard the voice of God, and God had told me that I was going to be all right.

It is a few years later and I am bustling around a kitchen in a large old convent, once a resort hotel, again on the Rhode Island shore. I am there to help my friend Mary Ann prepare some meals for a twelve-step retreat she is running over the weekend. Mary Ann is a C.N.D. (Congregation of Notre Dame) sister.

While we work, we chat, and as is her way, she asks about my personal life, which is often in turmoil. I am learning how to be a "single" and am making big mistakes. One of those mistakes is very much on my mind this morning. The man I am in love with seems to be rejecting me, and I am feeling confused and frightened at the prospect of another abandonment.

"Wait," says Mary Ann, as I prepare to leave, "let's talk for a moment," and, although she has twenty-five visitors arriving in thirty minutes, she takes me out to the beach where we walk back and forth for a while and I pour out my soul. I talk, she listens.

When I am through she gives me loving and practical advice.

From Mary Ann I have learned about the art of listening; in fact, in her nonobtrusive way, she has taught me many lessons. Some of these "lessons," I am lately learning, are part of the charism of her order, derived from the mystery of Mary's Visitation to Elizabeth. No one visits better or in a more artful way than Mary Ann and her congregation.

Another aspect of their order's charism is "matchmaking." It seems that their foundress, Marguerite Bourgeoys, housed young girls, as well as novices and professed religious, in her first convent in Montreal. There she carefully monitored the relationships that developed with the young men who came to call and often encouraged appropriate marriages. Among the numerous friends who gather around Mary Ann and the other C.N.D. women who live with her in their large old house in Providence are several young professional women who are struggling to cultivate and maintain sound relationships in the hopes of marrying. They invariably find a ready and patient guide in Mary Ann. As did I during that difficult time. Her advice couldn't save the relationship, but her friendship has been constant. We are still walking on beaches.

Twenty years after my visit to the beach at Matunuck with Bob, I am on another beach, this one in Scarborough, Maine. I am alone this time and it is a bright cold day in early December. Although the cold bites, I am grateful that there is no battering wind. I am lonely and troubled, having suffered a number of setbacks having to do with the move I have recently made to Maine. Still unattached, I am used to being the sole author of my life by now, but there are times when I long for a companion to help smooth the way. Today is one of those days; I am feeling vulnerable and unsettled.

The Voice of God

Again, there is little ocean action; all I can hear besides the cawing of sea gulls is the sound of gently breaking waves. The sound accompanies me as I make my way to a secluded cove at the end of the beach. The cove is one of those complex micro-environments, filled with possibilities. Barnacles cling to the sides of large black granite boulders, and the incoming tide washes the water in intriguing swirls around them. Eventually, the small strand of beach I stand on will disappear, but now, as I stand there and watch, it is mid-tide, and the drama of it simply intrigues me. There is still time.

I stand in silence, waiting. And that is when I hear the voice, as sure as if someone were standing next to me.

"See, Jean?" says the voice, "I have been with you; I have been constant." It is the voice of God. And then I see it, the constancy that has kept me from disaster for the past twenty years, and loaded me up with the love of my family, success in my endeavors, and release from difficulties. I am in awe for a while listening to the swish of the water curling through the rocks, feeling the cold calm air on my face and the wan winter sun, recalling the words. My angst has been removed; once again I feel relaxed and confident. I will survive this transition in one piece.

When I tell this story later to my spiritual director, I am crying. Suddenly I am remembering the beach in Matunuck with Bob and the reality I experienced there of the constancy of God. And I realize that, there it is again, the word "constant." I brush away my tears and look at my director in amazement, and he tells me, smiling gently, that I have had "a religious experience." Yes. (Later, in checking Roget's *Thesaurus,* I found that, besides the peaceful wave sound, Roget defines susurrus as "soft voice, low voice, small or little voice," as the "still, small voice.")

But I want to return once again to the beach scene in John's gospel. There is Jesus and there are the seven disciples sitting with him around a charcoal fire eating breakfast at dawn on their last day together. In this setting they renew their declarations of love for one another and make commitments for the future. I see in this picture the kind of loving intentional community that I feel is so necessary for all of us and for single adults especially. Jesus modeled community for us innumerable times in the gospels. Along with a reflective attitude toward life and an intimate prayer life with God, also modeled in him, it forms the threefold basis of the balanced lifestyle we are calling focused living.

But Peter and the others at this point, even after three years spent in Jesus' company, were still underdeveloped in all these areas, beginners as are we. It is only later that we see them in Acts evolving rapidly under the nurturing tutelage of the Holy Spirit. This maturation process reminds me of what Mary Field Belenky and her team of researchers found in their studies on women, and the work the adult educator Paulo Freire did with illiterate peasants in Brazil.

Until Belenky's research was published, it was commonly assumed that the classroom experience was about the same for female students as it was for male. Her studies proved otherwise. Learning for most women, the research said, is adversely affected by conditions set up prior to their entering the classroom and that have nothing to do with education. In most societies, boys are traditionally enculturated to behave independently, confidently, and autonomously, and to have opinions on many matters, which they freely express without fear of intimidation or recrimination. Girls, on the other hand, are trained to be relational, constantly alert to the needs of others, and expected to put their best energies into serving those needs. Thus conditioned, especially as they move into adolescence, they tend to defer to the more assertive male, who, because of his self-confidence, appears to "know" more than they do. In the presence of these "betters" they are rendered speechless, inarticulate.

But they can change if they have a positive educational experience guided by teachers who are affirming and sensitive to the situation. There are five levels of development. First, they are silent and consider themselves incapable of learning. Then they become receivers of knowledge, but absorb it without comment, criticism, or complaint. In the next phase, what Belenky calls "subjective knowledge," they begin to integrate this knowledge with their own personal experience, and apprehend new knowledge or information subjectively, somewhat as the disciples did when they questioned how they fit in with Jesus' plans. How does this have meaning, they want to know, in the context of what I know from my life? There is a lack of maturity in this way of knowing, even a pomposity, unless prodded gently into the next higher level of learning in which they apply a strictly objective approach, "procedural knowledge." The final and fifth step in the process from silence to articulation is the ability to integrate and weave together what they have been taught with what they know intuitively and experientially, what Belenky and her colleagues call "constructed knowledge." They now have the capacity to make unique contributions in those areas that interest them.

Paulo Freire was charged with eliminating adult illiteracy in Brazil in the mid-1950s. He set out to meet the challenge armed with theories and methods he had developed as a doctoral student and professor of education at the University of Recifé. The traditional formal ways of teaching, he believed, thwarted spontaneity and passion in learners and made them compliant and easily exploited by authoritarian political, social, and economic systems. As wisdom comes from the people, even those we call ignorant, the learners themselves, he believed, should determine what subject matter is most relevant to their experience. It is they, not those who have power over them, who should determine the matter of their education and what exactly they need to learn. What Freire's adult literacy eventually demonstrated to the marginalized Brazilian peasants was that they were poor and inarticulate because they were being oppressed and that, therefore, they needed to work to change the autocratic systems in Brazil. As a result, the programs were shut down and Freire exiled for fifteen years. His theories, however, have thrived and are influential worldwide. Later, under a more democratic government, he returned to Brazil and, at the time of his death in 1997, was director of schools in São Paulo.

I am struck by commonalities between the women Belenky studied, Freire's illiterate adults, and any marginalized population, whether they be women, the illiterate poor, the disabled, gays or lesbians, and, in this case, single people in the church. Any of these could be intimidated by those who have a sense of autonomy and freedom resulting from privilege, whether it be a strong education, political or physical power, social status, financial security, or any other entitlement.

We single adults, men and women alike, in our poorly defined relationships with church, family, and society, are like the silent women in Belenky's study and the illiterate peasants Freire empowered. At least for the moment, we, too, are voiceless; at the same time, we are moving toward informed articulation. With this new awareness we can become vocal and influential in those areas that affect our lives—our relationships, our families, our workplaces and communities, our world, our churches. It is my hope that we can move through a process, from speechlessness to articulation and contribution, by telling our stories, by beginning to develop an objective overview, by replacing our tendency to blame with a more realistic "seeing how it is," by forming intentional community, and by focusing our attention on our own spiritual development. Then, not only will we be empowered to effect change in this system we call church, even more important, we will become advocates for the disadvantaged in other systems. As Tolstoy said, "It is by those who have suffered that the world is advanced."

Joseph of the coat of many colors says it well. At the pinnacle of his life, at the height of his powers in the land of his slavery, he tells his brothers who had scorned and rejected and betrayed him—and who are now beholden to him—that he sees his early distress as providential, and himself as selected "to serve God's purpose." Like Joseph, Hannah, the mother of Samuel, suffered ignominy by society's standards but rose to proclaim the prophetic call to solidarity with the poor, a message that was repeated by Mary at the time of her own call to greatness, the same message that Jesus would repeat in his first sermon. We, too, can point to a better way and, through our suffering past and renewed present, show others in our spheres of influence how to take charge of their own spiritual well-being through intentional community, prayer, and self-reflection.

Again, Dorothy Day is our model. She was a socially committed world citizen and intensely devoted to her church, although often in loyal dissent with it. Not only was she passionately devoted to caring for the poor and marginalized, she was equally committed to the development of her spiritual life and to the formation of community in her Catholic Worker houses of hospitality. To follow her example, we must become as she was, single-minded; the words she spoke in an interview with Robert Coles must become our words. Reflecting on her conversion to Catholicism, she said, "My conversion was a way of saying to myself that I knew I was trying to go someplace and that I would spend the rest of my life trying to go there and try not to let myself get distracted by side trips, excursions that were not to the point." Like her, we must avoid the "side trips" and not be "distracted" by those who would bring us down or who have allowed the system to take them over and have become immersed in materialism, frenetic activity, endless "lonely wanderings," mindless "do-gooding," or pietistic churchiness. Ours is the way of vibrancy, the active life, as Teresita Weind says, not the agitated life.

Bernard Lee and Michael Cowan, in *Dangerous Memories,* their seminal book on intentional Christian communities, claim that we are in times that demand the creation of a new metaphor, a theme or concept that gives a framework for the way we speak of ourselves and our experiences. Formerly, we thought of church as institution with all the attitudes and structures implied in that definition. The new metaphor, the one that members of the church need today, say Lee and Cowan, has already been given, and given by the church herself. The Second Vatican Council gave Catholic Christians a new root metaphor for themselves: "You are the People of God." Catholic Christians, then, should be working collaboratively with, not under orders from, the ordained clergy. We, the unnamed new minority—soon to be a majority?—of single adults who are Catholic, can play a significant role as the church struggles to reconstruct herself.

Time for Empowerment

But first we need to speak out about our unnamed place in the church and demand that our voice, our unique expression, be heard. For too long we have been like the mute and mumbling Hannah whose behavior was misinterpreted as drunken babble, like uneducated inarticulate women, like oppressed peasants. But now our time for empowerment has arrived. We have found a way to reach authenticity, a way to author our lives, so that we, like Hannah, like Dorothy, like Merton, like Belenky's women and Freire's illiterate adults, and, yes, like Jesus, can pave the way for others who have been silenced.

My storytelling, my plan, my vision, and my challenge are over for now. But, before a final goodbye, let's revisit the people we met in Chapter 1, the cast of characters in the demimonde, and see what they might be up to—and what you might be up to—in an imagined future.

There are, as you remember, eleven of them, just about the right number, for an intentional community, and representative of the shapes and sizes of single adults in today's world. They all live in a small New England city not far from a parish to which each is loosely connected. No one knows any of the others. Nancy is a school guidance counselor but really wants to be the bed and breakfast hostess she is on weekends in her large old Victorian house. James, who is gay, misses church but won't go because of old wounds. Ellen works with the hospice movement and would like to be a mother, but her long-term relationship with her boyfriend, whom she thinks she loves, is too volatile even to consider the subject. Linda and Jane have just bought new "starter" houses in the hope of assuaging their past hurts; each has recently suffered a broken engagement. Rosemary and Mike came to town as Jesuit volunteers and have stayed on to work in social service agencies. Their spirituality was formed in the Catholic colleges they attended and they are homesick for the life back then, when it was OK to be openly religious or traditionally moral. The "out there" world they now belong to seems harsh by comparison. Charlie is an older man, recovering from alcoholism and guilt over his broken marriage. Terry, too, is older, a career woman, very busy with a long work week and heavy traveling schedule. She finds comfort in the company of her dog, Tyke. Joe, a widower the age of Terry and Charlie, spends a lot of time with his children and grandchildren, but isn't willing to risk heartbreak in a relationship. Sally is the mother of Sarah and solely responsible for her. She maintains a low profile.

These people all don't go to church for many reasons. Charlie feels left out when he goes because he sees so many married couples there; besides, he is new to the city and the parish. Terry is too exhausted on weekends, those when she is in town, to bother. Rosemary and Mike go sometimes but don't know anyone there. Linda and Jane are planning to go one of these days when they get things settled in their new homes. Ellen's boyfriend is very hostile on the subject of religion and she doesn't want to stir up his anger during their weekends together. Nancy is too busy with her bed and breakfast. Joe likes to be with his family on Sundays although both he and they are finding the regularity tedious.

But one by one they all found their way into the church and saw that a discussion series around issues of interest to single people was beginning. The notice specifically said that people of all ages and gender preferences were welcome. They began to go to the meetings, at first occasionally, then regularly. Initially, they were relieved to find that it was not a social gathering, that the meetings were prayerful, that the focus was on issues of spirituality, that there was no apparent leader and no "study material" to prepare. The topics were ones that were relevant to their situations—how to create a sense of home, how to bring balance into their work commitments, what good books were out there to read, how to pray in ways that were refreshing. Gradually they began to bond and became friends outside of the meeting times. Some of the things they do: taking walks with Tyke, helping Nancy dig a garden, going to movies, attending James's concerts. Linda and Jane really hit it off and help each other make choices on how to decorate their new homes.

When the discussion series ended they decided to stay together and form an intentional community. They meet every other week to read and reflect on the Sunday gospels. As a group they have begun to support the parish; they all go to the same Mass on weekends and volunteered to collect bedding and household equipment for a refugee family the parish recently sponsored. All in all everyone is feeling much more relaxed, grateful for new comfortable friendships, and happy to be worshiping again.

And that is about all anyone can wish for; it is what I wish for you. Good-bye for now. Good luck.

Bibliography

Introduction

Day, Dorothy. *The Long Loneliness*. San Francisco: HarperSanFrancisco, 1981.

Nouwen, Henri. *Reaching Out: The Three Movements of the Spiritual Life*. Garden City: Doubleday, 1975.

Social Life—no references

Sex Life

Bailey, Derrick. *Sexual Relations in Christian Thought*. New York: Harper, 1959.

Goergen, Donald. *The Sexual Celibate*. New York: Image Books, 1979.

Norris, Kathleen. *The Cloister Walk*. New York: Riverhead Books, 1996.

Parish Life—no references

Feeling Invisible

Buber, Martin. *I and Thou*. New York: Scribner, 1958.

Buchmann, Christina and Celina Spiegel, Editors. *Out of the Garden: Women Writers on the Bible*. New York: Fawcett Columbine, 1995.

Day, Dorothy. *The Long Loneliness*. San Francisco: HarperSanFrancisco, 1981.

McPherson, Mary Oliver. *Conjugal Spirituality: The Primacy of Mutual Love in Christian Tradition*. Kansas City: Sheed and Ward, 1994.

Merton, Thomas. *Eighteen Poems*. Trustees of the Merton Legacy Trust, 1997.

Shannon, William. *Something of a Rebel: Thomas Merton, His Life and Works, An Introduction*. Cincinnati: St. Anthony Messenger, 1997.

The Focused Life

"In the Company of the Risen Christ" (Dick Westley Talks to Teresita Weind). Call to Action Spirituality/Justice Reprint. May/June, 1995: 1-6.

Benedict. *The Rule of St. Benedict*. Trans. Anthony C. Meisel and M. L. del Mastro. Garden City: Doubleday, 1975.

Chittister, Joan. *The Rule of Benedict: Insights for the Ages*. New York: Crossroad, 1996.

223

Egan, Eileen. *Dorothy Day and the Permanent Revolution*. Erie, PA: Benet Press, 1983.

Dennis, Marie Adele. *A Retreat With Oscar Romero and Dorothy Day: Walking With the Poor*. Cincinnati: St. Anthony Messenger, 1997.

Hammarskjöld, Dag. *Markings*. Trans. Leif Sjoberg and W.H. Auden. New York: Knopf, 1964.

Meister Eckhart. *Meditations With Meister Eckhart*. Santa Fe: Bear, 1983.

Reflective Living

Benedict. *The Rule of St. Benedict*. Trans. Anthony C. Meisel and M. L. del Mastro. Garden City: Doubleday, 1975.

Caprio, Betsy and Thomas Hedberg. *Coming Home: A Handbook for Exploring the Sanctuary Within*. New York: Paulist, 1986.

Chittister, Joan. *Wisdom Distilled From the Daily: Living the Rule of St. Benedict Today*. San Francisco: HarperSanFrancisco, 1990.

de Chardin, Teilhard. *The Phenomenon of Man*. New York: Harper & Row, 1959.

———*The Divine Milieu*. New York: Harper & Row, 1957.

de Waal, Esther. *Seeking God: The Way of St. Benedict*. Collegeville, MN: 1984.

Dillard, Annie. *Teaching a Stone to Talk: Expeditions and Encounters*. New York: Harper and Row, 1982.

Fox, Matthew. *Original Blessing: A Primer in Creation Spirituality Presented in Four Paths, Twenty-Six Themes, and Two Questions*. Santa Fe: Bear, 1996.

Howard, Kathleen. *Praying With Benedict*. Winona, MN: St. Mary's Press, 1996.

Jung, Carl. *The Portable Jung*. Ed. Joseph Campbell. New York: Penguin, 1971.

Meister Eckhart. *Meditations With Meister Eckhart*. Santa Fe: Bear, 1983.

Merton, Thomas. *A Thomas Merton Reader*. Rev. Ed. New York: Image, 1996.

Norris, Kathleen. *Dakota, a Spiritual Geography*. New York: Ticknor and Fields, 1993.

Palmer, Parker. *The Active Life: Wisdom for Work, Creativity, and Caring*. San Francisco: Harper & Row, 1990.

Rohr, Richard. *Everything Belongs: The Gift of Contemplative Prayer*. New York: Crossroad, 1999.

Teresa of Avila. *Interior Castle*. Trans. and edited by E. Allison Peers. New York: Doubleday, 1989.

Commitment to Prayer

Artress, Lauren. *Walking a Sacred Path: Rediscovering the Labyrinth as a Spiritual Tool.* New York: Riverhead, 1995.

Bergan, Jacqueline Syrup and S. Marie Schwan. *Take and Receive Series.* Winona, MN: St. Mary's Press.

Brooke, Avery. *How to Meditate Without Leaving the World.* Noroton, CT: Vineyard Books, 1975.

Callahan, William. *Noisy Contemplation: Deep Prayer for Busy People.* Hyattsville, MD: Quixote Center, 1994.

Froehle, Virginia. *Called Into Her Presence: Praying With Feminine Images of God.* Notre Dame, IN: Ave Maria, 1986.

Keating, Thomas. *Open Mind, Open Heart: The Contemplative Dimension of the Gospel.* Rockport, MA: Element, 1991.

Moore, Thomas. *The Re-Enchantment of Everyday Life.* New York: HarperPerennial, 1996.

Nhat Hahn, Thich. *Being Peace.* Berkeley, CA: Parallax, 1987.

Nolan, Albert. *Jesus Before Christianity.* New York: Orbis, 1976.

Ochs, Carol. *Jewish Spiritual Guidance: Finding Our Way to God.* San Francisco: Jossey-Bass, 1997.

Reiser, William. *Looking for a God to Pray to: Christian Spirituality in Transition.* New York: Paulist, 1994.

_____*To Hear God's Word, Listen to the World: The Liberation of Spirituality.* New York: Paulist, 1996.

Rupp, Joyce. *The Cup of Our Life: A Guide for Spiritual Growth.* Notre Dame, IN: Ave Maria Press, 1997.

Ryan, Thomas. *Prayer of Heart & Body: Meditation and Yoga as Christian Spiritual Practice.* New York: Paulist, 1994.

Savary, Louis, Patricia Berne, and Strephon Williams. *Dreams and Spiritual Growth: A Judeo-Christian Way of Dreamwork.* New York: Paulist, 1984.

Sellner, Edward. *Mentoring: The Ministry of Spiritual Direction.* Notre Dame, IN: Ave Maria, 1990.

Teresa, of Avila. *Interior Castle.* Trans. and edited by E. Allison Peers. New York: Doubleday, 1989.

Participation in Intentional Community

Allaire, James and Rosemary Broughton. *Praying with Dorothy Day.* Winona, MN: St. Mary's Press, 1995.

Fischer, Kathleen. *The Inner Rainbow: The Imagination in Christian Life.*

New York: Paulist, 1983.

Griebler, Marianne and Felicia Wolf. *Keeping the Conversation Going: A Method of Community Formation and Process*. Chicago: Institute of Pastoral Studies at Loyola Univeristy, 1995.

Lee, Bernard and Michael Cowan. *Dangerous Memories: House Churches and Our American Story*. Kansas City: Sheed and Ward, 1986.

Palmer, Parker. *A Place Called Community* (Pendle Hill Pamphlet No. 212). Wallingford, PA: Pendle Hill, 1977.

Westley, Dick. *Redemptive Intimacy: A New Perspective for the Journey to Adult Faith*. Mystic, CT: Twenty-Third, 1981.

———*Good Things Happen: Experiencing Community in Small Groups*. Mystic, CT: Twenty-Third, 1992.

Whitehead, Alfred North. *Process and Reality*. New York: Macmillan, 1969.

Friendship With Silence and Solitude

Chittister, Joan. *The Rule of Benedict: Insights for the Ages*. New York: Crossroad, 1996.

Dillard, Annie. *Teaching a Stone to Talk: Expeditions and Encounters*. New York: Harper and Row, 1982.

Merton, Thomas. *A Thomas Merton Reader*. Rev. ed. New York: Image, 1996.

Nouwen, Henri. *Reaching Out: The Three Movements of the Spiritual Life*. Garden City: Doubleday, 1975.

Palmer, Parker. *To Know as We are Known: A Spirituality of Education*. San Francisco: Harper & Row, 1983.

A Spirituality of Home—no references

Hospitality as a Way of Life

Chittister, Joan. *Wisdom Distilled From the Daily: Living the Rule of St. Benedict Today*. San Francisco: HarperSanFrancisco, 1990.

deWaal, Esther. *Seeking God: The Way of St. Benedict*. Collegeville, MN: 1984.

Nouwen, Henri. *Reaching Out: The Three Movements of the Spiritual Life*. Garden City: Doubleday, 1975.

Proper Balance in Work

De Grote-Sorensen, Barbara and David Sorensen. *Six Weeks to a Simpler Lifestyle*. Minneapolis: Augsburg, 1994.

Dominguez, Joe and Vicki Robin. *Your Money or Your Life: Transforming Your Relationship with Money and Achieving Financial Independence*.

New York: Penguin, 1992.

Fox, Matthew. *The Reinvention of Work: A New Vision of Livelihood for Our Time.* San Francisco: HarperSanFrancisco, 1993.

Hammarskjöld, Dag. *Markings.* Trans. Leif Sjoberg and W.H. Auden. New York: Knopf, 1964.

Norris, Kathleen. *The Quotidian Mysteries: Laundry, Liturgy, and "Women's Work."* New York: Paulist Press, 1998.

Stability

Chittister, Joan. *The Rule of Benedict: Insights for the Ages.* New York: Crossroad, 1996.

Study of Sacred and Spiritual Resources

Dechanet, J.M. *Yoga in Ten Lessons.* New York: Cornerstone, 1968.

Moore, Thomas. *The Re-Enchantment of Everyday Life.* New York: HarperPerennial, 1996.

_____*Care of the Soul: a Guide For Cultivating Depth and Sacredness in Everyday Life.* HarperPerennial ed. New York: HarperPerennial, 1992.

Norris, Kathleen. *Dakota, a Spiritual Geography.* New York: Ticknor & Fields, 1993.

_____*The Cloister Walk.* New York: Riverhead, 1996.

Sinetar, Marcia. *Reel Power: Spiritual Growth Through Film.* Ligouri, MO: Triumph, 1993.

Welch, John. *Spiritual Pilgrims: Carl Jung and Teresa of Avila.* New York: Paulist, 1982.

Wiederkehr, Macrina. *The Song of the Seed: A Monastic Way of Tending the Soul.* San Francisco: HarperSanFrancisco, 1995.

Preferential Option for the Poor

Hellwig, Monika. "Good News to the Poor: Do They Understand it Better?" *Tracing the Spirit: Communities, Social Action, and Theological Reflection.* Ed. James E. Hug. New York: Paulist, 1983.

Kubick, Art. "A Preferential Option for the Poor: Prayer." *Living Prayer* March-April 1988: 3-6.

Meister Eckhart. *Meditations with Meister Eckhart.* Santa Fe: Bear, 1983.

Merton, Thomas. *No Man is an Island.* Garden City: Doubleday, 1955.

_____*Conjectures of a Guilty Bystander.* Garden City: Doubleday, 1966.

Nolan, Albert. *Jesus Before Christianity.* New York: Orbis, 1976.

_____"Four Stages of Spiritual Growth in Helping the Poor." *Praying* 15 (1987): 8-12.

Reiser, William. "With the Poor, With Jesus." *Praying* 65 (1995): 11-12.

_____*To Hear God's Word, Listen to the World: The Liberation of Spirituality.* New York: Paulist, 1996.

_____*Looking for a God to Pray to: Christian Spirituality in Transition.* New York: Paulist, 1994.

Ryan, Thomas. *Disciplines for Christian Living: Interfaith Perspectives.* New York: Paulist, 1992.

Disciplines in Daily Life

Elgin, Duane. *Voluntary Simplicity: Toward a Way of Life That is Outwardly Simple, Inwardly Rich.* Rev. Ed. New York: William Morrow, 1993.

Foster, Richard. *Freedom of Simplicity.* San Francisco: HarperSanFrancisco, 1971.

Heffern, Rich. *Adventures in Simple Living: A Creation-Centered Spirituality.* New York: Crossroad, 1994.

Kellner, Kim. "Journey to Freedom." *Radical Grace.* April-May, 1997.

Lissner, Jorgan. "Reasons for Choosing a Simpler Lifestyle." *Radical Grace.* April-May 1993: 5.

Ryan, Thomas. *Disciplines for Christian Living: Interfaith Perspectives.* New York: Paulist, 1992.

Woods, Rebecca; "Laying on of Hands." *Radical Grace.*

Living a Personal Rule

Benedict. *The Rule of St. Benedict.* Trans. Anthony C. Meisel and M. L. del Mastro. Garden City: Doubleday, 1975.

Chittister, Joan. *Wisdom Distilled From the Daily: Living the Rule of St. Benedict Today.* San Francisco: HarperSanFrancisco, 1990.

_____*The Rule of Benedict: Insights for the Ages.* New York: Crossroad, 1996.

_____*Seeking God: The Way of St. Benedict.* Collegeville, MN: 1984.

Pennington, Basil. *Lessons from the Monastery that Touch Your Life.* New York: Paulist, 1994.

Thompson, Marjorie. *Soul Feast: An Invitation to the Christian Spiritual Life.* Louisville: Westminster John Knox, 1995.

New Wineskins

Cameron, Julia and Mark Bryan. *The Artist's Way: A Spiritual Path to*

Higher Creativity. New York: Putnam, 1992.

Conway, Jill Ker. *Road From Coorain*. New York: Random, 1990.

_____ *When Memory Speaks: Exploring the Art of Autobiography*. New York: Vintage, 1998.

Day, Dorothy. *The Long Loneliness*. San Francisco: HarperSanFrancisco, 1981.

Dlugozima, Hope, James Scott, and David Sharp. *Six Months Off: How to Plan, Negotiate, and Take the Break You Need without Burning Bridges or Going Broke*. New York: Henry Holt, 1996.

Hammarskjöld, Dag. *Markings*. Trans. Leif Sjoberg and W.H. Auden. New York: Knopf, 1964.

Keen, Sam and Anne Valley-Fox. *Your Mythic Journey: Finding Meaning in Your Life through Writing and Storytelling*. New York: Putnam, 1973.

Merton, Thomas. *Seven Storey Mountain*. New York: Harcourt, Brace, 1948.

O'Heron, Edward. *Your Life Story: Self Discovery and Beyond*. Cincinnati: St. Anthony Messenger, 1993.

Progoff, Ira. *At a Journal Workshop*. New York: Dialogue House, 1975.

Ryan, Thomas. *Disciplines for Christian Living: Interfaith Perspectives*. New York: Paulist, 1992.

New Vows

Chittister, Joan. "Vows." *New Dictionary of Catholic Spirituality*. Collegeville, MN: Liturgical, 1993.

New Rituals

Bergan, Jacqueline Syrup and S. Marie Schwan. *Taste and See: Prayer Services for Gatherings of Faith*. Winona, MN: Saint Mary's Press, 1996.

Chittister, Joan. "Ritual." *New Dictionary of Catholic Spirituality*. Collegeville, MN: Liturgical, 1993.

Cronin, Gaynell Bordes. *The Best of Holy Days & Holidays: Prayer Celebrations with Children*. Cincinnati: St. Anthony Messenger, 1997.

De Ferrari, Patricia. "Ritual." *New Catholic Encyclopedia*. Palatine, IL: J. Heraty, 1989.

Fischer, Kathleen. *Women at the Well: Feminist Perspectives on Spiritual Direction*. New York: Paulist, 1988.

Howard, Julie. *We Are the Circle: Celebrating the Feminine in Song and Ritual*. Collegeville, MN: Liturgical Press, 1993.

Rupp, Joyce. *May I Have This Dance?* Notre Dame, IN: Ave Maria, 1992.

_____*Dear Heart, Come Home: The Path of Midlife Spirituality.* New York, Crossroad, 1996.

Schaffran, Janet and Pat Kozak. *More Than Words: Prayer and Ritual for Inclusive Communities.* New York: Crossroad, 1994.

Somé, Malidoma. Lecture, Portland, Maine. March, 1997.

Conclusion

Belenky, Mary Field, Nancy Rule Goldberger, Jill Mattuck Tarule, editors, *Women's Ways of Knowing: The Development of Self, Voice, and Mind.* New York: Basic, 1986.

Coles, Robert. *Dorothy Day: A Radical Devotion.* Reading, MA: Addison-Wesley, 1987.

Freire, Paulo. *Pedagogy of the Oppressed.* New York: Sheed and Ward, 1972.

Lee, Bernard and Michael Cowan. *Dangerous Memories: House Churches and Our American Story.* Kansas City: Sheed and Ward, 1986.

OF RELATED INTEREST...

Traits of a Healthy Spirituality
Melannie Svoboda, SND

Describes 20 indicators of a healthy spirituality such as self-esteem, friendship, courage, tolerance, joy and forgiveness, and demonstrates how to use these signs to determine where we stand in terms of our Christian spirituality. Includes meditations, questions for reflection, and prayers.

ISBN: 0-89622-698-0, 144 pages, $9.95

A Single Mother's Prayerbook
Ginger Farry

Here are the prayers of a real mom who called upon God in child-rearing situations and in times of loneliness and frustration. Through them readers can learn the truth that the author discovers in her own journey...that we are never alone and that God is present, walking with us through every tear, every disappointment, every glass of spilled milk, and every joy. These prayers validate concerns while they give meaning to losses—because they are permeated with a consistent sense of hope.

ISBN: 0-89622-973-4, 64 pages, $7.95

Alone But Not Lonely
A Spirituality of Solitude
Donna Schaper

These meditations help us confront the causes of our loneliness and journey with us to a point of solitude. They define and differentiate loneliness and solitude in order to refresh and renew us to reconnect us to our real lives and to God.

ISBN: 0-89622-956-4, 96 pages, $7.95

Healing Wounded Emotions
Overcoming Life's Hurts
Martin Padovani

Describes how our emotional and spiritual lives interact, and challenges readers to live fuller, more satisfying lives. Chapters cover anger, forgiving, guilt, change, self-love, depression, compassion, affirmation, and more.

ISBN: 0-89622-333-7, 128 pages, $7.95

Available at religious bookstores or from:

TWENTY-THIRD PUBLICATIONS
PO BOX 180 · 185 WILLOW STREET MYSTIC, CT 06355 · 1-800-321-0411
FAX: 1-800-572-0788 BAYARD E-MAIL: ttpubs@aol.com

Call for a free catalog